PEMBROKESHIRE
HISTORIC LANDSCAPES FROM THE AIR

Figure 2 (above). The uncompromising symmetry of the barracks at South Hook Fort, Herbrandston (built 1859-65), on the north side of Milford Haven (RCAHMW, AP-2006-1176).

Figure 3 (opposite). St Justinian's Chapel and St Davids Lifeboat Station from the north, overlooking Porthstinan (RCAHMW, 96-cs-0199).

PEMBROKESHIRE
HISTORIC LANDSCAPES FROM THE AIR

Toby Driver

Comisiwn Brenhinol Henebion Cymru

Royal Commission on the Ancient and Historical Monuments of Wales

COMMISSIONERS

ISBN 978-1-871184-29-7

British Library Cataloguing in Publication Data.
A catalogue record for this book is available from the British Library.

Comisiwn Brenhinol Henebion Cymru
Royal Commission on the Ancient and Historical Monuments of Wales
Plas Crug, Aberystwyth, Ceredigion, SY2 1NJ

Telephone: 01970 621200   *Fax:* 01970 627701
e-mail: nmrwales@rcahmw.gov.uk
Web page: www.rcahmw.gov.uk

Figure 1 (page i). Mynydd Preseli, winter landscape looking north-west over Foel Trigarn hillfort (right) towards Mynydd Carn-ingli (left background) and the north Pembrokeshire coast (RCAHMW, 99-cs-0201).

CONTENTS

Figure 4. The confluence of the Western Cleddau (right) and Eastern Cleddau (left) at Picton Point, looking south along the historic Daugleddau estuary fringed with castles, quays and country houses (RCAHMW, AP-2005-2144).

ACKNOWLEDGEMENTS

Any Royal Commission publication is the result of a team effort, combining the skills and expertise of all its members of staff. I would therefore like to thank the past and present Secretary and staff for all their advice and assistance in the long preparation of this book. In particular, Fleur James has put in countless hours completing the scans of the aerial photographs. Layout was by John Johnston, with Owain Hammonds, the main maps and graphics by Charles Green, with copy editing and publications guidance by David Browne. Louise Barker lent her considerable expertise to produce the geology and Ramsey Island maps and the plan of Banc Du. Tom Pert contributed his technical skills in air-photo mapping and 3D landscape visualisation to reproduce many of the digital scenes and archaeological maps, including the LIDAR views and those of Mynydd Carn-ingli. My predecessor Chris Musson took many of the Royal Commission aerial photographs in this book as Investigator: Aerial Photography, prior to his retirement in 1997 (see list in appendices).

Pembrokeshire is a county where many different interests overlap and where so many individuals and organisations have researched the archaeology and history before me, particularly Terry James, Chris Musson, Professor J. K. St Joseph and David Wilson, all of whom pioneered archaeological aerial reconnaissance in west Wales. I owe a deep debt of gratitude to the several friends and colleagues who agreed to give up their time to read the whole or parts of the draft book text: Dr Peter Wakelin, Professor Ralph Griffiths, Dr Llinos Smith, Stephen Hughes, Chris Musson, Ken Murphy, Roger Thomas, Polly Groom, Phil Bennett, Neil Ludlow, Dr Siân Rees, Dr Kathryn Roberts, Dr Stephen Briggs, Medwyn Parry and David Browne. All have considerably enriched the text with their careful reading, detailed regional knowledge and pointers to obscure sources. I would particularly like to thank Terry and Heather James for their detailed comments and learned advice on all aspects of Pembrokeshire's archaeology and history. In addition, Derek Elliot of the Central Register of Air Photography for Wales helped to unearth many of the historic aerial photographs. I have tried to incorporate all suggestions for amendments but the responsibility for the final version rests with me alone.

I have enjoyed many flights out of Haverfordwest (Withybush) Airport, and thanks are due to the owners, John and Gwen Rees, and the many pilots who have flown me and my predecessors over the years, including Gwyndaf Williams, Jo Rees, Cliff Day, Dave Phipps, Dan Surridge and others. My thanks also to Professors Geoffrey Wainwright and Tim Darvill for collaboration on the SPACES project; Marion Page and Richard Jones at Cambria Archaeology for sourcing aerial photos and digital data; Professor David Austin for information on the Carew Castle Project; Helen Winton and Martyn Barber for information on the early view of Stonehenge and Adrian James and the Society of Antiquaries of London for permission to reproduce it; Rose Desmond at the Unit for Landscape Modelling; Mike Woodward for the Terrence Soames view of Milford Haven; Martin Dean, Archaeological Diving Unit Surveys, for permission to reproduce the image of The Smalls lighthouse; Julie Gardiner, editor of the *Proceedings of the Prehistoric Society* (PPS) for permission to reproduce the map of Skomer by the late John Evans from *PPS* 56, 1990; Melissa Turner at the Environment Agency for the supply of LIDAR images; and Neil Fairburn of RSK ESNR Environment for information on archaeological discoveries along the LNG pipeline route. I would like to acknowledge the history of research in the county by the Dyfed Archaeological Trust, now Cambria Archaeology, since its inception in the 1970s. Their Historic Landscape Characterisation reports for Pembrokeshire have been an invaluable resource. Various lectures to local history groups over the years in Pembrokeshire have allowed photographs taken from the isolation of an aircraft to be shown to, and discussed with, local people on the ground. The feedback on particular pictures has always been rewarding. I must also acknowledge many years of learning from the wider community of aerial archaeologists. My final thanks to my family, Becky, Aric and Charlie, who have once again put up with the extra time required to finish a project over a number of years.

The Royal Commission dedicates this book to the memory of Terry James FSA (1948-2007), a pioneer of aerial photography, a notable historian of west Wales and a valued colleague at the Royal Commission.

Figure 5. St Davids Cathedral and walled close, seen in the last light of a May evening in 1989 (RCAHMW, 895501-16).

FOREWORD

In about 1146 an eminent Welshman – Giraldus Cambrensis – was born in Manorbier Castle in south Pembrokeshire. Not generally given to understatement, he described his home county in terms which might be regarded as extravagant except by those of us who share his love of the county and its people. West Wales he considered to be the most beautiful and powerful region west of Offa's Dyke, Pembrokeshire as its finest part and Manorbier as its most pleasant spot. Coming from Angle by way of the Gwaun Valley I may contest his advocacy of Manorbier but not his general thesis. It was these attributes - percipiently recognised by Gerald – which led to the designation of the Pembrokeshire Coast National Park in 1952. As a result, 58,000 hectares – just one-third of the county – is carefully managed for future generations to enjoy, on account of its physical beauty and rich heritage. Viewed from a satellite in space and essential to our appreciation of Pembrokeshire is its peninsular character. The indented coastline means that the influence of the sea is all-pervading and there are few parts of Pembrokeshire more than ten miles distant from tidal water. Movement by water – whether by sea or river – would have been many times easier than travelling across land and these advantages combined with abundant natural wildlife, fertile agricultural land, stone and timber for implements and buildings and essential minerals made Pembrokeshire a thoroughly desirable area for settlement over seven millennia.

Set in this beautiful context the numbers and variety of monuments and landscapes are outstanding. Six thousand years ago the earliest farmers extracted stone from the north of the county to make their polished axes. A millennium later the famous connection of Preseli with Stonehenge was established with the transportation of the bluestones from north Pembrokeshire to build the first Stonehenge on the Wiltshire plain. The northern part of Pembrokeshire has huge potential to deepen our understanding of the early Celtic Church, whilst in the south the spectacular results of Norman settlement saw the establishment of castles and a settlement pattern which still exists today. Across the county are the remains of quarries, mines, coastal fortifications, harbours and airfields testifying to the rich industrial heritage and strategic importance of the county up to the present.

The medium of aerial photography is a perfect tool through which to depict this richness of scenery and settlement. It provides vivid images of the familiar, discovers new sites and unsuspected aspects of what is already known and sets them all in their landscape context. Toby Driver has exploited this potential with outstanding success through the many aerial photographs he has chosen, backed up with well-researched text. The photographs – largely from the rich aerial archive of the Royal Commission on the Ancient and Historical Monuments of Wales – are a delight. The text interprets them for scholar and the public alike and with the vivid images tells us the story of Pembrokeshire over 30,000 years from cave dwelling to airfield, thus bringing the beauty of the county and its rich heritage to a wider audience. The book deserves and will receive an international audience not only for the information it contains but the sheer pleasure of turning the pages. The Royal Commission deserves our thanks for producing such a lovely volume, and Toby Driver for writing it.

GEOFFREY WAINWRIGHT
March Pres
January 2007

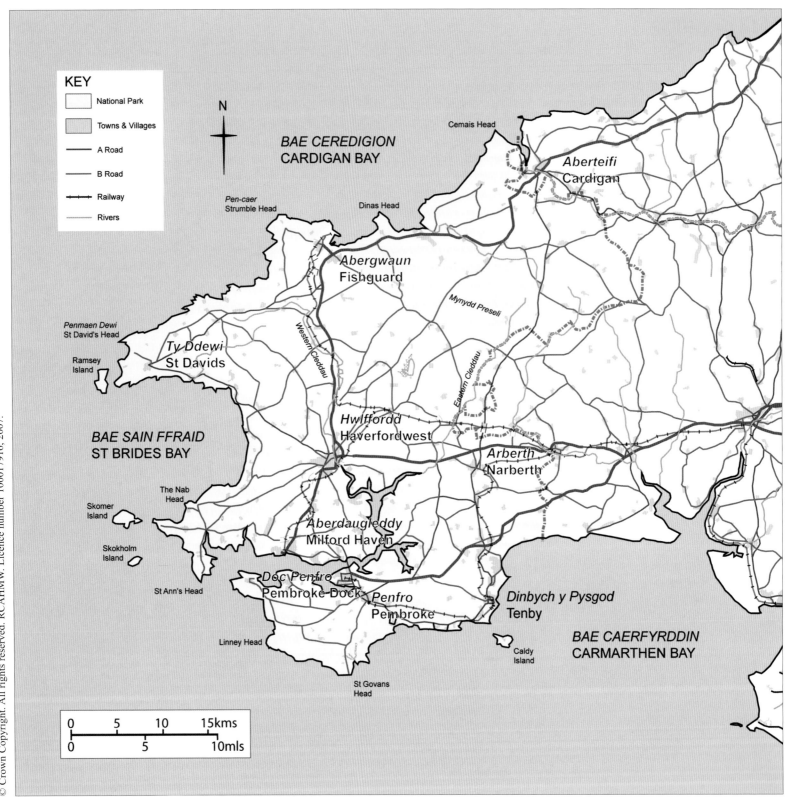

KEY

National Park

Towns & Villages

A Road

B Road

Railway

Rivers

N

BAE CEREDIGION
CARDIGAN BAY

Cemais Head

Aberteifi
Cardigan

Pen-caer
Strumble Head

Dinas Head

Abergwaun
Fishguard

Mynydd Preseli

Penmaen Dewi
St David's Head

Western Cleddau

Ty Ddewi
St Davids

Ramsey
Island

Eastern Cleddau

BAE SAIN FFRAID
ST BRIDES BAY

Hwlffordd
Haverfordwest

Arberth
Narberth

The Nab
Head

Skomer
Island

Aberdaugleddy
Milford Haven

Skokholm
Island

St Ann's Head

Doc Penfro
Pembroke Dock

Penfro
Pembroke

Dinbych y Pysgod
Tenby

Linney Head

Caldy
Island

BAE CAERFYRDDIN
CARMARTHEN BAY

St Govans
Head

| 0 | 5 | 10 | 15kms |
| 0 | | 5 | 10mls |

CHAPTER ONE

HISTORIC LANDSCAPES FROM THE AIR

The historic landscapes of Pembrokeshire are among the most diverse and fascinating in the British Isles. Within the winding boundaries of this far-westerly county of Wales, bordered on three sides by sea, are traces of some of the oldest settlements in Britain. Defences of brick and concrete from the last two centuries share coastal headlands with prehistoric forts of earth and stone. Across unenclosed moorlands ancient field boundaries, some first laid out between four and six thousand years ago, bear witness to once productive farmlands in what are now marginal environments. Beneath the grass and crops of modern fields lie hidden settlements, long-since ploughed away but rediscovered by aerial photography. The physical echoes of people's relationships with the Pembrokeshire landscape repeat many of the same themes, from prehistory to the recent past: defence, farming, worship and settlement.

Hundreds of Pembrokeshire's historic sites lie hidden from view either on private land, on inaccessible peaks and cliffs, or simply buried by centuries of cultivation. Only from the air can the true extent of Pembrokeshire's rich heritage be appreciated. This new perspective reveals concealed monuments and allows us to appreciate more familiar ones from a unique point of view.

Since the end of the Second World War decades of aerial survey have steadily revealed the complexity of Pembrokeshire's historic landscapes. This book travels out across the sea to the furthest islands off the Pembrokeshire coast. It returns over steep cliffs fringed with promontory forts and indented with quays, passing inland to mountain summits and their

Figure 6. Porthgain harbour seen from the south-east in July 2000. From the late nineteenth century slate, and later granite, was quarried from the coastal headland. Clay from the same quarries made bricks, baked on the harbour's edge and then exported to south Wales and Ireland (RCAHMW, DI2006-0522).

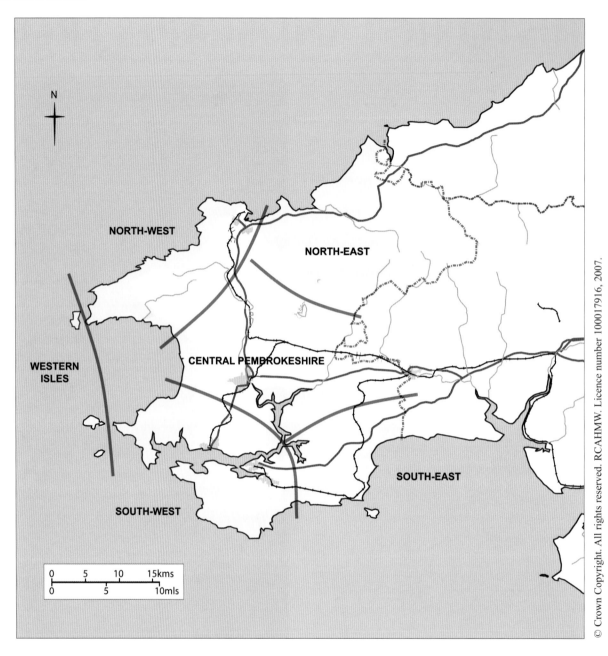

Figure 7. The six regions of Pembrokeshire which are described in the main sections of this book (RCAHMW).

lonely burial mounds. Rising high above familiar villages and towns, prehistoric and medieval fields are apparent, forming the structure of the landscape still in use today. Hidden along quiet valleys or in the lee of mountain slopes are abandoned farmsteads and quarries that tell of prosperity and decline in recent centuries. Through older aerial photographs, some taken more than half a century ago, it is possible to see long-vanished wartime airfields, or Milford Haven before the oil refineries arrived. This book tells the story of the landscapes of Pembrokeshire, and their people, from the earliest times to the very recent past.

The book illustrates the landscapes of Pembrokeshire region by region, where evidence of different ages lies close together, like a document amended and over-written. Distinct blocks of

Figure 8. Failed enterprise. Geometric farmstead on Waun Clyn-coch (SN 101 311), below the snow-covered peak of Foel Feddau, on the southern flanks of Mynydd Preseli (RCAHMW, DI2006 0578).

landscape are described, whether coastal or inland, urban or upland. The boundaries between the chosen regions are blurred, for to draw a hard line between them would be misleading. No landscape can be isolated from the environment around it, and the lives of people in adjacent regions were always interdependent. Nevertheless, each distinct region of Pembrokeshire has its own stories to tell.

ARCHAEOLOGY FROM THE AIR

Figure 9 (below). 'Stonehenge, as seen from a War Balloon', from the pioneering aerial photographs taken by Sharpe in 1906. These earliest-known aerial photographs of an archaeological site in Britain illustrate strengths of the technique still relevant today, notably the power of the elevated perspective and the effects of drought to highlight details of buried or vestigial structures through differential plant growth (reproduced from Archaeologia 60, pt. 2 (1907), pl. LXIX. DI2006-0031. By kind permission of The Society of Antiquaries of London).

In the twenty-first century airborne imagery has found its way into all our lives. On television and the Internet it is an increasingly familiar device for capturing people's attention. High-resolution satellite imagery, once an exclusive resource, is now commonplace on evening news bulletins to show world locations or the impact of natural disasters. Yet in most forms the aerial view becomes little more than a passive illustration, showing the position and layout of buildings in a town, or providing a rolling background to a television narrative. However, used analytically to extract information about lost or buried landscapes at the extremes of light and season, aerial photography can push forward or sometimes fundamentally re-write certain chapters in Welsh history.

The first aerial photographs of an archaeological

site are thought to have been those taken of the Forum excavations in Rome, in June 1899, by Giacomo Boni and two engineer officers of the Italian Army, from a tethered balloon at a height of 300-500 metres. In a letter to a friend Boni recounted:

'I have been three times on the Military Engineers' balloon 400m above the Palatine and the Forum Romanum…. The sight was wonderful…. The Coliseum, the Constantine basilica looked like wood models!' (quoted in Ceraudo 2005, 74).

In Britain the earliest-known aerial photographs of an archaeological site are of Stonehenge, taken late in 1906 from an army war-balloon by Lt. Philip Henry Sharpe whilst he was stationed at Bulford Camp. Sharpe's pioneering photographs, one oblique and

Figure 10. The dramatic power of parching to reveal our buried past at Carew Castle. The view on the far left, taken on 13 April 1995, exploits low sunlight to highlight the earthworks of the outer ward fronting the castle and the rock-cut ditch and foundations of the outer gate. The view on the left, taken on 8 July 1995 in one of the hottest, driest summers in three decades, shows the grass cover parched yellow to brown, except in the damper soil of buried rock-cut ditches (crossing left to right) of a pre-existing promontory fort (RCAHMW; April (left) DI2006-0559; July (right) DI2006-0558).

one vertical, demonstrated for the first time the power of the elevated perspective in clarifying the layout of the complex stone settings at Stonehenge. The parched grassland around the monument also helped to highlight otherwise invisible elements of the surrounding prehistoric earthworks, including vestigial pits, ditches and trackways.

Aerial reconnaissance can be used to record changing historic landscapes through pictures of such diverse subjects as field patterns, chapels, townscapes and parkland. It can also aid the management of monuments. Protected sites of national importance include medieval castles, standing stones and early industrial remains. All are parts of a working, changing landscape, and their condition can be recorded by over-flying them on a regular basis. Such work forms a key part of the Royal Commission's flying programme. Using photographic sources dating back to the 1940s with new computer software, archaeological remains can be mapped precisely to reconstruct entire landscapes that may have been destroyed or ploughed away. For all these reasons, aerial photography is a long-established method for national archaeological survey throughout the British Isles and worldwide. International training schools designed to foster new programmes of aerial survey in countries as diverse as Hungary, Poland, Italy and Finland have ushered in new eras of archaeological discovery and advanced new frontiers for the discipline.

Figure 11. Bulliber Camp, also known as Warmans Hill or Castle Lady Fort, an Iron Age hillfort south of Castlemartin, on the 8 April 1938, taken by the 210 photo reconnaissance squadron of the Royal Air Force based in Pembroke Dock. (210. 349.1.95, 8.4.38. 1503; Crown Copyright MoD/1938. DI2006-0044).

In telling the story of Pembrokeshire from the air, the author can draw on a considerable legacy from earlier aerial archaeologists. Aerial photography in Pembrokeshire dates to the earliest years of the twentieth century. The long military presence in the county, particularly leading up to and including both world wars, led to the acquisition of numerous early aerial views, first from airships and then from aircraft, mostly during training sorties. The establishment of a Royal Naval Air Service airship station at Sageston in the south of the county resulted in some of the earliest aerial views anywhere in Wales, including shots of Pembroke Dock from 1915 (Evans 2001). Aerofilms also visited the county in the inter-war years and, together with private flyers and entrepreneurs, published aerial views and postcards of locations like St Davids for the tourist market. These earliest photographs were taken on large, single, glass plates mounted in unwieldy cameras.

Collections of aerial photographs taken between the 1920s and 1940s by the Royal Air Force, private companies (often producing postcards), and even the Luftwaffe, are more common in archives today. Pembrokeshire's archaeological monuments were often recorded in the course of reconnaissance training, providing rare glimpses of how these sites appeared up to 70 years ago and more. In terms of dedicated archaeological recording, the Cambridge University Committee for Aerial Photography (CUCAP) made its first sortie over the south of the county in July 1948. These flights formed part of a wider programme of reconnaissance by Professor J. K. St Joseph and later David Wilson which spanned the British Isles and parts of Europe, amassing a rich aerial archive (see St Joseph, 1961). Aerial views of Pembrokeshire's archaeology and landscapes taken by Roger Worsley and Studio Jon began to appear in a number of county publications and guides from the 1960s (see Rees 1963, Beazley 1976), but more regionally-targeted work focussed on the archaeology and history of the county began in earnest in 1978 following the establishment of the Dyfed Archaeological Trust in late 1974.

In the early years of the Dyfed Archaeological Trust simply getting airborne to photograph archaeology proved difficult. Terry James hitched lifts with Doug Simpson, who was engaged in non-archaeological aerial photography, and monuments were photographed as and when possible. There was little chance to get rapidly airborne on optimum days to exploit changing light or seasonal conditions. In 1979 the Carmarthenshire Antiquarian Society paid for a three-hour flight which resulted in the 1980 book *Ancient West Wales from the Air* by Terry James and Doug Simpson, summarising achievements to date. During the early 1980s funding for aerial reconnaissance in west Wales continued to waver, although flights were conducted over early church sites and Roman roads during parched summer conditions. The summer of 1984 saw exceptional drought conditions across the inland grasslands of Pembrokeshire and Carmarthenshire, rarely repeated since. Discoveries of scores of prehistoric and

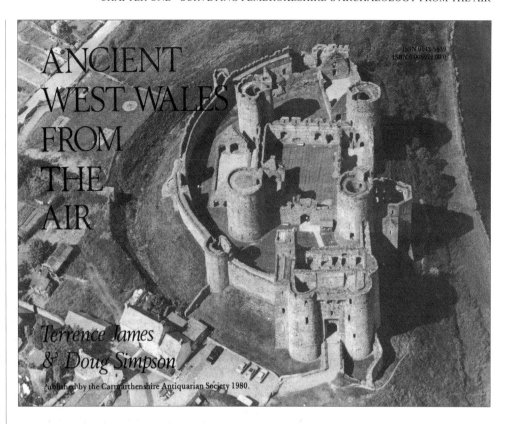

Roman settlements as cropmarks showed the dramatic impact this method of survey could have on understanding the development of west Wales through the millennia. These were published as a major article in *Archaeology in Wales* in 1984, combining descriptions and maps of significant discoveries with analyses of the summer's drought and rainfall conditions and dates of silage cropping, all of which affected the visibility of the buried archaeology. The impressive results from only fourteen hours of summer flying were presented at a conference in Cardiff that winter. They helped to add weight to the growing calls for a full-time aerial archaeologist in Wales, and in 1986 the Royal Commission appointed its first Investigator for Aerial Survey, Chris Musson. The Royal Commission began reconnaissance work across Pembrokeshire and the rest of Wales, together with the regional flyers, building an impressive image archive for the county and continuing the discovery of Pembrokeshire's past. The author took over this work in 1997.

Figure 12. Ancient West Wales from the Air, published in 1980, was the first book to showcase archaeological aerial views of Pembrokeshire and showed the enormous potential for aerial recording of the archaeology of Wales (Reproduced by kind permission of the Carmarthenshire Antiquarian Society and Terry James).

THE PRACTICE OF AERIAL RECONNAISSANCE AND REMOTE SENSING

The discipline of aerial archaeology encompasses a wide variety of survey and recording activities, from actual reconnaissance to interpreting and mapping sites from the photographs taken. Aerial reconnaissance is widely used around the world and is part of the wider discipline of 'remote sensing',

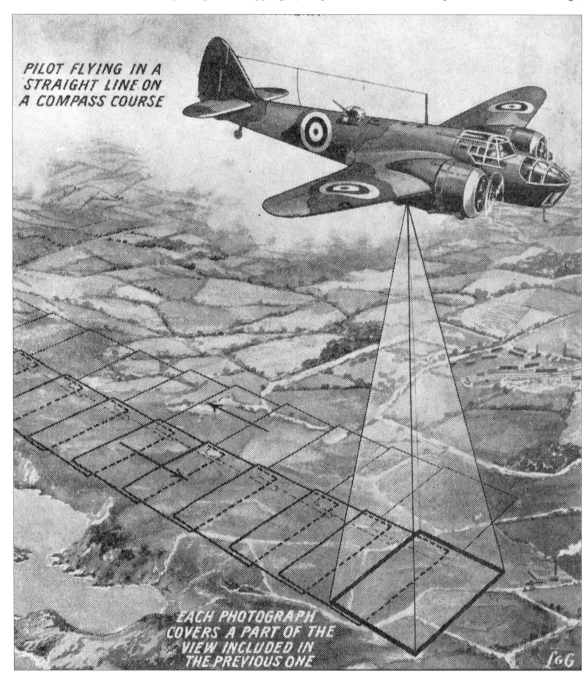

Figure 13. Vertical aerial photography. An illustration of the process originally published in a 1942 guide to Britain's fighting forces. A Bristol 'Blenheim' Mark IV long-range bomber is engaged in vertical photographic reconnaissance. Each photograph has a consistent overlap with the previous one allowing pairs of prints to be viewed in stereo. Photographs taken by the RAF in this manner during and after the war form a major component of British aerial archives and a significant research resource for archaeologists today (Britain's Wonderful Fighting Forces, Chapter IV, Figure 5. © IPC+ Syndication).

surveying archaeology in the landscape without actually touching it, as one would do in an excavation. Aerial imagery can be either oblique, taken from a light aircraft or helicopter, or vertical, taken from a specially modified survey aircraft. In countries where costs are prohibitive or such activities may be illegal, archaeologists can use kite aerial photography (KAP) or even model aircraft.

Changing technology continues to bring new possibilities. Airborne laser scanning, or LIDAR (LIght Detection And Ranging), chiefly undertaken in Britain by the Environment Agency and Cambridge University, was developed to provide digital terrain models for calculating flood-risk, but the data is now being used for archaeological recording. Accurate to a few centimetres, LIDAR data can produce a virtual landscape, with a virtual sun directed to show up every slight bump or dip on the ground surface and extraneous trees and hedges digitally removed to provide an uncluttered view. Satellite imagery becomes ever more refined, the current 60-centimetre resolution approaching that

Figure 14. Comparison of oblique (left) and vertical (right) photographs of Pembroke castle and town. Oblique photographs taken out of an aircraft window are targeted at subjects selected by the archaeologist or photographer and are easily understandable, but other features of interest may be missed, falling just outside the frame. Distortions are present caused by variations in the topography, and tall buildings or hills may hide objects from view. The vertical view is more like a map and not as attractive for illustration. The image quality can be variable, and the conditions are not always ideal for identifying archaeological sites, but a sortie taken in exceptionally clear conditions, as here, provides a first-class visual record. Although there are some distortions, mapping is more straightforward. When viewed with a stereo pair, scenes can be looked at in three dimensions in considerable detail (RCAHMW, DI2006-0556; Crown Copyright MoD, 1946, 106G UK 1625 4355).

offered by the 9-inch square negatives of historic vertical aerial photographs taken by the Royal Air Force. The multi-spectral range of satellite imagery can also allow examination of landscape features using visible and invisible light spectra. Satellite imagery is a vital resource for those working in parts of the world where flights are difficult or prohibited. Costs of both LIDAR data and high resolution satellite imagery are still high, but in future this technology may be more widely accessible.

Figure 15. LIDAR image of Haverfordwest Priory from the south-east; not a picture but a digital height model compiled by a scanning laser mounted in a passing survey aircraft in February 2004. This is a highly detailed record of every building, tree and undulation in the ground. It shows the raised beds of the reconstructed medieval gardens (centre left, next to river) alongside the priory ruins, as well as other earthworks and terraces above the priory. The cruciform plan of St Thomas Hospital workhouse can be seen at upper left. The airborne laser cannot show the underside of structures like bridges, thus the road and railway bridges crossing the Western Cleddau appear as solid blocks. LIDAR points the way to future possibilities of aerial imagery (© Environment Agency copyright, D0031908. All rights reserved. View generated by RCAHMW)

AERIAL RECONNAISSANCE: TAKING TO THE SKIES

For most archaeological aerial reconnaissance a four-seater Cessna 172 aircraft is the preferred platform. The high wing allows an unimpeded view of the ground and costs are relatively low. Helicopters are fast and allow hovering over chosen subjects, but their regular use would be prohibitively expensive for archaeological purposes.

The archaeologist usually sits on the left-hand side of the aircraft and takes photographs through the open window. There is little spare room, yet the archaeologist must carry at least two cameras (for back-up), maps, films or memory cards, batteries and spare lenses, and a GPS or Global Positioning System. In excellent weather a plentiful supply of film or memory cards and extensive map coverage for every eventuality permits whole days spent in the air, with six or more hours of photo-reconnaissance and cross-country stops at airfields for food and fuel.

Figure 16. Cessna 172 at Haverfordwest Airport, the standard aircraft for archaeological aerial photography. Cessna 172s have four seats and high wings allowing excellent views of the ground. The aircraft pictured can fly for three hours before landing for fuel, allowing a safe reserve for emergencies or re-routing to an alternative airport (RCAHMW, DS2006-120-001).

Figure 17. A cramped working environment. The cockpit of the Cessna 172 showing the left-hand seat routinely used by the aerial photographer. Room for equipment is limited once the photographer is strapped in and wearing headphones to communicate with the pilot. For winter flying, often in sub-zero conditions, hats, a very thick jacket and gloves reduce the working space still further. Parachutes are not worn or carried (RCAHMW, AP-2006-1640).

Figure 18. Returning to Haverfordwest Airport after a summer flight. On the flight back to the airfield the aerial archaeologist will be packing away equipment, making notes and reflecting on possible discoveries, whilst also preparing to write a summary flight report. The vertical view on the left shows Haverfordwest in winter, photographed in a steep turn before landing. The flying archaeologist is heavily reliant on the skill and experience of the pilot to manoeuvre the aircraft (RCAHMW, (above) AP-2004-0868; (left) AP-2005-2771).

Reconnaissance is highly reactive to weather and seasonal conditions. The archaeologist prefers clear, sunny weather, and when these conditions arrive it is important to get airborne as quickly as possible. Flights are planned in detail prior to take-off against a flying map annotated to show every known site of archaeological or historical interest, but they must often be re-planned in transit to avoid shifting cloud, fog patches or areas of haze and poor visibility. Times of flights will vary with the seasons. During winter and early spring clear, low light, ideal for the photography of earthwork monuments, will last throughout the day. During late spring and into summer low light suitable for earthwork recording will vanish by 10 o'clock in the morning and will not return until 5 or 6 o'clock in the evening. However, bright, flat, summer light with few shadows can be ideal for the photography of upstanding buildings and townscapes unimpeded by contrasting light and shadow.

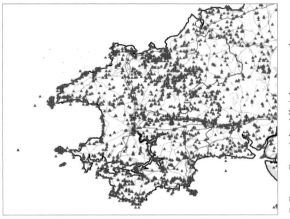

Figure 20 (above). This distribution map shows all oblique aerial photographs taken by the Royal Commission since the flying programme began in the mid-1980s. Particular clusters are visible, notably around Skomer and Ramsey Islands and an east-west line between Haverfordwest and Whitland following the course of the Roman road. Maps like this are invaluable in planning strategies for future reconnaissance. (RCAHMW).

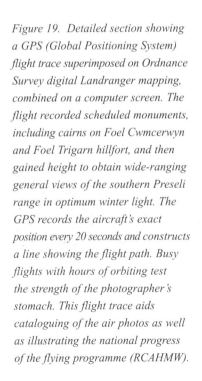

Figure 19. Detailed section showing a GPS (Global Positioning System) flight trace superimposed on Ordnance Survey digital Landranger mapping, combined on a computer screen. The flight recorded scheduled monuments, including cairns on Foel Cwmcerwyn and Foel Trigarn hillfort, and then gained height to obtain wide-ranging general views of the southern Preseli range in optimum winter light. The GPS records the aircraft's exact position every 20 seconds and constructs a line showing the flight path. Busy flights with hours of orbiting test the strength of the photographer's stomach. This flight trace aids cataloguing of the air photos as well as illustrating the national progress of the flying programme (RCAHMW).

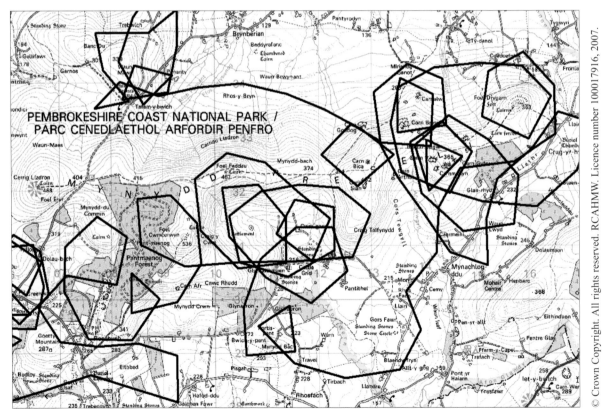

CROPMARKS AND SOILMARKS, SHADOWS AND FROST

Misconceptions persist in popular histories about the sophistication and complexity of the prehistoric landscape, its settlements and agricultural economy. Descriptions abound of a thickly forested, primeval land before the Roman invasion, with 'Celtic' tribes living a primitive existence hunting wild animals in the wooded valleys and retreating to hilltop refuges in times of strife. This long-held view, where the Roman invaders are credited with bringing a civilising influence to the prehistoric populace, bears

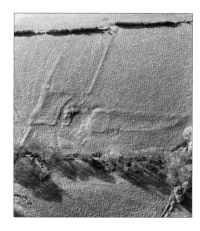

Figure 21 (above). Earthworks of a deserted farmstead at Trellyffaint, north of Nevern, picked out in winter sunlight. The rectangular house platform is surrounded by turf-covered remains of a sunken yard, outbuildings, trackways and field plots. The farm could date back to the medieval period, but is currently undated (RCAHMW, 2002-cs-0721).

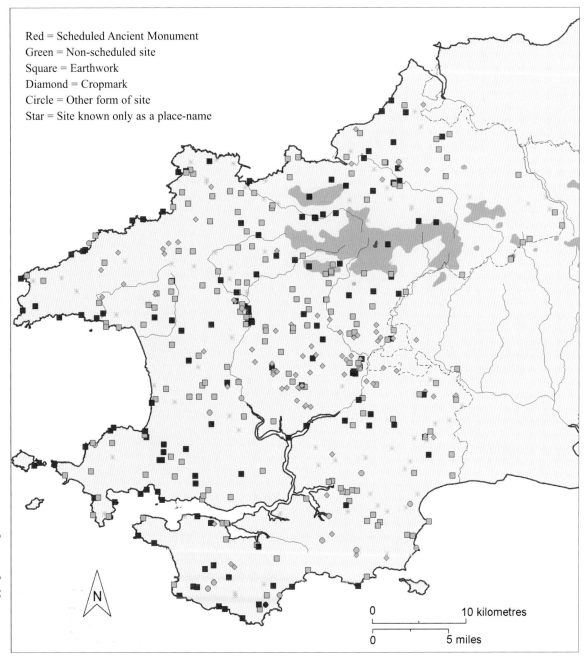

Red = Scheduled Ancient Monument
Green = Non-scheduled site
Square = Earthwork
Diamond = Cropmark
Circle = Other form of site
Star = Site known only as a place-name

0   10 kilometres

0   5 miles

Figure 22. Prehistoric hillforts and defended enclosures in Pembrokeshire. The survival of upstanding earthworks (squares) and plough-levelled cropmarks (diamonds) illustrates the extent of Pembrokeshire's buried prehistoric landscapes. Many more buried settlements doubtless await discovery, some indicated by place-names (stars) (map by Ken Murphy, © Cambria Archaeology).

13

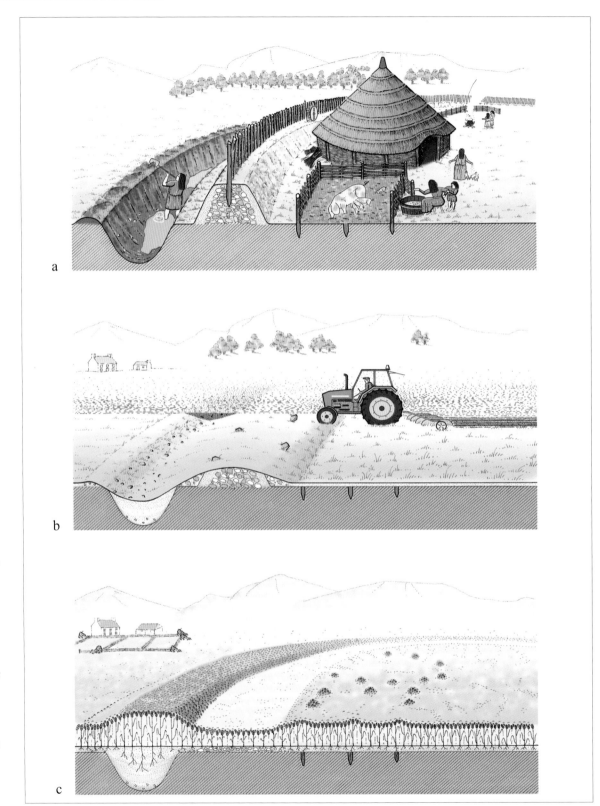

Figure 23. How cropmarks form: from Iron Age farm to low earthwork and then to modern farmland. This sequence illustrates how certain elements of a prehistoric farmstead, particularly the enclosure ditch, defensive rampart and postholes, can survive as below-ground features and affect the way that an arable crop or grassland grows during a dry spring and summer.

Key: a: late Iron Age farmstead around 100 BC. b: remains of farmstead survive as a low earthwork under grass which is then cultivated in recent decades. c: years of cultivation for arable crops have completely levelled the enclosure, but below-ground remains of the ditch and rampart footing produce cropmarks (RCAHMW).

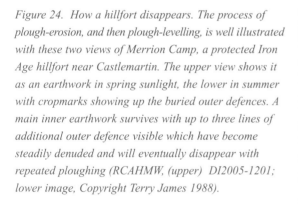

Figure 24. How a hillfort disappears. The process of plough-erosion, and then plough-levelling, is well illustrated with these two views of Merrion Camp, a protected Iron Age hillfort near Castlemartin. The upper view shows it as an earthwork in spring sunlight, the lower in summer with cropmarks showing up the buried outer defences. A main inner earthwork survives with up to three lines of additional outer defence visible which have become steadily denuded and will eventually disappear with repeated ploughing (RCAHMW, (upper) DI2005-1201; lower image, Copyright Terry James 1988).

Figure 25. The transience of cropmarks: Post-coch defended enclosure, north-east of Nevern in north Pembrokeshire (SN 110 411), photographed following partial harvesting of the field in July 2006. Once the cropmark is fully harvested, the site will vanish again until the next dry summer (RCAHMW, AP-2006-3915).

Pembrokeshire and the rest of Wales was settled. Similar advances in understanding are related to ensuing centuries and into the present day.

In parts of Pembrokeshire aerial photography has shown that the density of prehistoric defended settlements was similar to that of farms today. At ground level nothing may remain to show the position of prehistoric farmsteads or Roman villas, but beneath the topsoil buried ditches, wall footings and other features may survive. Crops growing on well-drained lowland soils can reveal the shapes and positions of these buried remains in dry summers. Cropmarks occur when plants growing over old ditches or postholes respond to the more fertile, damp soil and nutrients they retain, growing taller, thicker and greener. Conversely, those growing over buried stonework and walling will quickly ripen and turn yellow or parch in response to the shallow soil and lack of nutrients. These differences in growth revealed between the months of May and August are

little relation to what we now understand about the long development of the Welsh landscape. The extent and character of the buried prehistoric settlement is often not appreciated. Archaeological aerial reconnaissance, coupled with ground-based investigation, has long been a major force for change, pushing forward our understanding of how

Figure 26 (above). This defended prehistoric farmstead at Myrtle Grove, Cresselly, is one of many in the fertile farmland between the Daugleddau Estuary and the coast at Tenby. The red plough soil reveals the stony material of the buried rampart spread by the plough, and the darker circle of the prehistoric defensive ditch. Other darker patches nearby may represent worn trackways approaching the fort, or areas of formerly boggy ground (RCAHMW, 95-cs-1366).

Figure 27 (right). Getting the timing right. These two views show the prehistoric concentric farmstead near Brechfa, east of Penffordd. At top right in 1990 an experienced aerial archaeologist might just have spotted the semi-circular cropmark in the centre of the field, and the faint positive cropmarks in the adjacent field. Returning during the dry summer of 1992 (bottom, right), with both fields put down to the same, responsive arable crop, a stunning cropmark reveals both the inner settled enclosure, where the round houses may have stood, and the outer enclosure, which probably formed a corral (RCAHMW; top image, DI2006-0555; bottom image, 905528-12).

best seen from the air. Prolonged droughts may reveal buried sites which have never previously shown, and years of crop rotation or summer rain may render them invisible for a decade or more. Once harvested, the physical mark in the crop vanishes, so aerial photographers must race through a four- to six-week window of opportunity to capture the crucial images.

Sites may also show from the air as soilmarks after fields are ploughed in the autumn and spring. Wall footings, road surfaces or hillfort ramparts will be caught by the plough, leaving visible stony scatters in the topsoil; damper soil from buried ditches will show as dark lines. Soilmarks can vividly show the outline of buried forts or buildings after ploughing, but they are essentially records of the ongoing destruction of a site as features become ever more dispersed in the plough-soil.

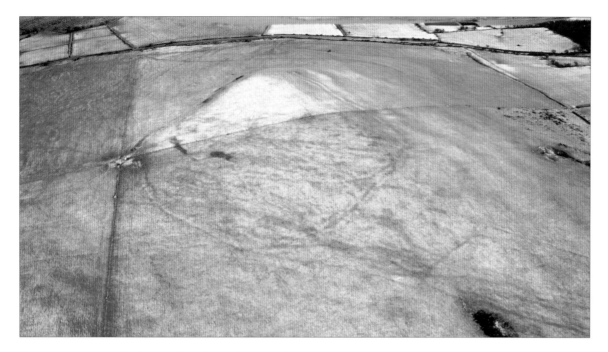

Figure 28 (left). Banc Du Neolithic enclosure, above New Inn in Mynydd Preseli, with a light dusting of snow highlighting very slight remains of its intermittent ramparts and ditches (RCAHMW, 2004-cs-0271).

A great many of the archaeological sites in Pembrokeshire survive as grass-covered 'lumps and bumps'. Some earthworks are prominent and well preserved, like the many medieval mottes (castle mounds) or Iron Age hillforts. Others are far less well preserved. Vestigial earthworks are best photographed under low, raking sunlight to reveal their patterns in light and shadow. During the summer months late evening shadows can provide ideal conditions, but vegetation can obscure some

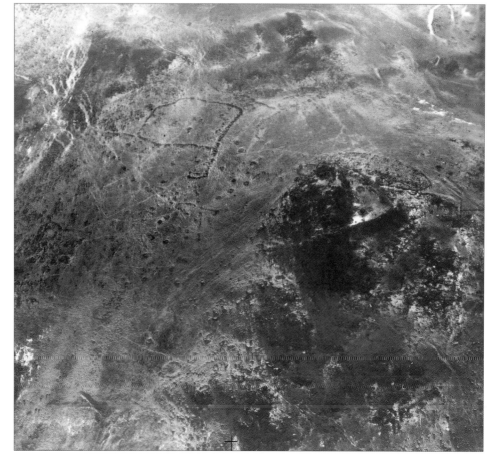

Figure 29. Carn Alw, Mynydd Preseli. The complex upland landscape which survives across Mynydd Preseli has been worked and re-worked by generations of farmers, each building fields, clearing stones into characteristic cairns, and enclosing their homes and farms with stone walls. This winter view from January 1970 with a dusting of snow on the higher ground shows all these features particularly well, along with the small fort of Carn Alw which clings to a triangular crag, centre-right. A similar view in the height of summer, with flat light, would show far less of this striking ancient landscape (Copyright reserved Cambridge University Collection of Air Photographs, BAM 063, DI2006-0033).

Figure 30. Getting the right light: two views of the late-seventeenth-century historic garden earthworks at Landshipping on the Daugleddau estuary; the garden is comprised of terraces, raised walks, ponds and former planting beds. Both views were taken in low winter light with low vegetation and bare trees to maximise the visibility of the earthworks. However, in the top view taken in 1993 the light shines along the main earthworks, casting few useful shadows. In the bottom view taken in 1995 low light strikes across the garden, throwing surviving earthworks into sharp relief. The contrast is dramatic. In the centre of the lower view even rows of small mounds, thought to be the former sites of fruit trees, are visible in the grass (RCAHMW, 93-cs-0217 and 95-cs-1275).

detail. During winter, especially after the first fall of snow, grass and bracken are low and many upland earthworks can be photographed with breathtaking clarity. The outlines of very faint earthworks become much clearer from the air if photographed in sharp frost or under a light dusting of wind-blown snow. In Wales the amount of new discoveries made during earthwork recording in the hills and mountains is comparable in number to the summer discoveries of cropmarks in lower-lying areas.

Without the addition of these aerial discoveries our understanding of the nature and extent of early settlement in Pembrokeshire, and the rest of Wales, would be severely limited. This is also the case across Britain and Europe. Taken together, the landscape contains rich evidence for thousands of years of human endeavour, and aerial photography remains one of the key ways for re-discovering this evidence. Only when we know an archaeological site exists can we take steps to record or preserve it, so that future generations may learn something of the history and development of the landscape they inherit.

Figure 31 (above). Seeing through the water: a submerged pile-built structure on a sand bank in Sandy Haven Pill, just west of Herbrandston, with a moored catamaran for scale. The two parallel lines of piles, with multiple re-builds at one end, may be the remains of an old jetty but their exact date and function remain a mystery (RCAHMW, 2002-cs-0787).

Figure 32. Captured in the extremely dry summer of 1975, this cropmark enclosure (dark circle, centre) lies south of Islands Farm, nearly 3km north-east of St Florence in south Pembrokeshire (at SN 102 030). It is probably an Iron Age defended farm with a short 'antenna' entrance corridor formalising the approach on the far side. The parching of the grassland is so severe that curving bands of subsurface geology can be seen snaking across the fields, partly masking the archaeology (Copyright reserved Cambridge University Collection of Air Photographs, BTQ 006, 2 July 1975, DI2006-0038).

Figure 33 (above). Looking remarkably like the cropmark of a circular barrow or ditched enclosure, with a rectangular enclosure nearby, these are marks caused by dressage exercises. Repeated riding of the same circuits has compacted the ground in a stubble field, encouraging lush grass growth after rain. This example was photographed near Aberporth in Ceredigion (RCAHMW, DI2006-0568).

Figure 34. Aerial archaeologists learn to look for characteristic shapes in the landscape, and these oval depressions close to Pentre Ifan Neolithic burial chamber, with their central 'mounds' and outer 'ditches', could be interpreted as burial mounds, especially if photographed under grass. However, the culprit is still in shot: a movable, oval cattle feeder. When in position it will leave a central mound while cattle wear away a ditch around it. These marks may remain in pasture for months, or even years (RCAHMW, DI2006-0563).

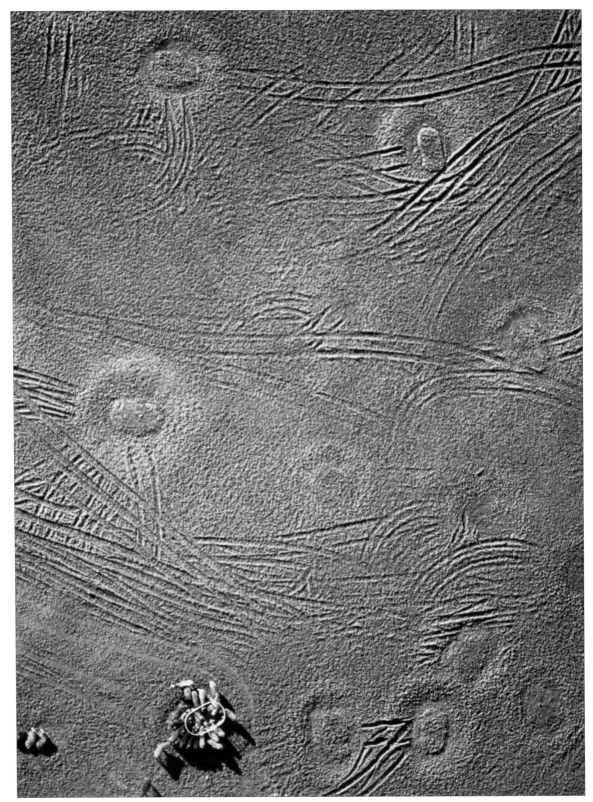

The value of an aerial photograph showing a new archaeological site has not been fully realised until it has been interpreted and mapped. Aerial photographs can be difficult for the non-specialist to interpret, and when planning ground fieldwork, such as an excavation, it is useful to have an accurate plan to work from.

For these reasons mapping archaeology from air photographs is an essential task. It is easy to make the case for mapping cropmarks, because there is usually little surviving at ground level to show where the buried site is. However, mapping earthworks can also be rewarding: a well preserved upland landscape of field boundaries, clearance cairns and house sites (seen for example at Carn Alw) may have been well visited by archaeologists over the years, or even partially surveyed in the field, but detailed air photo mapping will often discover vestigial elements almost invisible at ground level. These could include relict plough ridges or old field boundaries which may be obscured by tussocky grass. Crucially, working from vertical air photographs from 60 years ago, one may be able to map early field systems or archaeological earthworks since lost to agricultural improvement, forestry or development.

Transferring a plan from a distorted oblique view to a scaled map used to be achieved by drawing a geometric grid or 'mobius network' on clear film over the photo. This was then transferred to a paper map, and the archaeological detail could be copied from one to the other. Since the early 1990s computer rectification programmes have been the standard method. The Royal Commission began its programme of archaeological air photo mapping in

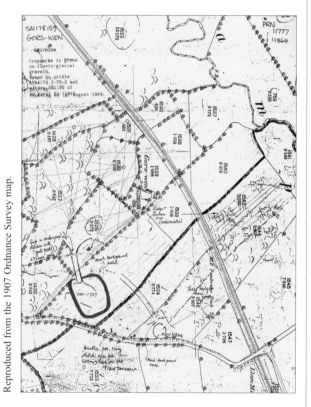

Figure 35 (above). Mapping aerial archaeology the traditional way. Cropmarks of a concentric antenna enclosure, or Iron Age farmstead, near Gors Wen farm between Lampeter Velfrey and Whitland. The site was discovered during aerial reconnaissance by Terry James in 1984 and mapped by hand using a mobius network, first constructed on the oblique aerial photograph, then transferred to a paper map with annotation. The plan of the cropmark was finally drawn up with an accuracy of between 3-5 metres (Courtesy of Terry James).

Figure 36 (below). Mapping aerial archaeology: the oblique aerial photograph shows a prehistoric enclosure at Glancleddau, west of Llandissilio in eastern Pembrokeshire. Key 'control points', like field intersections, visible both on the air photo and the digital map, are first identified. A specialist computer programme then stretches the entire photograph to accurately fit the map. By drawing over the archaeology on-screen (here in red) and then deleting the photograph, an accurate ground plan of the buried archaeology is produced (RCAHMW, 905528-18).

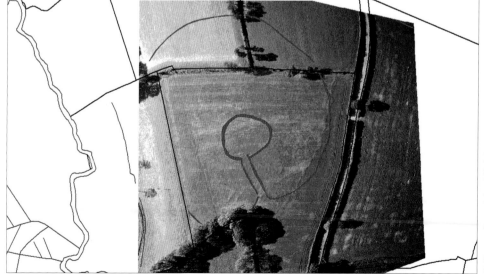

Figure 37 (right). Mapping upstanding archaeological remains from aerial photographs. Part of Carn-ingli common immediately south of Newport (at SN 057 378), showing a concentric prehistoric homestead with a recent stone-built sheepfold at the centre, surrounded by rectangular field boundaries and circular clearance cairns, where stone has been gathered into piles to improve the pasture for early agriculture (RCAHMW, DI2006-0560).

Figure 38 (below). The same part of Carn-ingli common, viewed from the north-west with the concentric homestead right of centre and Carn-ingli hillfort in the background. (View created by RCAHMW from Ordnance Survey Land-Form data).

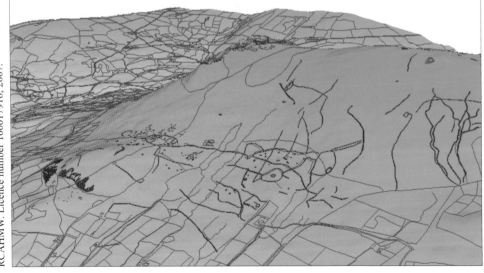

Wales in 1995 and led the way in its use of Ordnance Survey digital data. Today, air photo mapping continues to advance across Wales, giving a new understanding and comprehensive overview of its preserved or buried ancient landscapes. More recent integration of 'digital terrain models', which allow the map-maker to drape an air photograph over a virtual computer model of a hill or slope, has made the plans even more accurate.

Mapping of the Banc Du enclosure (*see* Chapter 5) by Tom Pert gave the project team of the Strumble-Preseli Ancient Communities and Environment Study (SPACES) the first accurate plan of this Neolithic hilltop enclosure. When they subsequently came to undertake centimetre-accurate ground remote sensing over the whole site to discover its buried plan, they found that the air photo map had been accurate across the site to one metre. The air photo mapping may take one or two hours for the whole site, whereas a full ground survey may take several days to complete.

Air photo mapping is used across Britain and Europe as a standard method of national archaeological survey, although it does not receive as much publicity as other, more high profile, survey programmes. The National Mapping Programme (NMP) in England is an ambitious air photo mapping project which commenced in the 1980s with a long-term aim of mapping all archaeological sites visible on aerial photographs. By 2005 32% of England had been covered. Similar programmes of air photo mapping are carried out by the Royal Commissions in Wales and Scotland. The interpretation of the photographs to produce such maps takes skill and experience, for example to separate artificial, man-made ditches from those caused by natural geological markings or recent field drains, or to separate the vestigial marks of Bronze Age round barrows from the foundations for circular searchlight batteries of the Second World War.

Figure 39. Charting change through repeated aerial photography at Bulliber Camp, Castlemartin Range. Overflying Scheduled Ancient Monuments (SAMs) across Wales at least every four to five years allows the Royal Commission to document changes to these nationally important monuments. A good example is demonstrated here. The top image shows the fort in March 1991. The foreground ramparts are relatively clear of vegetation; however, bracken and scrub have grown to obscure the eastern (left) and south (rear) ramparts. A recent programme of scrub clearance by Defence Estates has cleared this thick vegetation from most of the Iron Age ramparts, allowing them to be seen again (bottom, 2005). In these two views the results can be quickly compared and contrasted (RCAHMW, DI2006-0567; AP-2005-2645).

Figure 40. One fort, two fields. An aerial photograph is the perfect way to document the effects of differing land-use on the same monument. Woodland Rath, south of Broadhaven, is a prehistoric promontory fort built over two millennia ago which has been incorporated in the farming landscape with the construction of a substantial field bank, dividing it in two. In this view taken in spring 1991 lush improved grassland in the bottom half of the fort contrasts with worn grassland in the top (RCAHMW, DI2006-0557).

Figure 41. Making the buried past visible. Not in Wales but Austria; the plough-levelled Neolithic henge monument at Puch, lower Austria, was first discovered in 1981 from analysis of vertical aerial photographs at the Vienna Institute of Prehistory. The site was then surveyed using ground-based remote sensing equipment, resulting in a detailed picture of the buried ditches and palisade trenches. A final, innovative, stage was to work with the local community to mark out the site of the buried monument on the ground and then plant it in contrasting crops. When this was done, local people and school parties could clearly see this once lost site, exploring it on the ground for the first time in millennia. Similar initiatives in Wales could work well to show communities the places where their local prehistoric monuments have been long lost to the plough (Copyright: Aerial Archive, Institute for Pre- and Early History, University of Vienna).

DOCUMENTING PEMBROKESHIRE'S CHANGING LANDSCAPE

Pembrokeshire is constantly changing. Buildings, industrial structures, villages and townscapes have always formed key subjects for the Royal Commission's aerial photographers. One of the great strengths of the aerial perspective is its ability to bring coherence to complex patterns of buildings or structures which may be difficult or time-consuming to record at ground level. New roads, out-of-town superstores or housing developments can also have a tremendous impact on the overall shape and character of a community. Views of present-day Pembrokeshire, in all its urban, industrial and domestic variety, can be found throughout this book alongside more traditional archaeological and historical scenes.

Figure 42. Concentric housing development with a central green at Glebelands, Hubberston, Milford Haven (RCAHMW, DI2006-0564).

Figure 43. A sinuous pattern of slip roads serving a roundabout at Haverfordwest, captured in a near-vertical view (RCAHMW, DI2006-0549).

CHAPTER TWO

THE STORY OF PEMBROKESHIRE

Situated in the far south-west of Wales, at the southern end of the broad sweep of Cardigan Bay, Pembrokeshire looks west across St George's Channel and the Irish Sea. The county has a long history of greeting travellers, saints and merchants, and repelling or assimilating intermittent invaders. To historic seafarers the twin peninsulas of Pembrokeshire and Cornwall guided vessels into the mouth of the Bristol Channel. The changing coastline was at the same time full of inviting landing places and treacherous cliffs. Coves and beaches offered impromptu harbours, while the larger ports like Fishguard and Milford Haven continue to offer some of the best harbourage in the Irish Sea.

The west coast has its islands, among them Skomer and Ramsey, and the settlements which line the cliffs have weathered their share of winter storms. The north-west peninsula is Dewisland, where fertile farmland is fringed by a wild coastline. Less intensively farmed tracts of moorland at the western tip on St David's Head preserve rich remains of prehistoric fields and settlements. Similar ancient landscapes are found to the east across Pencaer/Strumble Head, Mynydd Carningli, the flanks and peaks of Mynydd Preseli and out to the islands of Skomer and Ramsey. At lower altitudes the moorland gives way to enclosed farmland, criss-crossed by deep, winding lanes and interspersed with small villages and farms. The agricultural land is predominantly set down to pasture for grazing.

Figure 44 (left). Pembroke Castle, formidable stronghold of parliamentary resistance in Pembrokeshire for the duration of the Civil War (RCAHMW, 915508-2).

Figure 45 (right). The fractured southern coastline of Rumsey Island, looking north across Ynys Cantwr to the island landscape beyond. The scale of the coastal scenery dwarfs an approaching speedboat (RCAHMW, DI2006-0520).

27

Figure 46 (above). The spire of St John the Baptist's church, Slebech (centre), east of Haverfordwest, rising from a central Pembrokeshire landscape beset by thick fog on a cold April morning in 2002 (RCAHMW, DI2006-0343).

Figure 47 (right). The old and the new; looking across south-west Pembrokeshire, from Roman's Castle Iron Age fort at Walwyn's Castle, in the foreground, to the Amoco oil refinery (RCAHMW, DI2006-0595).

To the south, the landscape within commuting distance of the towns of Haverfordwest, Pembroke Dock and Milford Haven is far more developed. Golf courses, leisure parks and dual carriageways are steadily transforming and traversing the longer-standing patterns first laid down by the Norman invaders and Flemish colonists of the Middle Ages. Modern oil refineries and historic docks fringe the deep-water port of Milford Haven, bringing heavy industry right to the heart of the Pembrokeshire Coast National Park. Nearby, Pembroke and Pembroke Dock are among the largest conurbations in west Wales and represent two distinct periods of settlement and defence of the Haven. Beyond, to the south of Pembroke, occupying the rugged coastal plateau between Castlemartin and Stackpole, is the Castlemartin range, used for tank and artillery training since 1938. In a juxtaposition typical of Pembrokeshire, grand medieval farm buildings and an early hermit's chapel stand close to abandoned tanks, shooting ranges and shell craters.

Although much is made of Pembrokeshire's natural landscapes, few corners of this westerly county have escaped intervention by man. Successive generations have sought to divide and own the land and all have left traces of their activities. The cliffs and islands are held by many as the best examples of Pembrokeshire's wilderness areas, constantly eroding and difficult of access. But even in these remote corners one is never far from forts, quarries, once-thriving farming settlements and flints worked by prehistoric peoples, often eroded on to the coastal path from buried land surfaces. Mountains and upland moor display from the air a continuation of the activity seen at lower altitudes; isolated standing stones, hillforts, quarries and wider-spreading patterns of trackways, peat-cutting and ridge-and-furrow cultivation. Farming from medieval times onwards, but most damagingly since the end of the Second World War, has eroded or buried these accumulated patterns of people's activities in the lowlands. With upland pasture improvement, seasonal ploughing and wholesale stone removal for land clearance, fragile traces of our past continue to

Figure 48. The triangular Iron Age fort at Carn Alw (centre), on the northern side of Mynydd Preseli, is dwarfed by its own dramatic shadow cast late on a summer's evening in July 1990 (RCAHMW, 90-cs-0604).

disappear. Initially upstanding foundations, walls and banks are reduced to earthworks which are still visible at ground level, but continuing erosion denudes earthworks still further, until they become imperceptible banks and hollows. Ultimately a site may be entirely levelled, but in the right conditions of lighting and season the aerial archaeologist can rediscover them.

THE ROCKS OF PEMBROKESHIRE

The 'geologist's paradise' (T. R. Owen) which is Pembrokeshire has attracted attention and speculation since George Owen's early descriptions in the seventeenth century. In a comparatively small region great swathes of geological history occur in close, near-parallel bands. Although all of

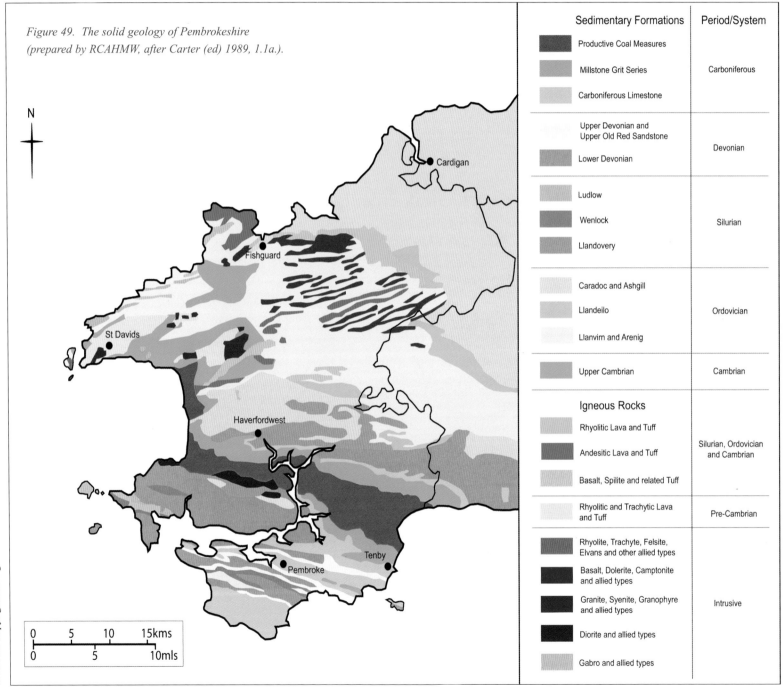

Figure 49. The solid geology of Pembrokeshire (prepared by RCAHMW, after Carter (ed) 1989, 1.1a.).

Sedimentary Formations	Period/System
Productive Coal Measures	
Millstone Grit Series	Carboniferous
Carboniferous Limestone	
Upper Devonian and Upper Old Red Sandstone	Devonian
Lower Devonian	
Ludlow	
Wenlock	Silurian
Llandovery	
Caradoc and Ashgill	
Llandeilo	Ordovician
Llanvirn and Arenig	
Upper Cambrian	Cambrian

Igneous Rocks	
Rhyolitic Lava and Tuff	
Andesitic Lava and Tuff	Silurian, Ordovician and Cambrian
Basalt, Spilite and related Tuff	
Rhyolitic and Trachytic Lava and Tuff	Pre-Cambrian
Rhyolite, Trachyte, Felsite, Elvans and other allied types	
Basalt, Dolerite, Camptonite and allied types	
Granite, Syenite, Granophyre and allied types	Intrusive
Diorite and allied types	
Gabro and allied types	

Pembrokeshire's geology was formed more than 295 million years ago, and belongs to the Palaeozoic era, the northern province is older still, with the rocks formed more than 395 million years ago. To the south of a line between Druidston on St Brides Bay in the west and Tavernspite in the east on the border with Carmarthenshire, the rocks are generally younger than 395 million years. The differential resilience of neighbouring bands of rock has allowed the sea to cut deep bays and inlets or to leave protruding headlands around the coastline, whilst thousands of years of weathering and erosion inland have left more resilient outcrops exposed across the northern region above the softer rocks.

The oldest rocks in the county belong to the Pre-Cambrian 'Pebidian' era and were formed about 1,000 million years ago. These occur in two main blocks in the north-west of the county between St David's Head and Wolf's Castle, and are also found in a restricted southern band running west between

Figure 50. Pre-Cambrian headlands of St David's Head, dominated by the steep igneous gabbro outcrops of Carn Llidi, with Ramsey Island and Grassholm beyond (RCAHMW, DI2006-0590).

Benton on the Daugleddau and Talbenny at the foot of St Brides Bay, surrounded by much younger rocks. The Pre-Cambrian rocks can be seen most spectacularly in the cliff exposures west of St Davids, along Ramsey Sound. The remainder of the northern province of Pembrokeshire, which includes the lowlands north of Haverfordwest and the higher hills around Mynydd Preseli and Mynydd Carn-ingli, is formed predominantly of Ordovician sedimentary rocks, the shale slabs and flagstones being used extensively for building in the region. These sedimentary rocks are broken by Ordovician igneous intrusions, such as dolerite, across north Pembrokeshire, and the different qualities of these bands of igneous and sedimentary rocks have helped to shape the cliffs and deep inlets of Pen-caer/Strumble Head and the north-west coastline. The shattered, exposed forms of the igneous intrusions can be seen as outcrops and crags all along the north coast, east from Carn Llidi on St David's Head to Pen-caer/Strumble Head, Mynydd Carn-ingli, and culminating in the famous weathered 'bluestone' outcrops of dolerite and rhyolite along the Preseli ridge.

Figure 51 (top). Gateholm Island, looking north-west to Wooltack Point with Skomer Island beyond. This early Cambridge University aerial photograph, taken on 30 June 1949, shows the possible early monastic community on Gateholm Island, marked by a patch of mist, as well as the patterns of Silurian sedimentary rocks in the cliffs (original photography held at Cambridge University Collection of Air Photographs, Unit for Landscape Modelling, CY67, DI2006-0041).

Figure 52 (left). Along the north coast between St David's Head and Pen-caer/Strumble Head: a common pattern of alternating resistant headlands of Ordovician intrusive rocks, with intervening bays eroded into softer Ordovician shales. This view is west of Porthgain at Ynys Barry, with Traeth Llyfn in the foreground and the bays of Porth Egr and Porth Dwfn beyond. The foreground promontory of Porth Egr is home to an Iron Age fort (RCAHMW, 2000/5505-12).

The rocks of the southern half of Pembrokeshire are generally younger and less resilient than those of the north, being largely sedimentary, but with exceptions in the Silurian igneous intrusions which form Skomer Island and continue east on the mainland to Dale. The geology of the southern province is dominated by three main bands of rocks: the Devonian Old Red Sandstone and the Carboniferous coal measures and limestone. The coal measures form much of the west coast of St Brides Bay and cross mid- and south Pembrokeshire in a broad band eastwards through the confluence of the West and East Cleddau on the Daugleddau estuary, continuing to the coast at Saundersfoot. These measures are the westernmost extension of the South Wales Coalfield and were exploited from at least the medieval period, providing for a healthy export trade in anthracite. From an aerial perspective the more southerly band of Old Red Sandstone dominates the landscape from St Brides and Dale in the west, across the Milford Haven waterway and east to cliff exposures around Manorbier, south Caldy and to the north of Tenby. The deep reds of the sandstone bands, notably the lowest formation of the Red Marls, add variable colours to the promontory forts and coastal defences around the Haven and show inland in newly ploughed soils. The landscape of this Old Red Sandstone region is low-lying, varied in topography and agriculturally productive. The Carboniferous Limestone occurs in the southernmost parts of Pembrokeshire, in successive bands to the east of Milford Haven, but most notably along the south coast forming much of the windswept plateau of the Castlemartin peninsula. The spectacular limestone coastal scenery, with its whitish-yellow vertical cliffs, isolated stacks and the natural arch of the Green Bridge of Wales, is justly famous and contrasts with the darker, more rugged cliffs and inlets along northern coasts.

Figure 53. Cliffs exposing Old Red Sandstone at Little Castle Point, with its promontory fort centre left, looking north-west (RCAHMW, DI2006-0594).

Figure 54. Fertile soils on Old Red Sandstone in south Pembrokeshire, near Great Nash, west of Llangwm (RCAHMW, DI2006-0592).

Figure 55. Old Red Sandstone cliffs at Greenala Point promontory fort, from the south-west, between Freshwater East and Stackpole Quay in south Pembrokeshire (RCAHMW, DI2006-0342).

Figure 56 (above). Eroding Carboniferous Limestone strata in the westernmost cliffs of St Margaret's Island, west of Caldy (RCAHMW, DI2006-0350).

Figure 57 (left). In 1811 Richard Fenton described St David's Head thus: 'The immediate head, called by the old geographers Octopitarum, here projects itself into the ocean, formidably broken and convulsed, and, as it were, defying the element that rages round it.' (RCAHMW, DI2006-0518).

EARLY HUNTERS ALONG THE PEMBROKESHIRE COAST

The story of human settlement in Pembrokeshire can be traced back many tens of thousands of years to the Early Upper Palaeolithic period (*c*.38,000-23,000 BC), when early humans still hunted for survival. Discoveries of tools, animal bones and occasional burials from caves tell us something about these early people, although they were not necessarily all cave-dwellers. Successive glaciations of Wales, the most recent between 20,000 and 18,000 BC, saw vast ice sheets scouring and shaping the solid geology. In archaeological terms this 'wiped clean' the pre-

existing record of human settlement, except where traces were preserved in deep caves like Pontnewydd in north-east Wales (dating back to the early Neanderthals, *c*.250,000 BC), or in those areas which stayed free of ice in south Pembrokeshire, south Gower, and parts of the Vale of Glamorgan.

In Pembrokeshire, caves like Hoyle's Mouth (*c*.38,000-23,000 BC) have provided the principal evidence of settlement, with bones of bear, horse, deer and hyena and flint tools found during numerous excavations between 1840 and 1990. Caldy Island

Figure 58. Nanna's Cave (centre) is set in dramatic sea cliffs on the north-east tip of Caldy Island and was explored by Brother James of Caldy. Originally, sea levels would have been far lower with the bulk of the water suspended in glacial ice. The Caldy caves would once have been situated on the edge of a hill, rising above the dry plain of the Bristol Channel. (RCAHMW, AP-2006-0151).

has three early caves of interest, with occupation dating back to the Late Glacial (*c*.12,000 BC). Following the retreat of the last glacial ice, nomadic bands of Middle Stone Age or Mesolithic hunter-gatherers recolonised the warming land, between *c*.8,000 BC and 5,000 BC. Sea levels were low and Britain was joined to the continent by a 'land bridge' until *c*.5,000 BC. A thick forest of pine and oak extended many miles into Cardigan Bay and Carmarthen Bay, the remnants of which are still visible as 'submerged forests' in peat exposures along coasts and estuaries. Mesolithic (*c*.8,000-5,000 BC) people left no visible monuments, but traces of their hunting camps are sometimes found. One of the most famous is The Nab Head, where Mesolithic hunters manufactured microliths, or miniature flint tools, along with larger axes. Very early craft objects include over 500 perforated shale beads and a carved shale object. This artefact is thought to be the only such carving from a Mesolithic context in Britain and may represent a Venus figurine or a phallus.

Figure 59. The Nab Head promontory, just north-west of St Brides, where Mesolithic flint tools were manufactured over 7,000 years ago (RCAHMW, DI-2006-0613).

MONUMENTS TO THE FIRST FARMERS

The gradual introduction of cereal farming from Europe around 4,500 BC changed the course of human history and forged the beginnings of complex societies. The Neolithic (*c.*4,500-2,500 BC) or New Stone Age period was a dynamic time. The growth of crops, and their harvesting and storage, meant that for substantial parts of the farming year people were not directly involved with food production. This freed time for craft activities and tool production, and encouraged communities to work together for the creation of megalithic tombs formed of massive stone slabs. A more settled way of life with villages, fields and communal tombs no doubt helped to crystallise emerging ideas of territory, land ownership and the importance of ancestors and homelands.

Stone chambered tombs (burial chambers; dolmens) date from the Early Neolithic (*c.*4,500-3,500 BC) and are the oldest standing structures to survive in Europe. Built from large stones, or megaliths, to hold the collected bones of generations, and usually covered by long or round cairns of stone, it is thought they were sited to look out over homelands and to ensure dead ancestors brought fertility and prosperity to the land. Along the Gwaun Valley in the north of Pembrokeshire is found a characteristic group of Portal Dolmens which includes the towering Pentre Ifan burial chamber. It is thought that these tombs, overlooking good landing places from the sea close to Newport, may have been built by incoming Irish settlers, although new ideas from overseas may have influenced indigenous populations. Other types

Figure 60 (bottom, left). Pentre Ifan Neolithic burial chamber, with its surviving long cairn, seen surrounded by sheep on a July evening in 1996 (RCAHMW, DI2006-0620).

Figure 61. Pentre Ifan (below): The massive, yet elegantly perched, capstone has attracted visitors and speculation for many centuries. It would once have been entirely covered in a long cairn of stones (RCAHMW, CD2005-602-011).

Figure 62. Cerrig y Gof, Newport. The unusual circular cairn with its five stone chambers commands sea views across Newport Bay to the north and is a rewarding site to visit, together with a cup-marked rock in the same field. Today it survives alongside the main A487 road between Dinas Cross and Newport (RCAHMW, DI2006-0601).

of burial chamber exist in Pembrokeshire, including ruined passage graves, like the impressive remains of Carreg Samson on the north coast, and unusual multi-chambered round cairns such as Cerrig y Gof near Newport, and also sub-megalithic-style tombs formed from natural slabs propped up on other stones, usually in the lee of a shattered outcrop like those on Carn Llidi.

Whilst ritual and burial monuments dominate the landscape of the Neolithic and Bronze Ages, the houses of the day are by contrast rarely discovered. Until recently only one settlement site in Pembrokeshire, Clegyr Boia, had been dated to the Neolithic period. In 2006 radiocarbon dates were obtained for the Banc Du enclosure in Mynydd Preseli, first discovered from the air. They confirmed it was also Neolithic, and provided the first dated settlement in these hills where Neolithic burial monuments are common (see Chapter 5). Other research (Vyner 2001) has suggested that many of the large, stone-built hillforts of the north Pembrokeshire

coast whose walls are made of substantial boulders may have their origins in the Neolithic, rather than the much later Iron Age.

As Wales entered the Late Neolithic (c.2900-2500 BC) religion and ways of life changed. Chambered tombs were either deliberately blocked or fell into disrepair, and changes in society are indicated by new pottery fabrics which came to be used in the home, as well as by new ritual and burial practices. The first new pottery type is termed Peterborough Ware, a decorated type quite different from earlier, plainer Neolithic 'bowls' but still made with round bottoms and thus suitable for placing in fires for cooking, or resting on a floor with a stand. Further advances in society are implied by the appearance of Grooved Ware around 2700 BC, the flat-bottomed vessels adorned with striking grooves and surface patterns. The appearance of pottery with flat bottoms may also indicate a new prevalence of furniture and tables within houses. Certainly this new pottery is associated with the rise of 'open' monuments, such as stone circles and timber circles, and the appearance of major late Neolithic 'henge' monuments, large enclosures defined by banks and ditches. Although stone passage graves were still being built at this time, the major shift in ritual practices was towards more public, less 'closed' or private, monuments, where many people could gather to observe ceremonies in the open air. Gors Fawr stone circle south of Mynydd Preseli is one of the best preserved of its type in Wales and has probably changed little in appearance in over 4,000 years. Another unusual, and comparatively rare, monument in Pembrokeshire which dates from this transitional time between the Late Neolithic and Early Bronze Age is the pit circle at Withybush, near Haverfordwest. This perfect circle of nearly 30 pits probably dates from 3,000-1,500 BC and could represent the foundations of a once impressive monument of upright timbers or stones (see Chapter 6).

Figure 63. Clegyr Boia Neolithic settlement, from the north-west, occupying a low outcrop between St Davids and the west coast (RCAHMW, DI2006-0584).

METAL WORKERS OF THE BRONZE AGE

Figure 64. The Ridgeway, seen here near Sunny Hill Farm in 1997, looking north-west towards the Daugleddau. This route, which follows the high ground west of Penally towards Pembroke, is thought to have prehistoric origins and is flanked by a number of Bronze Age barrows, (RCAHMW, DI2006-0359).

The considerable changes in society which are indicated by the new types of public monuments and new pottery vessels of the Late Neolithic continue into what archaeologists have termed the Bronze Age. In the Early Bronze Age (*c.*2,500-1,400 BC) new types of burial and ritual monuments appear in the Welsh landscape: cairns (circular mounds of stone) and barrows (circular mounds of earth) were types of funerary monument built to cover single or multiple cremation burials or inhumations (whole-body burials). Stone and timber circles also continued to be built in open, level areas and may have been used for community festivals, trading or religious ceremonies. Standing stones were erected during the Early Bronze Age and remain the most enigmatic types of prehistoric monument in the country. Whilst some may have been simple boundary markers or wayside monuments, others occasionally marked burials or stood at the centre of wider ritual structures of stone settings and buildings, as was revealed by excavations in the 1960s at the Rhos y Clegyrn standing stone on Pen-caer/Strumble Head. Excavations by the Dyfed Archaeological Trust at the Stackpole Warren standing stone also revealed an

Figure 65. A stone kerb encircles the round cairn of Garn Ochr/Dyffryn Stones (SN 059 284), between Henry's Moat and Rosebush on the southern flanks of Mynydd Preseli. Here the detail of a ground view is contrasted with the overview offered from the air, showing the cairn in its modern farmland setting (ground view, RCAHMW, DI2006-0597; aerial photograph; RCAHMW, DI2006-0586).

extensive complex. The monument was preceded by a timber structure, possibly a Bronze Age house, with the stone then erected along with another setting of timbers, surrounded by a fan-shaped setting of over 3,000 pitched stones (Fig. 280).

New styles of pottery were introduced to Britain with their origins in European traditions. Most importantly, perhaps, a knowledge of metal-working was evident for the first time. The Beaker period (*c*.2,700-1,700 BC), straddling the end of the

Figure 66. Gors Fawr stone circle, south-west of Mynachlog-ddu, looks out over heathland and bog (RCAHMW, DI2006-0615).

Figure 67. Snow-covered Bronze Age cairns on Foel Cwmcerwyn, a ridge extending to the south of Mynydd Preseli overlooking Rosebush village (RCAHMW, DI2006-0602).

Neolithic and the beginning of the Bronze Age, was a cultural phenomenon bringing with it new ideas of burial practices, metal-working, wealth and power from abroad. Beakers themselves were highly decorated, delicate pottery vessels, often bearing thousands of impressions on their surface in complex patterns and thought to have taken many days to make. They were radically different from the more bulky, functional domestic vessels which preceded them. It was once thought that the Beaker period represented an invasion from the European heartland of warrior archers, frequently found buried with a uniform 'artefact package', which included characteristic highly decorated 'beaker' urns, new barbed and tanged arrowheads, wristguards to protect the archer from the recoil of the bow string, and also bronze or copper-alloy daggers. Some writers have even argued that the barbs on the new arrowheads may have been designed specifically to kill other humans in combat. The Beaker culture, however, appeared not to bring any new monuments with it or signal any great changes to the economy of later prehistoric Britain. Therefore, the new people who arrived with their new beliefs may have been assimilated into British culture, rather than radically altering it.

In the Middle to Late Bronze Age (*c.*1,400-700 BC), while the familiar monuments of stone circles, cairns and barrows ceased to be built, few characteristic, visible monuments emerged to take their place. This was a time of growing populations and more intensive land-use, in which farms were established with clear territories and boundaries. Finds of swords, shields, axe heads and daggers appear to show a society increasingly bent on aggression and conflict, no doubt spurred on by population pressure and a desire to defend 'homelands'. Towards the end of the Late Bronze Age and at the beginning of the Iron Age it also

Figure 68. Remains of stone-walled enclosures, huts and straggling field boundaries on Bernard's Well Mountain, immediately south-west of Rosebush Reservoir in Mynydd Preseli. Although undated, there is the possibility that some of the enclosures represent Bronze Age upland settlement (RCAHMW, DI2006-0610).

appears that the climate deteriorated. The clearance of Wales's rich tree-cover probably began before Neolithic times, accelerating into the Bronze Age as the population expanded. The act of burning and clearing exposed fragile soils to the elements, increasing soil moisture and starting the growth of blanket peats. The weather was also becoming cooler and wetter. Established narratives describe this time as one of famine and growing social unease, with upland, inland communities leaving their homesteads and moving to the lowland peripheries in Wales, such as the Welsh borderlands and parts of coastal Pembrokeshire. However, it is difficult to be sure whether the heartlands of Wales would have been dramatically abandoned in the face of this climatic deterioration. The picture of surviving settlement and farming activity around the peripheries of the Welsh uplands during this Late Bronze Age/early Iron Age transition could reflect the extent of early settlement; however, it is as likely to have arisen from an historical pattern of excavation focused on more

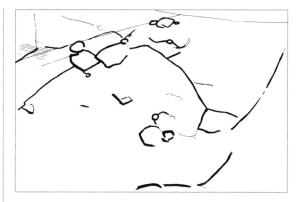

archaeologically attractive or productive regions. Future excavation at transitional sites in the heart of the mid-Wales hills may reveal better information about how later prehistoric communities 'rode out' the climatic storm. As the Late Bronze Age ended and the Iron Age began, charismatic leaders emerged, strong enough to unite growing groups of people and establish new defended homes and territories in the Welsh landscape.

Figure 69. Castell Mawr, a concentric hillfort commanding a level hilltop south of the main road between Eglwyswrw and Felindre-Farchog, just over a kilometre south of Castell Henllys. The interior is subdivided by an angled bank, suggesting more than one phase of occupation and alteration. An Iron Age promontory fort, Cwm-pen-y-benglog, can be seen beyond to the south. (RCAHMW, DI2006-0611).

Figure 70. Caer Penpicas, an Iron Age promontory fort lying immediately west of Trecwn in north Pembrokeshire. April sunlight highlights the low earthworks of prehistoric fields, or even a second defended enclosure, in the pasture beyond the fort (RCAHMW, DI2006-0607).

Before the Iron Age ritual and burial monuments formed the most visible features in the prehistoric landscape. In the Iron Age the situation was entirely reversed, with defended farmsteads and hillforts dominating the landscape, and burial and ritual sites all but absent.

The Iron Age saw a rise in the number of hillforts, usually heavily-defended hilltop enclosures with encircling stone ramparts topped with timber palisades and entered via well-defended gateways. Inside there were thatched round houses, store rooms, smithies and feasting areas. It was once believed that hillforts were built by invading immigrants to Britain, the earliest being constructed in southern England close to the Channel crossing, with later hillforts spreading out to the rest of England and Wales. We now know that hillforts were indigenous creations, although the long-term development of pre-Roman cultures was no doubt informed by developments in mainland Europe. Some hillforts were built during the later Bronze Age (*c.*900 BC),

and a handful of these are known from excavation, chiefly along the Welsh borderlands. The earliest known Pembrokeshire site is Dale fort, from the later Bronze/Early Iron Age, but a good many hilltop enclosures could be earlier. Future excavations will probably reveal early foundations at some sites, but the majority that we see were probably built in the final three centuries BC, as wealth from the land increased and particularly powerful leaders consolidated their territories.

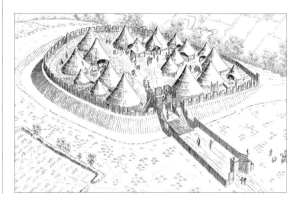

Figure 71. Reconstruction of an Iron Age hillfort at Dinas Fawr or Dinas Bran, just west of Drefach and Felindre in Carmarthenshire. It can be difficult to imagine what life was like at Iron Age forts and defended farmsteads. Today, earthworks can be quiet, overgrown places, while cropmarks can be even more difficult to interpret. Reconstructions like this one help us to imagine the bustle of everyday prehistoric life, with smoke rising from roofs and fields farmed on the surrounding hills. We can also appreciate the original complexity of the timberwork and massive gate towers which would not have been uncommon among the hillforts of south-west Wales (Neil Ludlow; © Cambria Archaeology).

Figure 72. Two hillforts of the Llawhaden group, seen from the north in low winter sunlight. Excavations have demonstrated that Broadway (foreground) was occupied in the eighth-fifth centuries BC, with Pilcornswell in a promontory position beyond occupied in the fourth-third centuries BC, with evidence for Early Bronze Age activity on the same site (RCAHMW 2003-cs-0228).

In the surrounding landscape were networks of smaller defended farmsteads and cattle corrals, linked by field systems and trackways. Where these are upstanding today they may be marked on maps as 'raths' or 'settlements' in gothic type. Many more have been ploughed away, only to be rediscovered using aerial photography from the 1960s to the present day, as this book demonstrates.

As the Iron Age progressed an emerging elite of wealthy landowners began to exert control over neighbouring smaller forts. Territories may have been formed or cemented by stronger chieftains to ensure control over land and agricultural resources. However, it is likely that these territories changed through time as successive leaders extended their networks of alliances with neighbours, raided and acquired land from their opponents, or were succeeded in power-struggles that seemed to shape Iron Age life in Britain. As chieftains died some may have passed their lands to their sons in the Celtic tradition of partible inheritance; such a practice may be visible in the landscape as close-set pairs of

Figure 73. Carn Alw: the pointed boulders and uncleared stones of the chevaux de frise, protecting the west and south sides of the hillfort. Beyond the well-defined edge of this stone defence, the surrounding moorland is relatively clear of stones (RCAHMW, 2006-cs-0024).

smaller hillforts reflecting ancestral ties, like those excavated in the Llawhaden group in the 1980s (see Chapter 6). However, the true nature of land-ownership may have been far more complex and fluctuating than a strict system of 'Celtic inheritance' would lead us to believe. Between 200 and 100 BC sophisticated 'ring forts' with elaborate defences appeared. Whilst many hillforts in Wales were abandoned during the Roman occupation, evidence suggests that ring forts in west Wales remained occupied and even prospered into Romano-British times.

The Iron Age is famously the time of the 'Celtic warrior', almost an archetypal figure of British prehistory. Much is recorded in writing by the Romans, who described the inhabitants of Wales as 'war-mad and quick to battle', usually fighting naked and daubed with blue woad tattoos. However, the Romans were skilled in political propaganda and may not have wished to describe the natives in a favourable light. Excavations at Castell Henllys revealed a cache of around 2,300 sling stones, piled behind the rampart as weapons against possible attack. Battles and skirmishes were a part of life in the Iron Age, but we should not imagine these people constantly at war. Increasingly impressive entrance defences and the gateways of even smaller hillforts served as powerful deterrents to would-be attackers, but also as statements of power and status to rivals. The small hillforts at Woodside and Drim in the Llawhaden group boasted elaborate gate towers. Additional protection outside the ramparts could be provided by a *chevaux de frise*, a curtain of upright stones designed to foil a charge by mounted soldiers. Fine examples of these extraordinary defences can be seen at Carn Alw in the Preseli mountains, while an excavated example at Castell Henllys appeared to incorporate quartz boulders for visual effect. It is likely that hillfort defences were more suited to the frequent feuding or cattle-raiding recorded within some chiefdoms. It is against this backdrop of irregular, low-level aggression and inter-clan rivalry that we should read the highly symbolic, but often structurally intermittent, defensive architecture of most Welsh hillforts, rather than suppose that they were all fortresses in a hostile landscape.

For the first time in prehistory we have names for the people in the landscape. The Roman geographer Ptolemy recorded the Demetae occupying much of south-west Wales, in the territory covered by the later county of Dyfed. It is likely that this was a name under which the disparate peoples of west Wales united in the face of the Roman conquest. A recent interpretation of the name Demetae by Andrew Breeze (2005) suggests it means 'the supreme cutters-down', alluding to a proficiency with swords and the ostentatious use of weaponry. The real territorial landscape was far more complex, based on smaller regions or even distinct localities in the west Wales topography, perhaps only tens of kilometres across. Although few names survive, the Romans listed St David's Head as Octapitarum promontory, which some have suggested might indicate the name of the 'Octapitae' people. If so, this could be the community which built the Iron Age promontory fort on St David's Head and farmed the fields on the surrounding headland. It is likely that other significant forts in the landscape, like Foel Trigarn or Garn Fawr on Pen-caer/Strumble Head, were owned by smaller communities with their own distinctive names and traditions.

Figure 74. Castell Henllys: we know that the Iron Age landscape, and even that of the preceding Neolithic and Bronze Ages, was well cleared and farmed and demarcated into territories belonging to particular chiefdoms. The houses too were impressive structures, as the authentic reconstructions at Castell Henllys demonstrate. Rather than being flimsy and poorly built, these strong and complicated structures have survived hurricane force winds unscathed while modern houses have been damaged (RCAHMW, DS2006-086-002).

Figure 75. Parchmark of the Roman road approaching Whitland recorded in 1992, three years before it was partly excavated in advance of a new bypass. Compare with Figue 77 (RCAHMW, 92-cs-0363).

Figure 76. The power of Romanisation: the partly excavated and restored Roman amphitheatre on the east side of Carmarthen/Moridunum. Along with bath houses and new towns, such lavish buildings would have been strange and wonderful sites in the countryside of the Roman period. Together with the effects of new market forces, such influences would have helped to 'Romanise' native communities and their leaders (RCAHMW, 2002-cs-0722).

In AD 43, hundreds of miles east of Pembrokeshire on the distant shores of Kent at Richborough, the Romans launched their final invasion of Britain. Under Aulus Plautius at least 22,000 Roman soldiers of four legions were landed on British soil, supported by an equal number of auxiliary troops, together providing an awesome invasion force of highly trained infantry soldiers and supporting cavalry. Initial campaigns against the Britons were swift and decisive, the Iron Age tribes being no match for the tactics of the Roman army. However, attempts to conquer Wales, then a westerly part of central Britain, were less successful. Through a combination of difficult terrain, some well-planned resistance and changing military priorities across the Roman empire, it was to be thirty years before west Wales was bought under full Roman control.

In the years following AD 47 the Roman general Ostorius Scapula made the first advances into what is now Welsh territory with the defeat of the Deceangli in Flintshire, whose homes were perhaps the distinctive forts of the Clwydian range, and waged a war against the Silures in south Wales which lasted until AD 51. This culminated in the defeat of Caratacus, a notable British king, at a battle in mid-Wales, thought by Webster (1981) to have been in the hills near Newtown on the Severn. A chain of Roman forts was established along the eastern borders of Wales to consolidate initial gains and to control and restrict patterns of movement and trade west into the tribal heartlands of Wales. It was to be nearly another decade before the Romans again attempted to push westward. Under Suetonius Paulinus the tribes in north and south Wales were largely subdued by AD 60, and it may have been that the whole of Wales would have followed shortly after had it not been for the revolt of Boudica. Only after Vespasian came to power in Rome in AD 69 was the conquest of Britain resumed. Governor Julius Frontinus completed a series of formidable campaigns between AD 74 and 78, moving great detachments of troops into the Welsh mountains and stationing them in marching camps on overnight stops. The closest marching camps to Pembrokeshire are those in the mountain country on the Brecknock/Carmarthenshire border. Following the conquest of Wales, a new road system was quickly established linking a network of more permanent

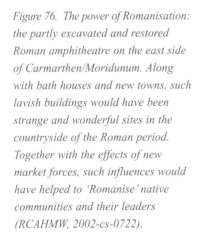

Figure 77. The Romans approaching Pembrokeshire. The line of the Roman road (highlighted) west of Carmarthen, pieced together from air photographs and reconnaissance, was confirmed on excavation at Pwll-yr-hwyaid, Whitland when the bypass was constructed in 1995. This view shows the road to the north of Whitland under excavation by Cambria Archaeology, with the excavated road surface, or agger, showing up as a light line cutting across the main sweep of the bypass (© Cambria Archaeology).

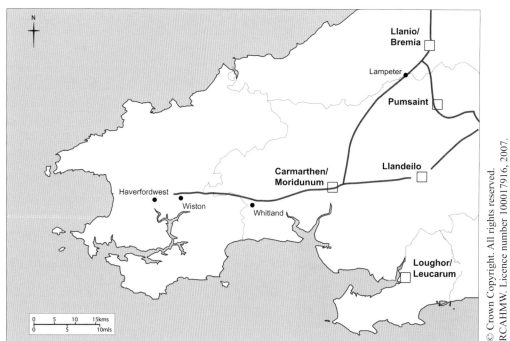

forts, usually established in lowland areas to subdue native communities.

Until recently it was not thought that Roman military engineering and civilian settlement had penetrated Pembrokeshire, west of the *civitas* capital at Carmarthen. It was believed that the Romans had not considered it necessary to subjugate the region, either because a comfortable peace had been struck with regional chiefs, or that the land was too poor or remote to invest with a network of roads and forts. However, the presence of the road into Pembrokeshire, along with numerous stray Roman finds such as coins and brooches, and excavated examples of 'Romanised' farmsteads thought to have been built by wealthy natives, show a level of Roman influence and trading in the county. Antiquarians had spoken of a Roman road west of Carmarthen linking a supposed port at St Davids, but much of this theory was based on a forged Roman document bearing false names of forts and stations (see Chapter 6).

In 1989 Terry James, then of the Dyfed Archaeological Trust, discovered a Roman road running west of Carmarthen while examining vertical air photographs. Excavations in advance of the construction of the Whitland bypass by Cambria Archaeology in 1995 revealed a well-built roadway, founded on brushwood and timber and re-surfaced several times with cobbles, slabs and gravel. As yet no convincing Roman forts or camps have been found west of Carmarthen served by the road, but the predictable nature of Roman planning tells us they should be there at regular intervals of around 15 miles or a day's march. In 2003 Mark Merrony excavated the site of a Roman villa at Ford, west of Wolf's Castle, first mentioned by Fenton in 1811. Fenton told how a farm labourer discovered stones and tiles in 1806 beneath a hedge and dug further to reveal a hypocaust, or under-floor Roman heating system. Merrony's research identified buried ditches and floor surfaces of a substantial building, thought to be a Romanised farmstead rather than a true classical villa. Considering the evidence, future discoveries of Roman military sites and civilian settlements may not be unlikely for Pembrokeshire.

Figure 78. The known extent of the Roman road network in west Wales, showing Roman roads (red line), Roman forts and fortlets (squares), and modern towns and villages (circles). The Roman road leads west of the civitas capital at Carmarthen/Moridunum as far as Wiston. Roman forts may be expected at regular intervals, every 15 miles, yet so far none has been confirmed to the west or north of Carmarthen. A Roman fort at Llandeilo, in the grounds of Dinefwr Park, was only discovered in 2003 (RCAHMW).

The centuries which followed the end of formal Roman rule in Britain in AD 410 were times of immense change and uncertainty. With no centralised authority or security, raids along the west coast were common. Although very few written records survive to tell us any history of the emergence of early medieval political systems during this time, finds of post-Roman settlements, religious communities, and a legacy of early Christian stone monuments provide glimpses of life in south-west Wales to illuminate what were once called the 'Dark Ages'.

It is thought by historians that much of the south-west peninsula was ruled by Irish dynasties during the fifth and sixth centuries AD, exploiting the power vacuum left by the Romans and providing some stability and protection for the populace. Sculptured commemorative stones give us a vital link with the names of leaders and dates of events from these early times. The Llandilo inscribed stones from Maenclochog, for example, record in Latin 'The stone of Andagellus, son of Cavetus. He lies here', inscribed in fifth-sixth century script (Rees 1992). Pembrokeshire has the highest concentration of early Christian monuments in Wales, and modern research has given us a greater insight into how these carved stones may have been used in the formative early medieval landscape.

The early Christian monuments of Wales were originally divided into four classes by V. E. Nash-Williams in 1950. Of these, group I comprises simple inscribed stones bearing ogam and Latin, probably dating to the fifth to seventh centuries. Group II includes cross-decorated stones which are thought to be later, from the seventh to ninth centuries. Group III encompasses the grand sculptured crosses of the region dating to the ninth to eleventh centuries. Many are found in Pembrokeshire churches, but it is thought that they may only have been brought to these sites in recent centuries for safe-keeping. Research by Nancy Edwards suggests that most of the Group I monuments were commemorative in

Figure 79. Excavations at West Angle Bay, 2005. The National Park Authority, Cadw and Cambria Archaeology commenced a project to research and excavate threatened early medieval cemeteries in the National Park. This has been spurred on by continuing coastal erosion which exposed the remains of coastal cemeteries in cliff sections on the south side of West Angle Bay and at St Brides. Excavations at West Angle Bay revealed a group of cist burials associated with a plough-levelled enclosure. The burials have been dated by radiocarbon to the eighth to tenth centuries AD. Two further groups of graves have been identified in the cliff-edge. The excavation of one such cist, a small stone-lined grave, is shown here (© Cambria Archaeology, courtesy of Polly Groom).

Figure 80. Some Iron Age hillforts were refortified by early medieval leaders. Beneath the medieval castle at Carew cropmarks show four large ditches cutting across the promontory, which probably belong to a pre-existing Iron Age promontory fort. Excavations have produced post-Roman pottery and radiocarbon dates for fifth to seventh century occupation. This Cambridge University view taken in 1949 shows the parchmarks of the buried ditches beyond the castle ruins (original photography held at Cambridge University Collection of Air Photographs, Unit for Landscape Modelling, CY 46, DI2006-0040).

function, marking individual graves and standing as visible symbols of land ownership or important boundaries. A number, including one from Castle Villa Farm, Brawdy, were sited on or near Iron Age hillforts in a deliberate attempt to reference the authority of vanished prehistoric leaders. Only with the appearance of the Group II cross-decorated stones do we have firm evidence for the arrival of Christian communities, particularly on or near the Irish Sea coast in south-west Wales. Some marked graves or kin cemeteries, others marked early church sites and formal cemeteries. The Group III monuments, which include some of the finest crosses like that at Carew, were associated with major monasteries and churches of the ninth to eleventh centuries.

Pembrokeshire is well known for the survival of early medieval cemeteries, usually marked by remains of slab-lined cist-graves, and possible early church sites preserved as circular or concentric churchyard enclosures. Research suggests that some Iron Age defended enclosures may have been re-used in the early Christian period, first as cemeteries, then developing into medieval church sites. Although these early ecclesiastical communities have often been referred to as clasau, this term probably refers to slightly later ecclesiastical communities established from the ninth century onwards. Excavations by the Dyfed Archaeological Trust at a plough-damaged earthwork enclosure at Caer, Bayvil (in 1979), to the north-east of Nevern, resulted in the discovery of an early medieval cemetery. This consisted of a series of dug graves and stone-lined cist graves, mostly orientated east-west. Although only narrow excavation trenches were opened to investigate small parts of the interior, the excavator, Heather James, estimated that the enclosure may contain up to 3,400

Figure 81. Carew Cross, Carew, a towering memorial to Maredudd, joint ruler of Deheubarth from 1033 until his death in AD 1035. The stone was photographed by Iain Wright of the Royal Commission as part of a project to re-photograph all early Christian monuments in Wales. The striking qualities of the image were achieved by photography at night, which enabled lighting, mounted on high scaffolds and powered by portable generators, to be critically positioned to show the carving to greatest advantage. This method has proved to give the best results for these subjects, on occasion showing up detail not previously known (RCAHMW, 990086.1).

Figure 82. Tenby north beach, from the north, on a summer evening in 2002. Prominent in the centre of the beach is Goscar or Gosker Rock, a term which means 'ploughshare' in Scandinavian and remains a good description of its shape. This demonstrates the longevity of place names, first assigned by Viking mariners and settlers, in modern Pembrokeshire (RCAHMW, DI2006-0355).

graves. Similar cist cemeteries are found throughout north and west Pembrokeshire, between Cardigan and St Davids, with a second cluster in south-west Pembrokeshire to the north and south of Milford Haven. A new survey of early medieval ecclesiastical sites in Pembrokeshire by Neil Ludlow for Cambria Archaeology formed part of a long-term study of similar sites across Wales funded by Cadw. Initial conclusions suggest the survival of over 150 such sites in the county. Together with early Christian monuments and placenames suggestive of further, undiscovered sites, they show the fluctuations in the establishment of power bases and cult centres in the post-Roman landscape of west Wales.

The western territory called Deheubarth was one of the three main divisions of Wales, and was itself divided into twelve further territories called cantrefi, each of which contained several commotes. Ruling dynasties operated from a llys, or court, and while a number of these early medieval courts in Wales have

been rediscovered or excavated by archaeologists, the sites of many more are hinted at by telling place-name evidence. Some Pembrokeshire villages may have been founded during this time, and historians studying village plans in south Pembrokeshire have identified possible pre-Norman settlements characterised by a radial pattern of houses and fields emanating from circular churchyards.

By all accounts, early medieval west Wales was a divided kingdom, wracked by battles, skirmishes and vendettas between dynasties and clans. Against this violent background, Deheubarth had the further worry of increasing Viking raids. Viking warriors represented a terrifying fighting force, and as expert mariners they navigated the dangerous waters and reefs around the Welsh coast, raiding coastal communities and religious establishments. The history of the Vikings in Wales has been documented by Mark Redknap (2000), following a campaign of new research and excavation by the National Museum of Wales.

Figure 83. The church of St Mary Magdalene, Llanfair Nant-y-gof, just south of Trecwn in north Pembrokeshire. The present church was built in 1855, replacing a medieval church, but the subcircular churchyard hints at a pre-conquest, early medieval religious foundation. Several earthworks within the churchyard, together with a large recumbent limestone slab which may have prehistoric origins, add to the archaeological potential of this isolated parish church (RCAHMW, AP-2006-1130).

Figure 84. The Smalls Reef with its graceful masonry lighthouse built in 1861 to replace a timber structure. Close by, a Viking ship came to grief on the rocks in the early twelfth century (Crown Copyright, Archaeological Diving Unit Surveys, DI2006-0587).

Coastal Pembrokeshire suffered heavily in the Viking raids, which occurred from the mid-ninth century onwards. Early raiders struck during the summer months, but following the establishment of settlements in Scotland, warriors began to over-winter in Wales and Ireland, leading to further clashes. The 'second Viking age' began in Wales about 950, following the death of Hywel Dda, and during the ensuing decades further raids were perpetrated from permanent settlements in north and east England. St Davids was raided eleven times between 967 and 1091, with bloody slayings of bishops and people. A tangible relic of these sea-borne raids along the Pembrokeshire coast is a late Viking brass sword-guard from the Smalls Reef, some 16 miles (26 km) west of Skomer Island. The sword-guard was found by sport divers in 1991 beneath a modern wreck and is one of the finest Viking finds known from Wales. The original sword,

along with the rest of the crew and boat, probably came to grief on a long-distance voyage sometime during the early twelfth century.

Today the most tangible legacy of the Viking age is the proliferation of Scandinavian place names in central and western parts of the county. Vikings named prominent coastal features, such as Skokholm, 'Pole' island, and Caldy, 'Cold Island', to aid navigation of the waters around the Bristol Channel, or to identify landing points for raids. Viking settlement names may also occur in inland Pembrokeshire, in the origins of place names like Wolf's Castle, Scollock and Scolton to the north of Haverfordwest. Here Norse speakers may have established semi-permanent settlements, but to date no archaeological traces of their houses or farms have been discovered. Future aerial reconnaissance may shed new light on this period of Pembrokeshire's history.

THE NORMAN LORDS

It was the Norman invasion of England in 1066, and the final subjugation of west Wales nearly thirty years later, which began to change permanently the landscape and people of what was later to become Pembrokeshire. The region emerged from a world of minor dynasties, which may have existed from at least the early Iron Age (c.700 BC), and came to embrace more familiar concepts of towns, boroughs, commerce and intensive agriculture and industry.

Following the Norman conquest of England, attempts to extend control over the far south-west were delayed for some years during the reign of the Welsh prince Rhys ap Tewdwr, who retained control over the medieval principality of Deheubarth in the face of Norman raids. King William I exerted political pressure against this indigenous rule when, in 1081, he made a pilgrimage through west Wales to St Davids with his army, as a pertinent show of strength to the populace. Full Norman control of the south-west quickly followed Rhys ap Tewdwr's death in battle in 1093. The advance was two-pronged: William fitz Baldwin approached from Devon to establish a castle at Carmarthen, while Roger de Montgomery marched from mid-Wales to establish castles at Cardigan and Pembroke.

The new medieval castles which appeared in Wales to consolidate Norman conquests were quite different from the pre-existing Iron Age hillforts and re-fortified settlements and courts of the early medieval period. Motte-and-bailey castles coupled a restricted castle mound (the motte) with a larger defended enclosure below (the bailey) for houses, workshops and ancillary structures, whilst ringworks were more like a large protected bailey, lacking the castle mound but with a heavily defended main gate. Where the castle was strategically well sited it was consolidated in stone, and so the great Pembrokeshire castles were born. These new fortresses naturally became focal points for traders and families to settle to serve the lord and to work on the lands. Norman settlement began to create new towns, with borough

status granted to established settlements like Haverfordwest and Pembroke. That said, the transition was long and bloody, with rebellions and setbacks preventing widespread social stability for some centuries.

Figure 85 (above). Medieval mottes, or earthwork castles, represent the less strategically important sites which were never consolidated in stone and were eventually abandoned. Pointz Castle (from the east, beyond the farm buildings) is a twelfth-century motte still standing about 4m (30ft) high with an outer ditch. It was built by Punch or Ponce (an alternative name for the site is Punch Castle), a tenant of the bishop of St Davids, and was later worked as a farm by the clergy (RCAHMW, DI2006-0583)

Figure 86 (left). Llawhaden Castle, a former timber castle on a circular ringwork rebuilt in stone in the early thirteenth century by the bishops of St Davids, and converted into an opulent bishop's residence by the early fourteenth century (RCAHMW, 2003-cs-1020).

Figure 87. Jameston medieval field systems, viewed from the north-west near Manorbier Newton, looking out to Manorbier Bay in the background. Genuine medieval open-field strips preserve a reversed S-curve formed from years of ploughing by teams of yoked oxen which needed to be manoeuvred and turned as they reached the end of the strip of land. (Hall 1987; RCAHMW, DI2006-0367).

Under Norman rule the landscape was fundamentally altered, particularly in the south of the county, following a large influx of peasant settlers and colonists, both Flemings and English, during the reign of Henry I in the early twelfth century. The *Brut y Tywysogion* (Chronicle of the Princes) records that the Flemings '...occupied the whole cantref of Rhos [south-west Pembrokeshire, south of Roch, north of Milford Haven and west of Haverfordwest]...and drove away all the inhabitants from the land'. The new Flemish lords tightened their grip on south-west Pembrokeshire. Wizo established a castle at Wiston, and Tancred (or Tancard) is thought to have founded

Haverfordwest around 1110. Terry James (1999) records that when the large community of Flemish farmers settled around Haverfordwest, '... the language was obliterated and Flemish gradually gave way to English as the modern language'. The agricultural prosperity of the Norman manorial system in this 'Little England Beyond Wales', Camden's *Anglia Transwallina*, is reflected today by the number of settlements which still retain the classic elements of a compact village plan, with greens around a substantial church, and systems of 'open' strip fields. Notable examples of open-field systems can be seen around Letterston, Templeton,

Angle and Jameston. While some of these may have been newly-established, historians agree that in parts of Pembrokeshire, particularly in the south around Manorbier, Norman lords took over existing estates of rich, cultivated land. The possibility even exists that great coaxial systems of narrow fields crossing much of the south Pembrokeshire landscape were first established in prehistory, with historic villages built on top of an older pattern.

The region was consolidated by a northerly chain of castles from Roch in the west to Narberth in the east, along a frontier zone and linguistic divide which in recent times has come to be called the Landsker. Markers along this divide, which include the Brandy Brook near Roch and Haycastle motte, graphically delineate the historic division between Norman south Pembrokeshire, which has historically been English speaking, and north Pembrokeshire, which remained Welsh in character. The linguistic divide across Pembrokeshire is still dramatic. The 1989 *National*

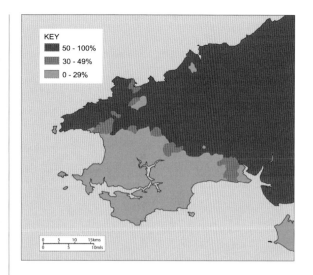
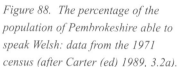

KEY

■ 50 - 100%
▨ 30 - 49%
▨ 0 - 29%

0   5   10   15kms
0   5   10mls

Figure 88. The percentage of the population of Pembrokeshire able to speak Welsh: data from the 1971 census (after Carter (ed) 1989, 3.2a).

Atlas of Wales summarises results of the 1971 census which show few Welsh-speaking parishes south of a line from Roch in the west to Pendine, Carmarthenshire, in the east (Fig. 88). The census records scattered Welsh speakers in south

Figure 89. Letterston, north of Haverfordwest. High view from the north-west in 2002 showing traces of medieval open-field strips fossilised in the modern landscape. Originally, as the name suggests, such field strips were part of an 'open' landscape undivided by hedges or fences. The principle behind the farming of such narrow strips was communal apportionment of land; thus each peasant would farm strips of land throughout the parish, all sharing good and bad land, with a general rule that no two strips lying together would be in the same ownership. Historical research has shown that many of these field systems may not have been entirely Norman in origin, and demonstrates instead the existence of prosperous pre-Norman estate systems which the new lords appropriated (RCAHMW, DI2006-0533).

Figure 92 (above). The ruins of St Dogmaels Abbey, close to the Teifi at Cardigan, founded in 1115 by Robert Fitzmartin and belonging to the austere Order of Tiron (RCAHMW, AP-2004-0810).

Figure 90 (above). On the line of the Landsker. Landsker border castles at Roch and Haycastle traditionally mark the linguistic and territorial boundary between Norman-controlled south Pembrokeshire and Welsh-held north Pembrokeshire. This view shows Roch Castle and village from the north in 2002 (RCAHMW, 2002-cs-0447).

Figure 91 (right). St Davids Cathedral, with the ruins of the once opulent Bishop's Palace nearby, set within an intact walled close dating from medieval times (RCAHMW, 91-cs-0259).

Pembrokeshire, in St Bride's, Angle and Stackpole, but the region is predominantly English-speaking.

Castles continued to change and evolve over the centuries. During the thirteenth century and later impressive defences were built and strengthened around towns such as Tenby and Pembroke. Raids by the Welsh no doubt spurred on these strategic improvements; in 1257 Llywelyn ap Gruffudd, son of Llywelyn Fawr, 'The Great', with the help of Maredudd ap Rhys Gryg, raided through Deheubarth, burning castles and towns at Newport, Narberth and Maenclochog. During the thirteenth century gatehouses were improved and strengthened, and new towers added along the walls of castles, but, following a period of stability after the Edwardian conquest of north Wales, the role of the castle as a military fortress began to decline.

During the mid-fourteenth century the Black Death was sweeping across Europe and affecting many parts of Wales. In its wake there was extensive depopulation, with many smaller villages and settlements deserted. Several earthworks of deserted or shrunken settlements in Pembrokeshire may be dated to this period, and aerial photography continues to highlight new examples. There was only a partial recovery in the economy and settlement pattern prior

Figure 93. The well-preserved medieval town walls of Tenby, running along St Florence Parade, give the town a continental air in summer. This view is from the south, with the tower of five arches at upper left, the old West Gate into the town (RCAHMW, 2002/5061-45).

61

Figure 94 (above). May sunlight casts shadows through the Bathstone mullions of windows from Sir John Perrot's Elizabethan north wing at Carew Castle, added to the medieval castle after he was granted governorship in 1558. Work on the wing was left unfinished after his arrest for treason in 1591 (RCAHMW, AP-2004-0019).

to Owain Glyn Dŵr's uprising (1400-10), which again plunged Wales into disarray. It was many decades before the country recovered from the effects of this rebellion, which had brought with it the destruction of some towns and cathedrals, the burning of crops and continuing rural depopulation. Following the revolt there was a new interest in refortifying older castles, and the period also saw the construction of fortified manors and tower houses, like that at Angle, although these remained rare in Wales. In the reign of Henry Tudor, born in Pembroke Castle in 1457, a number of Pembrokeshire castles were redeveloped as opulent residences of the local Welsh aristocracy, such as Sir Rhys ap Thomas. The fine and ornate range of rooms in the north wing of Carew Castle was redeveloped by Sir John Perrot in 1558, at a time when old fortresses were becoming fashionable residences.

The Acts of Union of 1536 and 1543 completed the administrative assimilation of Wales as part of the English state. The Acts saw the formation of the Welsh counties, the extension of English laws, and the further strengthening of the role of the gentry classes to develop their estates and become significant landowners. Great houses and estates from this period in Pembrokeshire include Haroldston (Fig. 257), to the south of Haverfordwest, and this may be the time when formal gardens along the Daugleddau, such as Coedcanlas (Fig. 264), were commenced. This process of land acquisition and estate building was further aided by the Reformation, which saw great transfers of lands formerly owned by the Church into Crown or private hands. The dissolution of the monasteries (1536-9) closed the great monasteries and Cistercian abbeys which had been established in the Middle Ages. Their once glorious buildings were largely destroyed and their estate lands sold cheaply. If the buildings were not demolished outright, they were comprehensively stripped of lead from their roofs and stone from their windows and walls, allowing dereliction and ruin to set in. It is the Reformation which we have to thank today for a surviving landscape of picturesque abbey ruins, rather than a complement of roofed historic buildings.

Figure 95 (right). Carew Newton village in south Pembrokeshire, from the north, showing earthwork banks and terraces of a possible shrunken settlement highlighted in low winter sunlight (RCAHMW, DI2006-0358).

After nearly 150 years of relative peace, the castles of Pembrokeshire briefly saw a return to their old roles during the Civil War, when the medieval walls provided ready-made strongholds for the competing forces of the parliamentarians and the royalists loyal to King Charles I. Following decades of abandonment, outdated medieval gateways were modified for guns and artillery with the provision of 'V'-shaped redans or ravelins outside the entrances to castles like Carew and Manorbier. Advancing forces would lay siege to a castle, or attempt direct attack by

undermining or blowing up its walls. A number of castles in Pembrokeshire saw active reuse, including Roch, Picton, Haverfordwest and Pembroke, although some changed hands between opposing forces several times with few hostilities. At the start of the Civil War in August 1642 most of Wales, including the gentry classes, came out in strong support of the king, although there remained widespread apathy. Only in the English-speaking parts of south Pembrokeshire did a well organised group of gentry families continue to hold out. They

Figure 96. The ruinous defences of Haverfordwest Castle, from the north-west, later used as the site of the town gaol (RCAHMW, 95-cs-1046).

established a parliamentary administration centred on the formidable castle and walled town of Pembroke which included Tenby and Haverfordwest. An exact understanding of the political situation early in the war in the south-west of Pembrokeshire is still lacking; the new royalist commander, the earl of Carbery, was welcomed in Haverfordwest in the spring of 1643, and during the summer of the same year he won back allegiance from most of the castles, towns and country houses in Pembrokeshire. The royalists began construction of a fort at Pill, just to the east of Milford, but this was taken back in a counterattack by parliamentarians under Colonel Rowland Laugharne the following year. Carbery's successive failures to capture Pembroke for the royalists caused him to lose his command in April 1644, while parliamentarians continued to dominate the Milford Haven waterway.

A new royalist leader, Col. Charles Gerard, took command in spring 1644 and launched a fierce and bloody offensive into south-west Wales, retaking castles at Laugharne, Newcastle Emlyn and Roch. Haverfordwest soon followed, but later in the year all these were regained by parliamentarians. Gerard returned in January 1645 with a force of over 2,000 men, besieging parliamentary troops in Cardigan Castle and forcing them to pull back to Pembroke and Tenby. Later, Gerard secured Picton and Carew castles but was soon recalled to England, and, with support for King Charles I steadily collapsing during 1645-6, parliamentarians were able to re-take much of Wales. One brutal skirmish took place on Colby Moor to the east of Haverfordwest in the summer of 1645. The parliamentarian Laugharne led 1,000 men out of Pembroke and was met by an army of 1,500 men at Haverfordwest, clashing on Colby Moor. Some 150 royalists were killed, with 700 captured. The Civil War ended in 1646, but a peaceful settlement between king and Parliament did not follow, and in 1648 the country was plunged into renewed war, with Pembroke unexpectedly becoming the scene of royalist resistance under John Poyer, the governor. In the face of this rebellion Oliver Cromwell marched west from London into south Pembrokeshire. He first took back Tenby, and, following a long siege, heavy guns were brought in to destroy the walls of Pembroke, which on 11 July 1648 surrendered to Cromwell. Because this castle had performed so well during the struggle, Parliament took steps deliberately to slight the defences during the years 1648-50, employing labourers to dismantle walls, setting explosives and stripping roofs. Cromwell ordered the partial demolition of Pembroke and Haverfordwest castles. Thus, once grand medieval castles were finally laid to rest as redundant ruins. The war left many scars. Civil disobedience and unrest was rife, agriculture was in disarray and there were food shortages among the populace. Somewhat cruelly, the plague struck west Wales between 1651 and 1653, affecting all parts. The effects were not long-lasting, but it was some time before settlements and religious houses regained some of their former prosperity and confidence.

Figure 97 (below). Colby Moor from the north, scene of the 1645 rout during the latter stages of the Civil War, and where around 150 royalists met their death (RCAHMW, AP-2006-0020).

PEMBROKESHIRE IN RECENT CENTURIES:
DIVISION OF THE RURAL LANDSCAPE

In the latter years of the seventeenth century the economic situation improved. Gentry houses were upgraded and extended to form the great houses and estates which we see today. In rural parts life was considerably more settled than during the preceding centuries of invasion, unrest, plague and depopulation, and settlement expanded. Crops were cultivated in the fertile lowlands of the county, while sheep grazing dominated the uplands and led to a thriving woollen industry and export trade in fleeces.

Around the coast the fishing industry prospered. Long-distance overland 'drovers roads', trade routes for the movement of cattle and livestock, passed through the more upland areas of Pembrokeshire; well-worn 'braided trackways' still survive as spectacular earthworks at Tafarn-y-bwlch and along the central ridge of the Mynydd Preseli.

Towards the end of the eighteenth century there was rural upheaval in Wales on a massive scale as the open-field system of agriculture, largely begun in

Figure 98. Braided trackways worn and reworn by centuries, perhaps millennia, of human and animal traffic, climbing the northern slopes of Mynydd Preseli from Tafarn y Bwlch. View looking south (RCAHMW, 96-cs-1007).

Figure 99 (below). One of the few areas of Parliamentary Enclosure in Pembrokeshire, looking north-west from Crymych, in the foreground, to Foel Trigarn and Mynydd Preseli. Regular planned fields enclosed formerly open ground, but the Acts were met with protest riots at Maenclochog in the 1820s (RCAHMW, DI2006-0576).

Norman times, was swept aside by a series of Parliamentary Enclosure Acts. Common lands and open hills were divided up between the stewards of the larger estates at the expense of 'squatters' who may previously have taken up residence in poor houses or founded 'squatter settlements' on the edges of the enclosed land. By 1760 certain Acts had begun to divide the open hills of north Wales into regular parcels defined by straight stone walls, and by the end of the century the process had accelerated to take in much of the unenclosed common land of Wales. By contrast, there were very few Acts of Parliament in Pembrokeshire, one of these being east of Mynydd

Preseli in the region of Crymych, which remained as open moorland until as late as 1812. Instead, the enclosure of the Pembrokeshire landscape was a more piecemeal process, with medieval open fields being fossilised as narrow field strips, and many tracts of open moorland preserved as common until quite recently.

Figure 100 (opposite). The grid of walls defining an abandoned farmstead at Carn Afr (SN 097 302), on the southern sweep of Mynydd Preseli east of Rosebush (RCAHMW, 99-cs-2308, DI2006-0579).

Figure 101. Popton Point, Angle, from the north, in 1995. One of a number of expensive and elaborate nineteenth-century forts built to protect Milford Haven from naval attacks which never came. The fort was reused from the early 1960s as the headquarters of British Petroleum. This aerial view shows the former sites of oil storage tanks, removed when BP closed the Ocean Terminal (RCAHMW, DI2006-0582).

In the last two centuries the landscape of Pembrokeshire has been influenced by the industrial revolution and the modernisation of coastal defences against the threat of invasion. From the early nineteenth century the Milford Haven waterway was radically transformed, from an advantageous harbourage fringed by farms, medieval castles and small ports, into a formidable centre for Royal Navy defence and shipbuilding. Sir William Hamilton commenced work on the construction of Milford, aided by the civil engineering expertise of his nephew Charles Greville, and initiated by an Act of Parliament in 1790. Quays, docks and other structures were established along with the town, but

these were rapidly superseded when the Royal Naval Dockyard was transferred from Milford to Pembroke Dock in 1802. Major sections of both these new towns were laid out in regular gridiron patterns of streets and terraced houses. In the same year as the Royal Dockyard was built Lord Palmerston instigated a national programme for the defence of Britain's main harbours. The Haven forts were built during the mid-nineteenth century, including the Defensible Barracks at Pembroke Dock, and many remain as spectacular, yet derelict, shells, testament to formidable engineering and architecture. They were reused and modified during the two world wars, which also left a legacy of twentieth-century

Figure 102 (above). Talbenny aerodrome west of Little Haven, from the north. One of a number of disused Second World War airfields in Pembrokeshire, each representing a considerable achievement in engineering and construction. Talbenny was opened in May 1942 and was chiefly home to squadrons of Wellington aircraft until its closure in August 1945 (RCAHMW, DI2006-0581).

Figure 103 (above). The former naval depot at Trecwn, virtually hidden from the outside world in a narrow valley south of Fishguard. It was built at the start of the Second World War as a munitions storage facility and has fifty-eight long storage tunnels dug into the hillsides, all served by a purpose-built railway network (RCAHMW, AP-2004-0874).

concrete coastal defences and airfields across Pembrokeshire. Until quite recently pillboxes and gun emplacements were seen as eyesores and many were demolished. Now we have come to appreciate that these buildings are some of the few tangible reminders within our communities of the great struggles of the Second World War and should be protected for posterity. A number of the larger wartime airfields are seemingly too massive to be used in any meaningful way, with a crumbling infrastructure of roads and buildings. Only at Brawdy and Withybush (Haverfordwest) have large Second World War airfields been continuously used and developed, although the runway at Brawdy is now effectively out of use.

Figure 104 (left). Planned housing of the naval town of Pembroke Dock, looking south-east over Park Street (right) and Meyrick Street (left), with the roof of Meyrick Street Methodist chapel prominent at centre-left (RCAHMW, CD2005-602-004).

69

Figure 105 (above). A tanker entering the Haven mouth below St Ann's Head, with winter sunlight on the water (RCAHMW, AP-2005-2755).

Figure 106 (right). Summerton quarry, a small-scale working on a hill overlooking Little Newcastle and Puncheston/Cas-Mael in north Pembrokeshire, with the Iron Age hillfort of Summerton Camp beyond to the north-west (RCAHMW, DI2006-0574).

70

The industrial revolution began to change the face of the Welsh landscape from the end of the eighteenth century, although smaller-scale extractive industries such as quarrying and anthracite mining had been practiced around the Pembrokeshire coast and inland since medieval times. Rural industries such as shipbuilding, quarrying, fishing and lime burning continued to thrive into recent centuries, and all have left a legacy of quays, harbours, lime kilns and, sometimes, the houses and hamlets of the workers who used them. The coming of the railway in the mid-nineteenth century revolutionised the movement of goods and people to and from the county and challenged the dominance of seaborne trade. In a series of rail building episodes the towns of Haverfordwest, Pembroke Dock and Milford were connected by 1863, and a later line to the Rosebush slate quarries was extended to connect to Fishguard by 1899. This was ultimately succeeded by a new line constructed in 1906.

Figure 107 (above). The single chimney stack marking Trefrane Cliff Colliery, which exploited the western limits of the Pembrokeshire coal field but was in operation for only six years before closing in 1905 (RCAHMW, 91-cs-0268).

Figure 108 (left). Bolton Hill Quarry at Tier's Cross, near Haverfordwest (RCAHMW, 2002-cs-0431, DI2006-0588).

71

Figure 109 (right). The awesome scale of the Texaco refinery at Rhoscrowther, looking south on a clear spring day in April 1995 (RCAHMW, 95-cs-1067).

Figure 110 (below). The Irish Ferries' Isle of Inishmore, unloading cars after docking at Pembroke Dock amidst foam and turbulence generated from her several bow and stern thrusters (RCAHMW, DI2006-0573).

As in the rest of Wales, the coming of the railways breathed life into a new industry, tourism, and today this is undoubtedly a major source of income for Pembrokeshire communities, if not the whole of rural Britain. Another significant change in the county has been the development of the oil industry, which arrived at Milford Haven in the 1950s and has occupied both north and south shores ever since. The establishment of successive oil refineries, a power station (now demolished), and the associated infrastructure in the heart of a National Park has not been without its problems. The worst in recent years was the tragic Sea Empress disaster of February 1996, when the holed oil tanker released approximately 72,000 tonnes of crude oil into the Haven and along the south Pembrokeshire coast, with the slick extending from Skomer in the north, south to St Govans Head and Caldy, and as far east as the Tywi estuary in Carmarthenshire. The fluctuating economic situation has also meant that apparently permanent installations of storage tanks and chimneys may grow or disappear year on year, often to be replaced by new factories, refineries or other buildings. Aerial photography remains one of the few ways to document these constant changes and reminds us how fleeting is the mark of man's hand on the enduring landscape of Pembrokeshire.

Figure 111. The annual County Show at Haverfordwest Airport in 2002, with runways providing the ideal setting for stalls and stands (RCAHMW, DI2006-0572).

Figure 112 (above). Built in 1998 as a weekend retreat by Future Systems architects, Malator House sits half-buried in the ground with a glass wall facing over the expanse of Druidston Haven and St Brides Bay. It is an innovative reinterpretation of the holiday home in a sensitive location and a welcome change from the normally drab domestic architecture of post-war Wales (RCAHMW, DI2006-0577).

Figure 113. The Pembrokeshire Coast Path is one of the great walks of Wales, but, although it was first proposed in 1953, it was not opened until 1970 following years of planning, construction and agreement on its final course. Today the path runs 186 miles (299 km) from Poppit Sands on the Teifi estuary in the north to Amroth at the southern border with Carmarthenshire. This view shows the path at Pwll-y-wrach, north-west of Moylgrove, with Careg Yspar beyond (RCAHMW, AP-2006-1100).

The Pembrokeshire Coast National Park was designated in February 1952 as Britain's first and only coastal park. Its role was not only to protect and conserve the extraordinary wildlife and landscape of the region, but also to provide a place of escape from Britain's cities for those seeking solitude, fresh air and outdoor life. In common with other National Parks in Britain, the boundaries designated reflected the limitations of 1950s landscape aesthetics. In seeking to protect the most beautiful, wild or untouched parts of Britain, urban and industrial areas were usually excluded. In Pembrokeshire this meant the heartland of the historic Milford Haven waterway, from Milford Haven to Pembroke Dock, and even Pembroke Castle and town were left out.

More recently this imbalance has been corrected with the designation of a series of Historic Landscapes by the Countryside Council for Wales, Cadw and ICOMOS, the International Council on Monuments and Sites. The first *Register of Landscapes of Outstanding Historic Interest in Wales* recognised the deep historic value of the Milford Haven waterway, its naval defences, towns and industries, in the same context as more traditionally valued historic landscapes like Skomer Island, Preseli and St David's Head with Ramsey Island. Since publication of this Register in 1998, Cambria Archaeology has worked to develop detailed characterisations of these and other landscape areas, making the results fully available online.

Figure 114. Families at Broad Haven beach, below Stackpole Warren in south-east Pembrokeshire, in early evening sunlight in August 2000. On hot summer evenings after a few hours of aerial photography, the author has often been tempted to head for the beach himself rather than write the flight report and start the long drive home (RCAHMW, DI2006-0353).

ISLAND LANDSCAPES: SKOMER, RAMSEY AND THE WESTERN ISLES

Scattered in the sea off western Pembrokeshire, separated from the mainland by narrow channels beset by turbulent currents and racing tides, are some of Wales' major off-shore islands and reefs. Unlike Scotland, Wales has few islands of any great size and those in Pembrokeshire are the focus of endless attention from geologists, ecologists, ornithologists, conservationists and archaeologists. Looking west the next landfall is the east coast of America, some 3,000 miles away, and the winter gales which drive in from the Atlantic are responsible in great part for the contorted forms of the battered shores. On clear days the islands can appear very close, including Grassholm with its white covering of nesting gannets lying 11 kilometres west of Skomer. The antiquarian Richard Fenton, writing in 1811, described a view from the west of Marloes which any visitor to the coastline bordering St Brides Bay can still enjoy on a clear day:

'From a knoll of some height for this part of the country… you have a most enchanting view of Bride's Bay, St David's Twin Mountains, and all the islands distinctly, Ramsey, Skomar, Skokham, Gatholm, at a great distance Gresholm, and at a still greater the lighthouse on the Smalls faintly seen in the horizon…'

Today the islands represent wild, marginal environments. Skomer is a National Nature Reserve and a Scheduled Ancient Monument, while the waters around it and Skokholm are designated as one of three Marine Nature Reserves in Britain. But the islands were very vigorously farmed even in Fenton's day. He writes that Skokholm (his Skokham) '… has pasture and arable land, is partly inclosed, and is well supplied with water, having several fine springs…' Two or three thousand years before Fenton's day, during the later Bronze or Iron Ages, some of the islands were actively farmed and settled. Remains of houses and fields on Skomer and Ramsey are typical of many similar remains which survive intact along the western seaboard of Wales. They are certainly of European archaeological significance and represent some of the best preserved pre-Roman farming landscapes in the British Isles, easily comparable to more famous examples in Wessex or Dartmoor. Together with the surviving landscapes of St David's Head, Mynydd Carn–ingli and Mynydd Preseli, these special places must be deeply valued for their cultural legacy, as well as for their flora, fauna and geology, and protected for future generations to marvel at and enjoy.

Figure 115 (opposite, page). Skokholm lighthouse, sited on the south-west point of the island, was originally opened in 1915. It looks out across some of the most dramatically coloured Old Red Sandstone cliffs in Pembrokeshire. (RCAHMW, 93-cs-0106).

Figure 116 (below). South Bishop and its treacherous rocks. Approaching the lonely rock of South Bishop from the east, March 2002. In 1839 a lighthouse was established on one of the larger of a treacherous scatter of islets and rocks known as the Bishops and Clerks, about eight kilometres south-west of St David's Head. Standing atop the 30.5 metre (100 feet) high rock. South Bishop preserves the oldest completely unaltered lantern in a working lighthouse in England and Wales. The lighthouse became automated in 1983 (RCAHMW, 2002-cs-0330).

Figure 117 (above). Fierce tidal races through Ramsey Sound, seen at The Bitches rocks, make for difficult crossings by boat between Ramsey Island and the mainland (RCAHMW, 2000-cs-0692).

Figure 118 (right). Eastern Skomer Island, looking south-east towards The Neck in winter 2001. Low February sunlight picks out the fields and hut groups of pioneering prehistoric communities who made Skomer their home. Whilst some of the fields are enclosed by well-built stone walls faced with boulders, others have become terraced into 'lynchets' by the use of the plough, a process whereby plough soil is moved downslope over many years of cultivation and forms earthen steps or terraces against the original boundary (RCAHMW, 2001-cs-0664A).

Figure 119 (left). The awesome spectacle of Ramsey Island's north-western cliffs, with their caves and inlets, seen as the aircraft turns on a cold winter's day in January 1994 (RCAHMW, DI2006-0589).

SKOMER ISLAND: A WINDOW ON THE PAST

Skomer Island (a Scandinavian word which describes the cloven shape of the island) ranks among the finest archaeological landscapes in Britain. Its comparative isolation from the mainland, and the limited impact of recent agriculture, has meant that considerable tracts of Skomer have not been ploughed or built on since prehistoric times. It is now famed for its wildlife and ecosystems, but on the unploughed parts of the island small huts, animal pounds, farmsteads and elaborate systems of fields survive from the Bronze and Iron Ages to show us the ways in which our prehistoric ancestors lived and worked the land. A detailed survey by John Evans, published in 1990, together with earlier survey work by W. F. Grimes, represent our main source of information.

The soils on Skomer are known to be fertile and were farmed in recent centuries. When prehistoric founding communities first made the crossing to Skomer it is thought the island would have presented a favourable habitat, with a light covering of oak woodland, an equable climate, and a number of freshwater springs and streams. Prehistoric settlements chiefly survive on the peripheries of the island. In the central area fields dating from the eighteenth century, and farmed until 1948, have largely obliterated any traces of earlier structures, in a pattern repeated endless times across mainland Pembrokeshire. Traces of life are abundant within

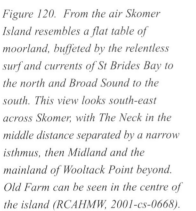

Figure 120. From the air Skomer Island resembles a flat table of moorland, buffeted by the relentless surf and currents of St Brides Bay to the north and Broad Sound to the south. This view looks south-east across Skomer, with The Neck in the middle distance separated by a narrow isthmus, then Midland and the mainland of Wooltack Point beyond. Old Farm can be seen in the centre of the island (RCAHMW, 2001-cs-0668).

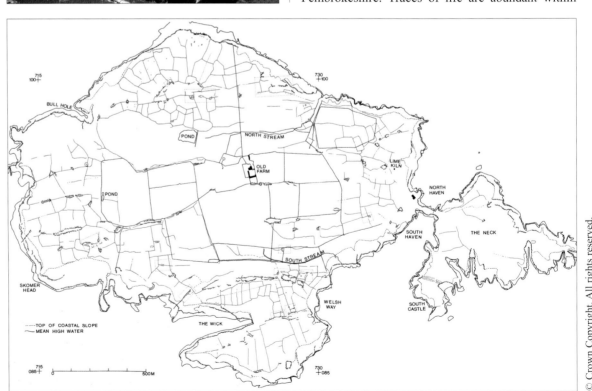

Figure 121. Plan of Skomer Island by John Evans (building on work by W. F. Grimes), showing relict field systems (in red) mapped from aerial photographs by Terry James (after Evans 1990, Figure 2. Reproduced by kind permission of the Prehistoric Society and Julie Gardiner; Crown Copyright).

these peripheral hamlets. Mounds of burnt stone close to houses are probably evidence for cooking sites, whilst funnel entrances to some farms, and isolated circular or D-shaped enclosures, are tangible evidence of stock management. Indeed, prehistoric fields, originally used for grazing sheep, cattle and even pigs, radiate outwards from the hamlets and their outcrops. A mixed economy of livestock and cereals would have been supplemented with coastal and marine resources: sea-birds and their eggs, seals and seaweed, plus a range of shellfish and sea-fish. In all, the Skomer families would have enjoyed a varied and nutritious diet. Groups of stone cairns along more remote coastal headlands may be burial monuments, or evidence for organised field clearance where they occur closer to farms. Siân Rees has noted that the Harold Stone stands as a prominent marker on the skyline as one approaches by sea. It may have been used as a transit marker to clear submerged dangers by those arriving from across the sea, although the

Figure 122. Southern Skomer, looking west, with South Stream on the right-hand side and the inlet of Welsh Way in the foreground. Terraced fields, cultivation ridges (centre foreground) and the circular 'pockmarks' of prehistoric huts can be seen on the right-hand side, parallel with South Stream (RCAHMW, 96-cs-0240).

81

Figure 123. At each of the cardinal points four main prehistoric communities can be discerned. Within each, single round huts and small farmsteads comprising two or more huts and animal pounds were built against rock outcrops, both for purposes of shelter and to be within easy reach of building stone. These two views show the northern part of the island with its field systems radiating from low outcrops. The detailed photograph shows two circular hut foundations and field walls around outcrops on the northern side of Skomer, John Evans's (1990) sites 7 (foreground) and 6 (background; RCAHMW, 2001-cs-0683 (overview) and 96-cs-0255 (detail).

possibility remains that it is a ritual standing stone.

There is little doubt that this would have been a rewarding place to live in prehistory, except during winter gales, but this way of life did not last. The fact that the settlements are clearly visible today and not confused by later periods of occupation tells a tale of abandonment. Archaeologists studying the settlement pattern have seen the potential for conflict, in particular between two closely-spaced hamlets on the isthmus of land between The Wick and Welsh Way on the south of the island where there were perhaps 'looming possibilities of competition for water, squabbles over boundaries and escaping stock…'

(Evans 1990, 252). At the same time, raw materials on the island like timber and peat became exhausted and the last families may have been forced to make the journey back across Jack Sound to start new lives on the mainland.

The richness and complexity of Skomer's archaeology only becomes fully visible from the air in winter or spring, when low ground vegetation and raking sunlight across this moorland table combine to reveal every bank and hollow before the growth of bracken. In late spring the patterns of fields and huts are enlivened by a carpet of bluebells, covering the whole island in purple and blue.

Figure 124. The Iron Age promontory fort of South Castle on The Neck, seen here from the east (left, background), may be contemporary with the farming settlements on the main island. Fewer field boundaries have been mapped on The Neck, but this air photograph shows additional prehistoric walls omitted on the original published survey (RCAHMW, AP-2006-0193).

Figure 125. Ramsey Island, with Ynys Bery in the foreground, from the south in winter 1994 (RCAHMW, 94-cs-0141).

Lying only some 700 metres west of mainland Pembrokeshire across a treacherous stretch of water known as Ramsey Sound, the slopes of Ramsey bear evidence of human settlement dating back some 4,000 years. Ramsey is thought to be either a personal Viking name, 'Hrafn's isle', or to mean simply 'wild garlic'. In Welsh it is known as Ynys Dewi, St David's Island, and also Ynys Tyfanog, St Tyfanog's Island. In legend Ramsey is the burial place of 20,000 saints; today it is a bird reserve managed by the Royal Society for the Protection of Birds (RSPB). The sea cliffs and grassy hills are home to a rich variety of wildlife, from major seabird colonies of guillemots and razorbills, kittiwake and fulmars, to deer and the largest colony of Atlantic grey seals in southern Britain.

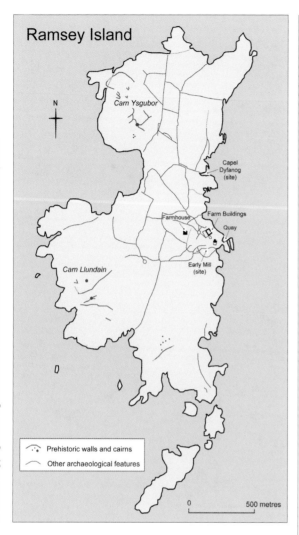

Figure 126. An archaeological survey of Ramsey Island carried out by Heather and Terry James for the RSPB in 1994, showing historic field boundaries, in black, and prehistoric boundaries and cairns, in red, climbing Carn Llundain and Carn Ysgubor in the west of the island (map by RCAHMW, after James and James 1994; redrawn by kind permission of Heather and Terry James).

Figure 127. Cliffs, coves and caves along Ramsey Island's south-western shores, north of Trwynmynachdy (foreground: RCAHMW, DI2006-0521).

As with Skomer, and perhaps Grassholm, there are traces of very early settlements on Ramsey. Both Carn Llundain and Carn Ysgubor have cairns on their summits which appear to be lofty burial mounds of the Early Bronze Age. More spectacular burial sites, facing the gales of the Atlantic Ocean, are hard to imagine. In 1811 Fenton first observed '…ancient lines of enclosure' on the slopes of Carn Llundain and mused that they might be of the same date as the summit cairns, but it was not until faint field walls

85

Figure 128 (above). The Farmhouse, on the eastern side of Ramsey Island overlooking The Bitches. Ramsey was the property of the bishops of St Davids until the early twentieth century, and the fields around The Farmhouse may conceal one of Ramsey's two reputed chapels and an early-medieval cemetery (RCAHMW, 97-cs-0205).

Figure 129 (right). Despite being only three kilometres long, the topography of Ramsey provides a wide range of habitats and landscape types. On the west side the two heather-clad rocky summits of Carn Llundain in the south and Carn Ysgubor in the north rise up above precipitous cliffs. Here, on Carn Llundain, sinuous low stone walls (left), thought to be of prehistoric date, are picked out in winter sunlight (RCAHMW, 94-cs-0158).

were seen during aerial photography by Terry James and, later, Chris Musson that their existence was confirmed. Field survey by Terry and Heather James during the 1990s for the RSPB showed that traces of these prehistoric field walls survive on the unenclosed slopes of both western summits. Those on Carn Ysgubor appear to be different in construction and, thus, perhaps older. Similar ancient walls have been mapped on the southern,

lower part of the island in an area deep-ploughed between the 1930s and 1950s for grain cultivation. The evidence suggests that fields may have been first laid out on Ramsey in the Early/Middle Bronze Age (*c.*2,100-1,500 BC), supporting island communities based in small hamlets and farms, as on Skomer, traces of which may have been erased by the later medieval fields and historic ploughing around The Farmhouse.

ACROSS THE SEA TO GRASSHOLM

The author and his pilot made the first archaeological flight to Grassholm Island on a clear, cold St Valentine's day in 2001. The eleven kilometres of open water from Skomer Island was crossed in a 2-seater Cessna, with pilot and photographer wearing life jackets, warm coats, hats and headphones and staying at altitude for safety. On reaching this small rock, barely 400 metres across, we were struck by the dense white covering of nesting gannets, which were also spiralling into the air below the aircraft, and the barren nature of the wave-bashed, rugged cliffs. Despite the extreme isolation of this island, the winter light showed up traces of enclosures, houses and shelters on the saddle of grassy ground between the gannets and the rocks, some first recorded in the middle of the twentieth century by the archaeologists W. F. Grimes and Douglas Hague.

Fragments of hand-made pottery of Iron Age type were found in 'ancient dwellings' on Grassholm before 1951, whilst further visits by archaeologists during the 1960s and 1970s provided surveys of a circular enclosure with radiating walls and a building platform. The surveyors concluded that the remains showed a serious attempt to set up a farmstead on Grassholm, rather than shelters associated with catching gannets. The prehistoric pottery shows potential for very early settlement on the island. There is the possibility that the main structures date from Viking or Early Christian times. Alternatively, they could have been used by shepherds into the twentieth century on occasional visits to de-pasture sheep. The island was used as a target for bombing practice by the United States Air Force during the Second World War, leaving bomb craters and shrapnel. Nonetheless, this new aerial photography of Grassholm, taken in low light, shows more structures than have been recorded by previous visitors. These may be undiscovered structures missed in the past when flat summer light and a covering of tussocky grass rendered them almost invisible.

Figure 130. Grassholm Island from the north-west, with its characteristic covering of nesting gannets, February 2001 (RCAHMW, 2001-cs-0688).

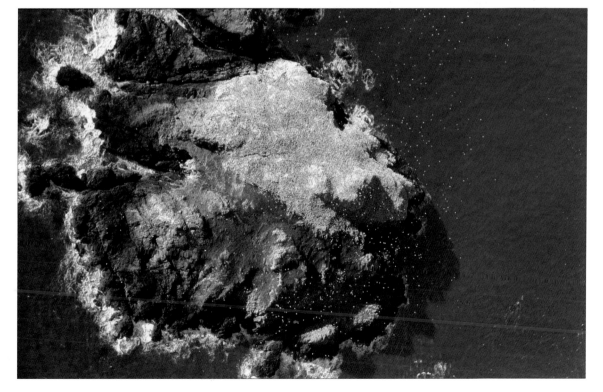

Figure 131. Grassholm, a detailed view from the south taken as the aircraft orbits, showing earthworks of walls and shelters on the south-east side of the island, and nesting gannets obscuring the north-west side. Compare with interpretation sketch (RCAHMW, 2001-cs-0690).

Figure 132. View along the southern cliffs of Skokholm Island from the west, winter 2001, with the lighthouse commanding The Head. The terribly isolated location of the lighthouse is evident in this view (RCAHMW, 2001-cs-0700).

Figure 133 (right). Skokholm from the north-east (left-background), looking out across Broad Sound from the mainland with Marloes Sands in the foreground at high tide, the medieval and earlier settlement at Gateholm Island jutting into the middle distance, and Skomer on the far right. Summer 2006 (RCAHMW, AP-2006-3332).

Figure 134 (below). Skokholm Island seen from the west, with Mad Bay in the foreground and Hog Bay opposite. Like Skomer and Grassholm, Skokholm is an important nesting site for seabirds, particularly Manx shearwaters and storm-petrels (RCAHMW, 2001-cs-0706).

CHAPTER FOUR

THE NORTH-WEST: ST DAVIDS TO PEN-CAER / STRUMBLE HEAD

The north-west peninsula of Pembrokeshire, extending from Pen-caer/Strumble Head to St David's Head and properly terminating in Ramsey Island offshore (see Chapter 3), is characterised by a craggy, indented coastline of steep cliffs and narrow inlets, fringing a fertile, level plateau intermittently broken by rugged outcrops. Despite being partly sheltered at the mouth of St George's Channel from the full ravages of the Atlantic Ocean, the exceedingly old rocks of this peninsula have been shaped by wind and waves for millennia. The stunted trees and bushes along the coast, together with the squat forms of the older cottages, reflect this long association with the worst of winter gales, yet lush vegetation and flowers thrive in the benevolent climate of spring and summer.

Approaching St Davids, Fenton wrote in 1811: '…the prospect in all its extent is enlivened by a view of the sea, its various bays, and diversified headlands…bounded in front by the bold rocks of St Davids and the islands; and in the rear by the blue range of the Presselly hills'. In common with much of the Pembrokeshire coast, the westward aspect of the St Davids peninsula has brought both prosperity and change. Porth Mawr, or Whitesands Bay, is the legendary gateway for embarkations and landings across the Irish Sea. The many Neolithic chambered tombs, some of them Portal Dolmens of the Irish Sea tradition, are frequently sited looking out to sea and may well reflect the Irish origins of their builders or at least acknowledge distant cultural influence. The Iron Age promontory forts, in which the Pembrokeshire coast is so rich, dominate the coastline and there is little doubt that the smaller irregular fields to the north of St Davids and on Pen-caer/Strumble Head, still part of the present-day farming landscape, originated in prehistory. The Roman navy certainly charted St David's Head, it being named Octapitarum Promontory on Ptolemy's map. With the Roman road west of Carmarthen appearing to head towards St Davids, it may be that this headland conceals a lost Roman port as indicated by finds of Roman remains by Fenton.

Tradition tells us that St David established an early Christian community or clas close to Whitesands Bay before founding a cathedral inland at the present site in the secluded valley of the River Alun. It is known that the Vikings carried out a series of raids during the tenth and eleventh centuries. St Davids was sacked four times by them, and it is probable that any vestiges of the original clas were destroyed. Under Norman control north Pembrokeshire was subdued by a chain of stone castles, together with smaller mottes supporting timber strongholds at St Davids and Pointz Castle near Brawdy. The English saw to the building of the great cathedral of St Davids and administered the Welsh province of Dewisland as an ecclesiastical domain.

Traces of more recent settlements and industries fringe a coastline rich in historic fishing villages, harbours and industrial archaeology. The coastal village at Porthgain is peaceful today but it lies at the heart of a derelict industrial landscape which, in its heyday, would have been alive with people, ships, smoke and noise. To the east the rocky headland of Pen Caer/Strumble Head retains a distinctive personality and air of remoteness, despite its proximity to the thriving ferry terminal at Goodwick. No doubt this air of solitude encouraged the French to launch the last invasion of British soil at Carreg Gwastad Point in 1797, a furtive act which contributed to a growing feeling of insecurity during the nineteenth century about the possible threat of a full-scale French invasion.

Figure 135. The deserted village of Maes y Mynydd, sited on the rather exposed northern flanks of St David's Head. Around the ruinous cottages are the fields which originally served this community. Local tradition suggests it was a Quaker settlement, with a cemetery (RCAHMW, 2002-cs-0325).

Figure 136 (opposite). St Davids Cathedral and Close, seen from the south-east over Goat Street in 1990. (RCAHMW, 905517-18).

Figure 137 (opposite). High view of the city of St Davids from the north in March 2002, showing traces of surrounding medieval strip fields (RCAHMW, DI2006-0524).

Figure 138 (left). Looking down on St Davids on 7 July 1946, with the cathedral in the centre of the view and the small, unmodernised city extending to the east. Curving patterns of medieval strip fields preserve the classic 'S' curve developed through years of ploughing by teams of oxen. Many of these have been built over as post-war housing has expanded. Granted city status by Queen Elizabeth the Second on 1 June 1995, and with a population of less than 2,000 inhabitants, St Davids is now recognised as the smallest city in Britain. Such historic vertical aerial views in the National Monuments Record of Wales exist of communities across Wales and are an invaluable record of post-war change (Crown Copyright, MoD/1946, 106G/UK/1625 3012).

Figure 139. The northern Dewisland coastline from near Porthgain (inlet, left foreground) towards St David's Head and Ramsey Island in the far distance, July 2000 (RCAHMW, DI2006-0532).

Figure 140. Traces of the Second World War. St Davids airfield was completed in 1943 for Coastal Command and used as a temporary home for detachments of Flying Fortresses before becoming a permanent base for Nos. 58 and 502 squadrons of Halifaxes. It saw service for the remainder of the war and eventually closed in the 1950s. The vast runways saw brief reuse for the National Eisteddfod in 2002. (RCAHMW, DI2006-0525).

The considerable antiquity of human occupation of this far-westerly peninsula of Britain cannot be overstated. The monuments and landscapes found here have been visited and praised by numerous early travellers and antiquarians, including George Owen, the Pembrokeshire antiquarian and historian writing in about 1600, the famous archaeologist Sir Richard Colt Hoare, who toured these parts in 1793, and

Figure 141. Clawdd y Milwyr promontory fort, St David's Head. On this battered, rounded headland, mostly comprising bare rock and washed by winter storms, an Iron Age promontory fort was constructed containing up to eight stone-built round houses on a saddle of ground. Six were excavated in 1898 by Rev. S. Baring Gould, the year before he investigated Foel Trigarn on Mynydd Preseli. Clearing the floors, he discovered spindle-whorls, used in weaving, pottery and blue glass beads, suggesting occupation in the Late Iron Age and Romano-British periods. More modern research has also suggested that fortifications like this could have far earlier origins, in the Neolithic or Bronze Ages (RCAHMW, 915505.13).

Figure 142. A stunning seaward view of St David's Head from the west-north-west, probably in 1961, with a bracken burn in progress on the main headland where the prehistoric field systems survive (undated print from the Grimes archive, Grimes 77, DI2006-0421. Copyright Reserved).

Figure 143. St David's Head from the south. The promontory fort was defended from the mainland by three ramparts built of rubble and substantial boulders, pierced by a passageway. The new survey identified a great defensive wall built inland, some distance away, cutting off about 25 hectares of the western headland (seen here crossing bottom left to top right). It appears to have been sited defensively, following key contours, and also has a central gateway. The suggestion is that this is an outer defence for Clawdd y Milwyr, turning it from a small promontory fort to one component of a massively defended headland (RCAHMW, 97-cs-0228).

Richard Fenton writing in 1811. The principal remains are preserved on St David's Head, an area of rough heathland bordering the coast which has not been farmed in modern times. They include a well-

preserved Iron Age promontory fort, a Neolithic chambered tomb, Coetan Arthur, and extensive relict field systems. Fenton eloquently described them thus: 'All over this dreary solitude there occur in every direction ancient inclosures seemingly the remains of the earliest population, druidical mysteries, and military operations.' In 1997 Ken Murphy, an archaeologist from Cambria Archaeology, carried out a survey of the entire headland, spurred on in part by a widespread bracken fire of 1996 which had revealed many previously hidden features. At the same time Chris Musson and the author flew several winter sorties to photograph these extensive field systems from the air, often recording faint wall lines and traces of ridge and furrow which were difficult for the ground archaeologists to see. This aerial information was mapped onto the results of the ground survey, giving a new plan of unparalleled clarity, the results of which are discussed in the captions of the following photographs.

Figure 144 (above). The 1996/7 bracken burn-off on St David's Head and Carn Llidi revealed ancient features so clearly that the aerial photography was able to record slight traces of cultivation ridges (parallel lines, centre), possibly dating from prehistoric times (RCAHMW, 97-cs-0242).

Figure 145 (above). Carn Llidi from the north-west, showing both rectilinear field boundaries and more sinuous lines running from the northern sea cliffs (foreground) to the slopes of the outcrop. The parallel field boundaries are thought to be prehistoric, and are interspersed with fields and enclosures of later, medieval date (RCAHMW, 97-cs-0246).

Figure 146 (left). The propped capstone of Coetan Arthur Neolithic chambered tomb (centre), amidst the boulders and outcrops of St David's Head (RCAHMW, 94-cs-0137).

Figure 147. Comparison with the sinuous, radiating field patterns still in use by modern farmers to the south and east of St David's Head suggests that these too have their origins in prehistory. This view looks north over Carn Hen (centre), with Carn Llidi rising on the right (RCAHMW, 89-cs-0249).

Figure 148. Clegyr Boia is a rocky outcrop rising from the coastal plateau to the west of St Davids. Excavations in the first half of the twentieth century confirmed occupation in the Neolithic and Iron Age periods. Dated Neolithic settlements in Wales are extremely rare, but the discovery of crude huts and Neolithic round-bottomed pottery confirms occupation of this rock 5-6,000 years ago. The name Clegyr Boia also associates this outcrop with the stronghold of a sixth-century AD Irish pirate named Boia, and the potential for post-Roman occupation here adds to the rarity and importance of this enduring settlement. Plastic covers protect Pembrokeshire potato crops beyond (RCAHMW, 91-cs-0258).

Figure 149. Whitesands Bay, more correctly Porth-mawr or the great gateway, is the traditional location for arrivals and embarkations from and to Ireland. This has long been the favoured site for the so-called Roman port of Menapia, originally proposed in a faked Roman itinerary, since debunked (see Chapter 6), and discussed many times since by Fenton, Sir Richard Colt Hoare and current historians and archaeologists. It is entirely possible that the great dune system of The Burrows/Y Tywyn on the coast at Whitesands conceals not only a Roman port but also the early Christian community originally founded by St David, before it was moved inland to the valley of the Alun. Stray sherds of Roman pottery or coinage from an established coastal settlement may yet be revealed to the eyes of walkers scouring the sand dunes (RCAHMW, 2002-cs-0461).

Figure 150. Caer Aber Pwll (Caerau) forts, west of Abereiddy, looking west. Complex coastal earthworks define a simple promontory fort to the east (bottom) and a more heavily defended promontory fort on the west (centre), both utilising the defensive potentials of the steep coastal cliffs. Several phases of occupation and rebuilding are probably represented by the many different ramparts and ditches which define the forts. The main, inturned, gateway to the complex west fort can be made out on the far side of the earthworks. Both are crossed today by the Pembrokeshire coast path (RCAHMW, 89-cs-0223).

The density of Iron Age promontory forts along the Pembrokeshire coast is scarcely matched elsewhere in Wales. Of the fifty-four promontory forts known, some occupy fairly level ground using sheer cliffs on one side to enhance their defences, while others employed massive banks and ditches to cut off entire promontories and enclose a settled area. Some have suffered so much at the hands of coastal erosion that only slivers of the original forts remain (see Great Castle Head and Flimston Bay, Chapter 7). Cambria Archaeology carried out two excavations towards the end of the 1990s at the badly eroded forts at Porth y Rhaw, Solva, and Great Castle Head, Dale, to learn more about the surviving fort interiors before they are lost to the sea.

Over the years archaeologists have debated the role of these coastal forts. Were they always sited on the edges of cliffs or have 2,000 years of coastal erosion made them that way? If originally sited to enclose treacherous cliffs, how did the inhabitants go about their daily lives without losing their foothold, or their livestock, over the edge? These are practical considerations if we are to visualise the residents of entire defended villages living with sea cliffs on three sides. The archaeologist Barry Cunliffe (2001, 9)

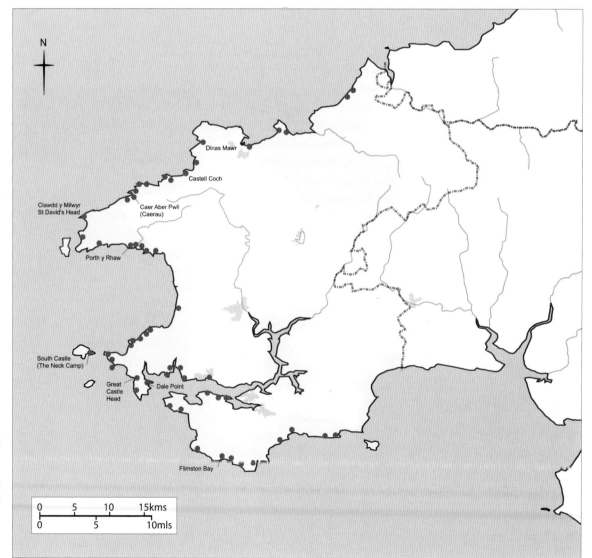

Figure 151. Locations of the 54 recorded coastal promontory forts in Pembrokeshire, from a survey and assessment by Cumbria Archaeology, showing key sites mentioned in this book (RCAHMW, after information from Crane 1999, illus. 1).

Figure 152 (right). Castell Coch, Tre-fin. Photographed on a May day in 1989, with lush grass and gorse bushes in bloom, this view looks south across the Iron Age promontory fort in the foreground, where two main ramparts cut across a narrow isthmus, to Tre-fin in the background (RCAHMW, 89-cs-0223).

questioned the whole role of prehistoric coastal forts, preferring to see them not as defended homes but rather as 'special places' in liminal positions between land and sea, perhaps where prehistoric communities would go to practice rituals and worship the gods of the sea. Ken Murphy (2002, 52-53) has also noted that while some promontory forts have easy access to the sea via coves and beaches, allowing inhabitants to exploit maritime resources below the fort, others are located on high cliffs many miles from a suitable access point, allowing little interaction with the maritime zone.

Recent excavations certainly suggest that at least some of these promontory forts were permanently occupied, with many different phases of settlement within the ramparts and evidence for metal and glass working. Rather than being solely Iron Age in date, it is now thought that a number were first constructed during the Later Bronze Age, while most continued in occupation well into the Roman period. However, some coastal promontory forts appear so striking or extraordinary, with little or no room for settlement (see Dinas Mawr, Llanwnda, below), that some other ritual purpose may indeed explain their construction.

Figure 153. Dinas Mawr, Llanwnda, Pen-caer. Looking down from the south-east, with gorse in bloom, the Iron Age promontory fort is visible as two substantial ramparts cutting across the promontory at the centre of the picture. The ramparts were once stone-walled and are pierced by central gateways, the inner lined with slabs. Although there are traces of at least one hut circle just inside the gate, most of Dinas Fawr comprises a towering pinnacle of rock, with little space for settlement. In instances like this, where much prehistoric effort was dedicated to defending a very restricted coastal promontory, it is hard not to wonder if there was some ritual or ceremonial use for the 'fort' positioned in a 'liminal' space between land and sea. Dinas Mawr resembles the Channel Island coastal site of La Pinnacle on Jersey, which was used for axe-making, settlement and ritual activities for thousands of years (RCAHMW, 96-cs-0594).

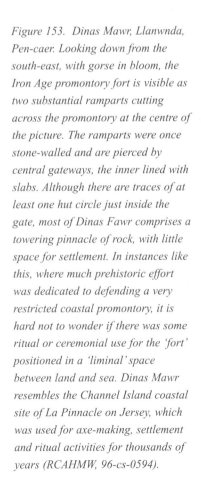

Figure 154 (above). Parc y Castell ring and bailey, St Davids. A medieval ringwork castle, with the remains of a rectangular outer bailey, survives in a concealed position on the north slopes of the River Alun, just west of St Davids, between the city and Porthclais harbour. Its origins are unclear and there is no recorded history, although some historians consider it may have been built by the bishops around 1115 to protect the early cathedral precinct from attack (RCAHMW, 2002-cs-0376).

Figure 155. St Davids Cathedral from the west on a bright May day in 2004, with visitors clustered at the south doorway (RCAHMW, 2004-cs-0657).

Figure 156 (below). Porth y Twr, St Davids. The original east gate into the Cathedral Close, which now functions as the bell tower. The gateway was re-roofed and restored in 2000 to serve as an exhibition area (RCAHMW, AP-2004-0143).

The westernmost peninsula of Pembrokeshire is dominated by the city and cathedral close of St Davids, spiritual home of the patron saint of Wales, which has stood as a place of religious sanctity and pilgrimage for well over a millennium. In medieval times it was said that two pilgrimages to St Davids were equal to one to Rome. The site of St David's original early Christian community, thought to have lain west of the city, has long been lost to history and archaeology and has passed into the realms of legend. This early community was short-lived, however, and was soon moved inland to the banks of the River Alun where the cathedral stands today. By the ninth century St Davids or Menevia was a famous Welsh monastery and a cult centre for followers of the saint. While the earliest sections of the cathedral date back only to the twelfth century, it is thought likely that the layout of the medieval cathedral close wall may have followed the line of the pre-existing religious enclosure.

The cathedral sits at the heart of a very old and largely intact close, encircled by a strong wall with fortified gates. The close contains the fine ruins of a once lavish Bishop's Palace, now a protected ancient monument, and a complex of houses and lodgings for the archdeacons and other clerics to the north of the cathedral. Also within the close are a cemetery, a silted fish pond and original tracts of meadow unencumbered by any later development or infilling. The entire complex is still bisected by the River Alun, which is crossed by a ford. When Fenton visited he wrote: 'This close was in circuit twelve hundred yards, had a walk round with a crenelled parapet. The entrance was by four handsome gateways or Porths, answering to the four cardinal points...' The present wall was probably that built by Bishop Bek (1280-93), and of the four fortified gates, Porth Boning on the north side, Porth Gwyn on the north-west, Porth Padrig to the south and the twin towers of Porth y Twr to the east, the latter can still be seen and still functions as a main entrance from the city.

Figure 157. Cross Square, St Davids. At the centre of the smallest city in Britain lies Cross Square. At the bottom of the picture the square, stepped base supporting the City Cross can be seen. This fourteenth-century monument featuring a wheel-head and octagonal shaft is thought to be a medieval preaching cross in, or close to, its original position at the heart of the city. (RCAHMW, AP-2004-0134).

COASTAL SHRINES TO EARLY SAINTS

The westernmost headlands of Dewisland, facing across the Atlantic, comprise some of the most dramatic and long-settled stretches of coastline in Wales. Among the reminders of St Davids' immense importance as a place of religious pilgrimage in the Middle Ages are two ancient chapels sited close to the cliffs' edges. To the south of St Davids city, overlooking Skomer Island and St Brides Bay, can be found St Non's Chapel, now represented by footings and a ruinous wall, but reputedly built on the site where St Non gave birth to St David. Just to the north-east is a covered holy well where water can still be taken. Though a significant place of pilgrimage in the medieval period, it fell into disuse after the Reformation and was used as a vegetable garden.

Arguably it has regained a role as a place of pilgrimage, solitude and reflection for the many tourists who now travel the coastal path or make the short walk from St Davids.

To the west of St Davids, overlooking Ramsey Sound and the St Davids Lifeboat Station, are the more substantial remains of St Justinian's Chapel (Fig. 3). Like St Non's Chapel, this was a place of pilgrimage for medieval travellers to St Davids and gathered donations which were passed to the cathedral. Like its smaller cousin, the present stone building may obscure an earlier structure many centuries older.

Siân Rees notes that the dedication to St Stinan, a little known Celtic saint, may indicate a pre-Norman establishment.

Figure 158. St Non's Chapel, St Davids, fringed in green grass, with the holy well and shrine to the left from which a stream issues (RCAHMW, 2002-cs-0388). Inset: ground view from the north showing its coastal setting (RCAHMW. 2006-cs-0020).

Figure 159. Solva, high view from the
north-east showing the limekilns at
Lower Solva/Solfach Isaf (bottom left)
and the housing of Upper
Solva/Solfach Uchaf to the right.
The Iron Age hillfort on Solva Head
occupies the promontory on the far
left (RCAHMW, 2000-cs-0697).

Figure 160. The southern Dewisland
coastline, from Solva in the foreground
to St Davids and Ramsey Island in
the distance (RCAHMW, 2002/5502-5).

The magnificent southern coastline of Dewisland is formed of some of the oldest rocks in Britain, with the Pre-Cambrian rocks at the western end changing to Middle and Lower Cambrian rocks eastwards towards Solva. The view from the air is breathtaking; jagged cliffs with arches and offshore rocks support Iron Age promontory forts like that at Caerfai, south of St Davids, or Porth-y-Rhaw to the east approaching Solva. The small quay at Porthclais, typical of many around the Pembrokeshire coast, allowed coastal traded goods to be unloaded and transported inland, while the impressive lime kilns at Solva are evidence of the rise in lime-burning during the nineteenth century. Today tourism has become the dominant coastal trade, and school groups of kayakers and 'coasteering' teams often prove to be irresistible targets for aerial photography amongst the sea swell and rocks.

Figure 161. A near-vertical view of Porth-y-Rhaw, the gnarled remains of a much-eroded coastal promontory fort to the west of Solva. Sweeping arcs of the banks and ditches cut off a protruding promontory from the coast, while the two 'horns' to left and right represent the remains of the interior. Circular depressions on the left-hand 'horn' are Iron Age house platforms. In response to ongoing coastal erosion which removed as much as three-quarters of the original fort, excavations were carried out during 1997-8 by Cambria Archaeology, focussed on the house platforms on the left-hand 'horn'. Circular footings of at least eight round houses were discovered, some having been rebuilt five times. The fort probably began life in the Early to Middle Iron Age, but occupation continued into the Roman period, attested by radiocarbon dating and finds of fine Roman tableware. Metal working was carried out on site, as was the manufacture of glass beads similar to those found on Foel Trigarn inland (RCAHMW, 96-cs-0182).

Figure 162. Once a focus for Neolithic rituals and a place of great sanctity for the communities who laboured to move the large stones into place, the ruinous burial chambers at St Elvis are now somewhat divorced from their original surroundings. The site appears to have once been two different tombs, each surmounted by a massive capstone (RCAHMW, 94-cs-0130).

Occupying the mouth of the River Solva, Lower Solva is set back from the sea along a narrowing inlet providing sheltered harbourage. This inlet has long been considered advantageous. Solva Head promontory fort has overlooked the harbour from the east since the Iron Age, and a Roman bronze bow brooch or 'fibula' of A.D. late-first-century type was also found here. Solva was once a vibrant fishing and trading port where in its heyday, between *c.*1750 and the mid-nineteenth century, it was recorded that there were some 30 trading ships, nine warehouses and a population of over a thousand people. Remarkably, emigrants once sailed from here to New York for a single fare of £3 but had to carry their own food. It was from the same harbour that equipment, cast-iron fittings and timber for the world's earliest pile-built lighthouse on the Smalls Rock were sailed in 1775/6 by Henry Whiteside, and also for the present stone lighthouse which was erected in 1858-61. Voyages to the notorious rock by the construction team often ended in failure due to changing wind conditions. A major role of the harbour at Solva was the importation of lime, and a number of kilns can still be seen. Today Solva is something of an artists' colony and a popular destination for summer tourists.

Figure 163. Kayakers navigate rocks and currents around Porth Coch Mawr, St Non's Bay, on the southern Dewisland coastline below St Davids (RCAHMW, 2002-cs-0386).

Figure 164. Evidence of the Sea Empress disaster. The oil tanker the Sea Empress was holed just outside Milford Haven on 15 February 1996, with the bulk of the heavy oil pollution spreading south and east of the Haven, away from the north Pembrokeshire coast. This view was taken on 27 February 1996 and shows a precautionary boom in place across the mouth of Solva Harbour, below Solva Head promontory fort (RCAHMW, 96-cs-0176).

The fine igneous rocks and softer shales which form much of the northern coastline of Pen-caer/Strumble Head, and occur in more confined bands west towards St Davids, were worked by a number of small quarries along the north coast of Pembrokeshire, which gave birth to a thriving export industry. Before the coming of the railways to Pembrokeshire the ship was of paramount importance in the transport of heavy loads to distant ports, and coastal villages like Porthgain developed impressive docks and industrial facilities. From the air the supporting industrial infrastructure can also be studied.

Figure 165. Porthgain. From about 1878 stone (slate, then granite) was regularly exported from Porthgain aboard the quarry company's six specially-built 350-ton coasters. Rock won from the coastal quarries above the port was transported by a network of tramways to a crushing and grading plant just above Porthgain. The crushed rock was then fed down into a series of brick hoppers which flank the harbour, whence it was loaded onto cargo vessels. Between 1902 and 1904 the harbour was enlarged to meet the demand of a flourishing trade. During the summer of 1909 one hundred and one shipments totalling 13,000 tons were made. Bricks for the hoppers were also baked on site and were later exported to Llanelli, with 'seconds' shipped to Dublin. In the inter-war years trade did not recover sufficiently and the crushing plant closed in 1931. Today, the brick hoppers are protected as Scheduled Ancient Monuments and the harbour has become a haven for tourists and industrial archaeologists ((above) from the east, RCAHMW, 91-cs-0238; (right) from the north-west, RCAHMW, 2000-cs-0691).

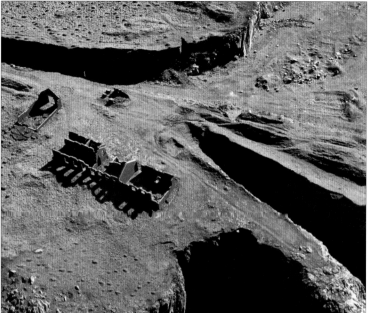

Figure 166 (above). Derelict industrial buildings, quarry face and inclines above Porthgain (RCAHMW, 91-cs-0241).

Figure 167 (top, left). Porthgain brick hoppers from the ground in 2002, showing their massive scale which can be forgotten in aerial views (RCAHMW, 2006-cs-0024).

Figure 168 (left). In their day the Porthgain quarries extracted stone not only from the headland immediately above the village, but also from half a kilometre or so west at the headland of Penclegyr, and west again on the headland close to Aber Eiddy village, where slate was quarried. This view of Aber Eiddy from the north shows the old barracks close to the beach, which used to house quarry workers (RCAHMW, 2002-cs-0319).

Figure 169 (right). Pen-caer/Strumble Head, landscape view from the east looking across Garn Folch in the foreground, with Garn Fechan and then Garn Fawr hillforts in the background. The small, irregular fields which survive in places on Pen-caer have their origins in prehistory (RCAHMW, 2003-cs-0362).

Figure 170 (below). Panoramic high view of Pen-caer/Strumble Head, taken from around 6,500 feet. Fishguard Harbour can be seen on the left, with the V-shaped Aber Felin bay below Carreg Gwastad Point in the centre foreground. In the far distance can be seen Ramsey (right) and Skomer (left) Islands (RCAHMW, 2000-cs-0499).

Pen-caer/Strumble Head is a prominent headland which breaks the line of the north Pembrokeshire coast, extending some way into Cardigan Bay. The southern part is largely comprised of softer Ordovician shales, successfully quarried for building stone in coastal exposures to the west, whereas more resistant bands of igneous, volcanic rocks rise in a series of craggy central outcrops and form much of the north of the headland. Around the coastline, in between these resistant bands, wave action has gouged inlets and bays into the softer shales, giving some respite to the otherwise vertical cliffs. Improved farmland characterises much of coastal north-west Pembrokeshire between St David's Head in the west and Mynydd Carn-ingli in the east. Only on Pen-caer do we see a return to the more ancient patterns of smaller field systems fringing the moorland, interspersed with chambered tombs, standing stones and monuments from early Christian communities. The central outcrops of Pen-caer are dominated by an impressive chain of rubble-built hillforts which overlook radiating blocks of fields first laid out in prehistory. To the north of these outcrops, and down to the formidable headlands surrounding Strumble Head lighthouse, Pen-caer retains a remote, distinctive character, far more ancient in appearance than its immediate hinterland. The single-track minor roads and hamlets remind us of what much of rural Pembrokeshire was probably like a century ago, and local people in the north-east always seem happy to retell their version of the famous French invasion of 1797 to visitors.

Figure 171. The great north Pembrokeshire hillfort of Garn Fawr occupies a prominent craggy outcrop at the west end of Pen-caer and dominates all approaches. A complex set of stony banks and ramparts formed of loose scree attests to a long and complex history. The site is notable in being one of the first British hillforts to be archaeologically surveyed, by Edward Lhuyd in about 1700. Following a field visit in 1921, Royal Commission surveyors pronounced it '...one of the most striking of the stone forts of the United Kingdom...' (Hogg 1973; RCAHMW, 2002-cs-0364).

Figure 172. On the southern flanks of Garn Fawr, is the defended enclosure of Ysgubor Gaer. This has a substantial inner bank and a wide-spaced outer rampart, partly preserved by later field boundaries. Its relationship to Garn Fawr is uncertain; it may have been a contemporary settlement or stock enclosure, or an independent fortification of the outcrop at another time in prehistory (RCAHMW, 89-cs-0206).

Figure 173 (above). The lighthouse on Strumble Head, Ynys Meicel, was built in 1908-9 to enable ships to navigate safely into Fishguard harbour, avoiding the treacherous rocky shore. It replaced an earlier light vessel moored in the south of Cardigan Bay. The island was formerly reached by an iron bridge from the mainland, but this was replaced with the current aluminium bridge in 1963. Today Strumble Head is automatically controlled from St Ann's Head to the south (RCAHMW, 2002-cs-0360).

Figure 174 (right). Aber Felin Bay below Carreg Gwastad Point (out of shot to the right), today marked by a memorial. This was the setting of the failed 1797 French landing, the last invasion of mainland British soil (RCAHMW, 96-cs-0610).

Figure 175 (below). Fishguard has a Scandinavian name, fiskigardr ('enclosure for catching or keeping fish'). The commercial port of Fishguard Harbour at Goodwick was largely constructed towards the end of the nineteenth century and the start of the twentieth. It was enclosed on the north side by a 2,500 ft breakwater which has a fine harbour light at its eastern end (RCAHMW, 2002-cs-0346).

Figure 176. One of the few pre-Second World War coastal defences to have fired shots in anger, Fishguard Fort occupies Castle Point overlooking Fishguard Harbour from the south-east. It was built between 1781 and 1785 and successfully warded off the French invasion force of 1797 with a single cannon ball, forcing them to land further along the coast of Pen-caer/Strumble Head. Today the fort stands restored with four cannon facing bravely out to sea (RCAHMW, AP-2005-1342).

Figure 177. The old fishing village of Lower Fishguard provides sheltered harbourage at the mouth of the River Gwaun (RCAHMW, AP-2004-0875).

CHAPTER FIVE

THE NORTH-EAST: CARN-INGLI, PRESELI AND THE TEIFI VALLEY

Mynydd Preseli and Mynydd Carn-ingli form two great blocks of unimproved upland moorland in the north of Pembrokeshire, sweeping east to west in an arc between Newport and Crymych and separated by the wooded valley of Cwm Gwaun. So special are these mountain tracts that the boundaries of the Pembrokeshire Coast National Park were drawn a considerable distance inland to include them. At the foot of these uplands the land changes from south to north. To the south rolling farmland cut by a series of deep valleys forms a busy, fertile plateau all the way to Haverfordwest and Narberth. To the north of Mynydd Preseli is a great expanse of bog, which gives way to a network of wooded valleys draining westwards to the sea at Newport, a medieval borough which still preserves its castle and medieval street plan. To the north-east, between Crymych and Llechryd in the Teifi Valley, the landscape is home to small villages, winding lanes and tracts of pasture extending to the boundary with neighbouring Ceredigion.

Despite their wild and remote appearance, the proximity of these hills to good farming land, ports, and communication routes has long made them a focus for human habitation. Along the high stretches of moorland, beset by hard frosts and dusted with snow during winter, can be seen a variety of rugged hillforts, lonely hilltop burial cairns, old quarries and abandoned farms, overlooked by shattered igneous rock outcrops. From the air these historic hills provide a never-ending source of monuments, sites, patterns and landscapes for photography, yielding different results in changing lights and seasons.

The quality and density of the archaeological sites on Carn-ingli and Preseli are unsurpassed in south Wales. Famous prehistoric monuments include the Portal Dolmen at Pentre Ifan and the Gors Fawr stone circle, both among the finest of their kind in Britain. Prehistoric settlements abound, most prominently in the great hillforts of Foel Trigarn in the east and Mynydd Carn-ingli in the west. The Carn Meini dolerite outcrops in the central Preseli range are the geological source of the famous 'bluestones' used at Stonehenge, reputedly transported to Wessex around 2,000 BC, although recent debates have challenged this theory. In between these very visible monuments lie scatters of boulders, disparate banks and ragged enclosures which represent the vestiges of prehistoric and later fields, farmsteads and stock enclosures. The aerial perspective can lend great clarity to these remains and has demonstrated the survival of extensive prehistoric landscapes on Mynydd Carn-ingli, on the hillslopes around Carn Alw, and on Bernard's Well Mountain to the south-west, near Rosebush reservoir.

Figure 178. An industrial legacy. High view of Rosebush quarries from the west, showing the quarries (centre), Rosebush village to the right, and the loop of the derelict Clynderwen-Maenclochog railway passing through forestry in the foreground. The slate quarries were closed by 1914 but still form an enduring sight. The main workings are characterised by stepped galleries from which slate was extracted and the great quantities of waste to either side, piled in tips. Rosebush village remains in the shadow of the quarries but now serves the needs of the tourist industry and those seeking the great outdoors (RCAHMW, 2002/5504-1).

Figure 179. Far older than the Egyptian pyramids, the slender Neolithic chamber at Pentre Ifan casts long shadows across the rectangular long mound behind it, actually the footings of a once tall stone cairn (RCAHMW, DI2005-0427).

Pentre Ifan is perhaps the finest surviving Neolithic tomb in Wales and forms one of a group of Portal Dolmens built around the tributaries of the Nevern Valley approximately 6,000 years ago. The tomb was excavated by W. F. Grimes in 1936-7, who thought that it was heavily influenced by prehistoric contacts with Ireland. More recent research suggests the tomb was an indigenous creation by the local communities but may have been nonetheless influenced by Irish culture and contact during a later stage of its use, when the long mound was extended. Finds from Pentre Ifan, as from other Welsh prehistoric tombs, were meagre, numbering a few sherds of pottery from a shouldered bowl and a triangular flint arrowhead. Its present appearance, as a gaunt freestanding structure supporting a delicately balanced capstone, may never have been witnessed by the communities who later used it. Instead, it is thought that the whole structure was covered in a massive mound or cairn of stones, with access to the chamber permitted only through the door or 'portal' at the south end.

Figure 180. An unusual view of Pentre Ifan, showing it as an integral part of its surrounding landscape. The tomb (upper right centre) survives as a fenced and restored monument in improved pasture, farmed and cleared of stones over many centuries. From the air one sees patches of deciduous woodland and occasional boulder-strewn hillsides which still survive in odd corners of the lower Preseli hills and must have covered much of Pembrokeshire in prehistory (RCAHMW, 2004-cs-0348).

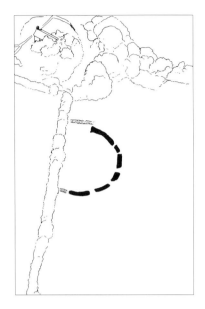

Figure 181. Bayvil is chiefly known for its tiny church, complete with bellcote, which sits in an isolated position within a circular churchyard. Aerial reconnaissance in July 1996 revealed an unexpected addition to its history. In the foreground can be seen a circle of rectangular pits showing as darker green cropmarks in ripening arable. This circle mimics the shape of the circular churchyard beyond but is far smaller and entirely different in construction. The pits suggest a Neolithic or Bronze Age ritual enclosure, similar to the Withybush pit circle near Haverfordwest. Originally, a circle of upright timber posts or stones may have stood here (RCAHMW, 96-cs-1418).

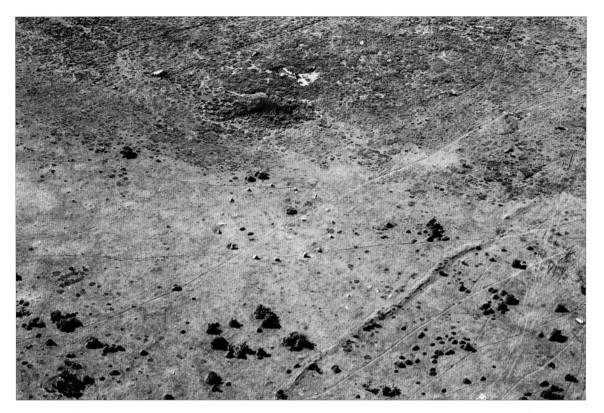

Figure 182. Gors Fawr stone circle. On the bleak fringes of Gors Fawr bog is this near-perfect circle of sixteen stones measuring about 22 metres in diameter. Eight of the stones are of spotted dolerite, the famous 'bluestone' sourced as being from the Carn Meini outcrops to the north. Recent geophysical survey by the SPACES project, searching for any buried structures which might lie hidden beneath the circle, revealed nothing. The conclusion is that this monument probably looks much the same today as it did to its late Neolithic or Bronze Age builders. Nearby is a pair of standing stones which appears to frame the distant Carn Menyn outcrop when viewed from the south-west. From the air the small stones of Gors Fawr blend with the expanse of naturally occurring boulders which litter these unimproved bog fringes. In his 1963 Shell Guide, Vyvyan Rees was unimpressed; 'Gors Fawr, the only recognisable stone circle left in the county, is very small beer'. It is, in fact, a remarkable survivor and one of the best of its kind to be seen in Wales (RCAHMW, 95-cs-2034).

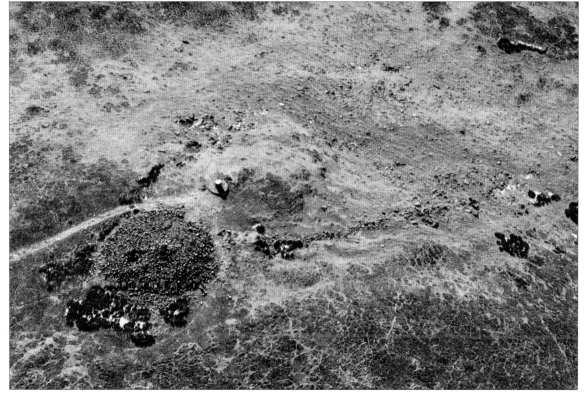

Figure 183. The grand stone cairn on the summit of Foel Eryr, thought to be a Bronze Age burial cairn, now accompanied by a concrete viewing post displaying a panorama for the benefit of walkers (RCAHMW, 93-cs-0180).

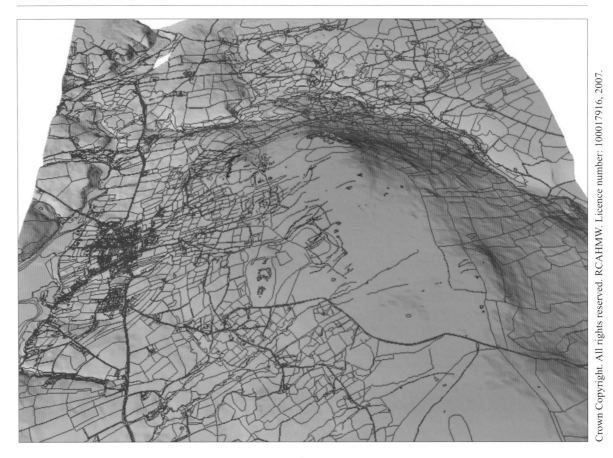

Figure 184. A virtual Pembrokeshire landscape of Mynydd Carn-ingli and Newport from the west. Newport lies at centre-left on the coastal plain, with the Gwaun Valley near Cilgwyn opening on the right side. In the middle distance are the uplands of Mynydd Carn-ingli, around Carn-ingli hillfort, with relict prehistoric and historic field boundaries and settlements mapped (in red) from aerial photographs (view created by RCAHMW from Ordnance Survey Land-Form data).

The great stone hillfort which crowns the scree-strewn summit of Mynydd Carn-ingli remains one of Pembrokeshire's great mysteries. The remains of ramparts, enclosures, huts and fields clearly have their origins in prehistory but, as yet, no excavations have shed light on the development of one of the largest hillforts in west Wales. Mynydd Carn-ingli is first recorded in the twelfth century as *Mons Angleorum*, reputedly the place where St Brynach met and discoursed with angels. It is not unusual that such a wild and remote spot should have attracted its fair share of visitors over the years. In his tour of Pembrokeshire, Fenton described it thus:

Carn Englyn... affords a most pleasing prospect of the bays of Newport and Fishguard,.... Its summit, *like that of most of the heights in this district, bears marks of early habitation, enclosures of various forms occurring amongst the wildest and most broken parts of it.*

The first detailed archaeological survey of the multitude of stone enclosures was published by A. H. A. Hogg in 1973, who was able to establish many aspects about the site which make it unusual in Welsh prehistory. The natural summit crags of Carn-ingli are enclosed by a long fortification formed of high, rough-built defensive walls. The earliest phases appear to be three conjoined enclosures on the highest point, which are probably the result of multiple periods of occupation and enlargement. The fourth and largest enclosure extends to the north onto lower ground and is crowded with stone-built

Figure 185. The expanse of Carn-ingli Common from the north-west towards the low summit of Carn-ingli hillfort in the middle distance. The distant peak of Foel Trigarn hillfort on Mynydd Preseli can be seen to the right. The overlapping patterns of prehistoric and historic field systems can be appreciated in this view (RCAHMW, 915501-02).

huts and pounds and even the remains of an old street or track. In all, the ramparts are pierced by twelve gateways, some through the cross walls which divide the successive enclosures, and some through the main outer walls. This is a very high number of vulnerable openings to defend if we assume the structure is an Iron Age hillfort, and it may be that parts of Carn-ingli date back far earlier,

to the Neolithic or Bronze Age. Another remarkable feature about the hilltop is the number of small pounds and platforms built on the slopes surrounding the fort, thought by Hogg to have been designed in prehistory to cultivate crops in the thin, stony soils.

Some researchers have suggested that parts of Carn-ingli were occupied during the early medieval

period, but Hogg cited the widespread, apparently deliberate, throwing down of walls and ramparts across the hillfort as evidence for systematic destruction by Roman invaders in the aftermath of the conquest of Wales. Such a dramatic interpretation, placing the Roman legions on the slopes of Carn-ingli in an attack on its inhabitants, might be questioned today.

All around Carn-ingli hillfort, particularly on the lower hillslopes to the north and west, survives a rich and well-preserved landscape of old field boundaries, clearance cairns, round huts and farmsteads which represents one of the great surviving prehistoric landscapes of southern Britain, unploughed in recent centuries. Aerial photography is a particularly powerful way to show the dense surviving remains of a prehistoric hillside as it was farmed and settled, probably dating to the Bronze and Iron Ages. Doctoral research by Alastair Pearson of the University of Portsmouth in the 1980s and 1990s suggested that many of these fields and worn trackways had their origins in the Bronze Age.

Figure 186. The multiple stone-built enclosures that make up Carn-ingli hillfort were probably constructed between the third and first millennia BC as a heavily defended fort and, in different times, the mountain base for a pastoral community. Settlement may also have continued into the post-Roman period (RCAHMW, 905521-12).

Figure 187. Carn Ffoi, a small Iron Age hillfort formed from scree-built ramparts linking pre-existing natural outcrops (RCAHMW, 96-cs-0127).

Figure 188. An overview of the slopes of Mynydd Carn-ingli, looking west, between Carn-ingli hillfort and Newport, showing a landscape of prehistoric clearance cairns, field boundaries and circular hut sites relatively untouched since they were first laid out (RCAHMW, 2004-cs-0255).

Figure 189. The Iron Age hillfort of Cas-fuwch, on the south-western side of Mynydd Castleblythe near Puncheston/Cas-Mael, with the ramparts highlighted by strong shadows and a hard winter frost (RCAHMW, 2004-cs-0221).

The expansive uplands which focus on, and surround, the peaks of Mynydd Preseli can be seen as a preserve of all of Pembrokeshire's human history. Here are found archaeological monuments and landscapes renowned across Wales and further afield. The following aerial photographs are intended to impart some of their breathtaking beauty and immense historical interest. Many archaeologists have been drawn to these north Pembrokeshire uplands over the centuries. Fenton provided early descriptions of numerous sites, while notable later projects included excavations at Foel Trigarn by Rev. S. Baring Gould (in 1899), at the Neolithic tombs of Pentre Ifan (in 1936-7 and 1958-9) and Bedd yr Afanc (in 1939) by

Grimes, and surveys of Mynydd Preseli by Drewett and students of the Institute of Archaeology, London, during the 1980s. Foel Trigarn was resurveyed by the Royal Commission in the late 1980s, while in 2002 an ambitious new programme of survey was commenced for the prehistoric landscapes of Strumble and Preseli by Geoffrey Wainwright and Timothy Darvill. The Strumble-Preseli Ancient Communities and Environment Study (SPACES) increased the known number of prehistoric monuments on the ridge between Carn Siân and Foel Trigarn by 300 per cent, and its new surveys of famous individual sites, like Gors Fawr, have helped to forge new understandings about prehistoric life in these hills and valleys.

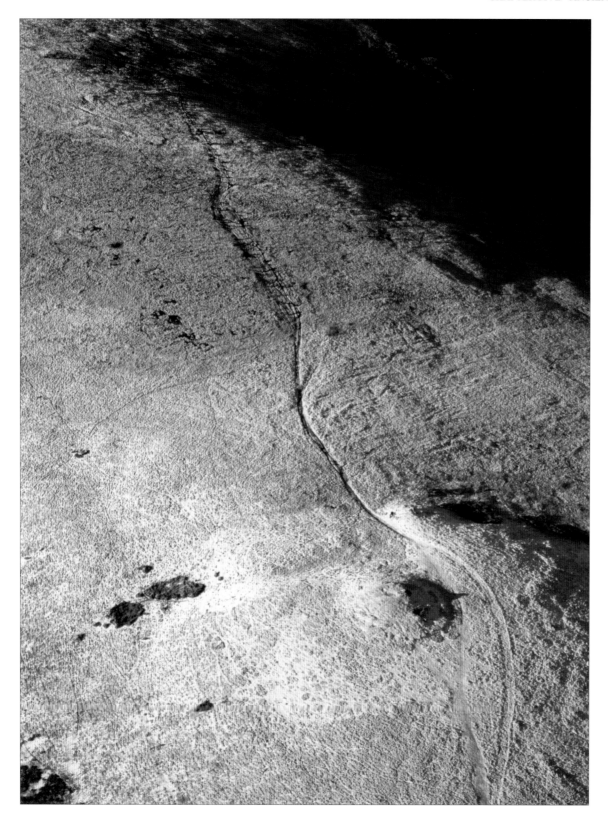

Figure 190. Bronze Age burial cairn at Foel Feddau, in the western part of Mynydd Preseli, under snow (RCAHMW, 99-cs-2311).

Figure 191 (right). Looking west along the low peaks of Mynydd Preseli in winter 1999, with Foel Trigarn hillfort in the foreground, Carn Meini in the left middle distance, and Foel Feddau in the far distance, dusted with snow (RCAHMW, 99-cs-2325).

Figure 192. Carn Meini or Carn Menyn. The shattered outcrops of characteristically white-spotted rhyolites and dolerites, known collectively as 'bluestones' for their colour when wet or freshly-broken, on the eastern arm of Mynydd Preseli above Mynachlog-ddu. View looking west, 2002 (RCAHMW, 2002-cs-1444).

Figure 193. High view of the Carn Meini outcrops, with Carn Menyn at the centre, from the north-west (RCAHMW, 2002/5504-3; DI2006-0529)

The Carn Meini outcrops on Mynydd Preseli have become famous in archaeological literature as the geological source for the 'bluestones' used at Stonehenge in Wiltshire. The 1.5- to 1.8-metre (5- to 6-feet) tall, narrow pillars formed a circle between the more massive Sarsen 'trilithons', or arches, which made up the main outer circle and the innermost stone settings. In 1923 petrological examination confirmed the scattered outcrops of Carn Meini on the south-west of Mynydd Preseli as the source of the distinctive blue-grey spotted dolerite with large white spots used in some of the earliest phases of the Stonehenge circles on Salisbury Plain. Indeed, a number of prehistoric monuments, including a ruinous cairn at Carn Menyn and Gors Fawr stone circle to the south, are also composed of this unusual

Figure 194. A bluestone pillar of Stonehenge dimensions found broken and abandoned in the process of being transported downhill from the Carn Meini outcrops by archaeologists of the SPACES project. Scale measures two metres (Copyright: SPACES. By kind permission of Professor Geoffrey Wainwright).

rock. Early investigators concluded that the known superiority of this same spotted dolerite as a raw material for Neolithic stone axes could have sparked off the massive human effort necessary to move the stones. The suggested route would have seen the blocks sledged overland to the upper reaches of the Eastern Cleddau, thence by sea along the Bristol Channel to the River Avon, and finally upstream to Stonehenge itself.

Some geologists and archaeologists have challenged this traditional view, proposing instead that glaciation, not human effort, carried the bluestones to Salisbury Plain. They cite finds of spotted dolerite in glacial erractics on Flat Holm and Steep Holm in the Bristol Channel as evidence for this geological movement. Archaeologists of the SPACES project have found an intense concentration of activity at Carn Meini, including prehistoric burial monuments and axe-flaking sites. Worked bluestone

pillars have been found broken and abandoned in transit down from the outcrops. Although these are of Stonehenge dimensions, they remain difficult to date, especially as the outcrops provided durable, conveniently-sized blocks in modern times for lintels and hearthstones and were quarried for building stone for at least two nearby chapels.

The continuing debate between the human or glacial transport of the Stonehenge bluestones has taken nothing of the romance and mystery away from the other-worldly landscape of shattered blocks and towering forms of Carn Meini. A lasting memory for the author is of getting lost amongst the outcrops in a thick fog in the early 1990s whilst researching the chambered tombs of Mynydd Preseli for an undergraduate dissertation. The gloomy fog-bound blocks were completely disorientating, and only a compass allowed safe navigation down the hill towards the path.

Figure 195. The Banc Du enclosure, from the west in winter 2002. Despite the earthwork being only a few centimetres high in places, this photograph shows many details of the enclosure ramparts which are barely visible at ground level. The curving prehistoric earthworks are crossed by lines of ridge-and-furrow cultivation (RCAHMW, 2002-cs-1734).

Occupying the summit of a low hill overlooking New Inn in Mynydd Preseli are the remains of an early defended enclosure first discovered from the air by Chris Musson in 1990. The enclosure uses steep rocky slopes on the east side as a natural defence, with ramparts completing the circuit on the more level ground to the west and north. New aerial photography in the winter of 2002 suggested that this was an unusual site. The rather meagre ramparts are built in short sections leaving gaps in between, quite unlike the more substantial, complete defences that one would expect from an Iron Age hillfort. This raised the possibility that Banc Du was an exceedingly rare Neolithic or Bronze Age hilltop enclosure. In 2005 a ditch section was excavated by the SPACES team, and radiocarbon dates from the initial silts which accumulated in the ditch show that it was open around 3,650 BC, during the Neolithic. The rampart was originally well built, with a stone-walled outer face and timber posts behind. A new

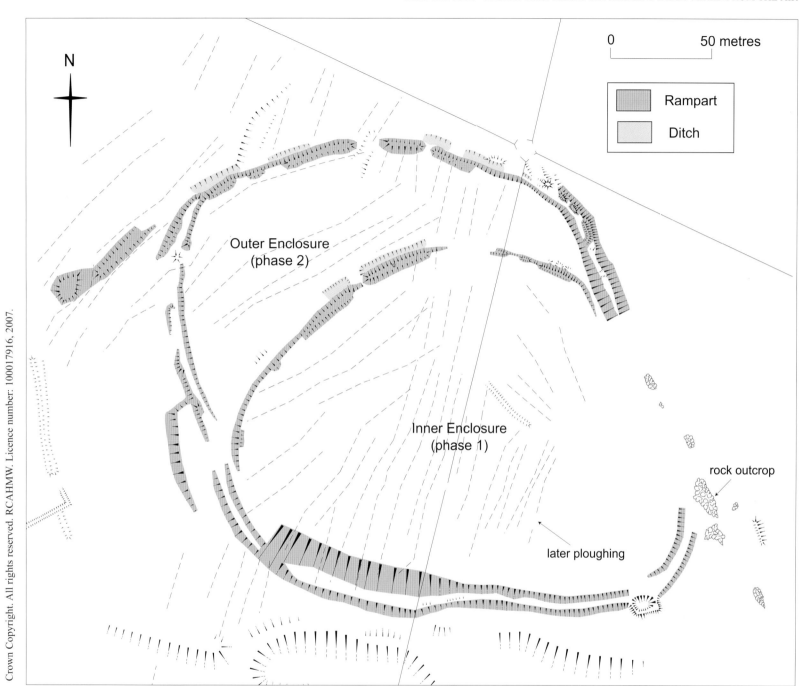

ground survey of Banc Du completed by the Royal Commission suggests that the original hilltop enclosure around the summit was enlarged with the addition of a second, wider enclosure at some point in prehistory. These discoveries are hugely significant. Banc Du is the first properly dated Neolithic enclosure in Wales and would have been contemporary with the great burial monuments of Mynydd Preseli, including the Portal Dolmen at Pentre Ifan. It is now entirely possible that other Neolithic enclosures await rediscovery and dating in the north Pembrokeshire hills.

Figure 196. Banc Du, a new survey completed by RCAHMW in 2005 (RCAHMW).

FOEL TRIGARN: AN IRON AGE REGIONAL CAPITAL?

Figure 197. Foel Trigarn hillfort: panoramic view from the east-north-east in 1989. The three great summit cairns are clear as is the second, outer enclosure and the third enclosure or annex in the foreground (RCAHMW, 895507-16).

Frequently photographed and one of the most visually striking Iron Age hillforts in Wales, Foel Trigarn occupies the easternmost ridge on Mynydd Preseli, its characteristic silhouette dominating much of the east Pembrokeshire skyline. Three main enclosures can be traced, defined by stone walls or stone-revetted banks, with traces of a ditch around the inner rampart. The earliest was probably that on the very summit, an oval fort set against natural cliffs on its southern side, enclosing 1.2 hectares and with main gates on the east, west and south sides. Attached to this first enclosure, and probably representing later periods of expansion, are a second enclosure on the north and east side which mirrors the outer ramparts

Figure 198. A hard frost and raking afternoon light in January 1999 yielded some of the most detailed images of the interior of Foel Trigarn ever taken. This view shows the fort from the north-east. The three summit cairns are punctured with countless later shelters, while some of the 88 certain and 20 possible house platforms which crowd the main, inner enclosure are visible. Two of the three main gateways into the fort can be seen as breaks in the rampart on the left and right (RCAHMW, 99-cs-2321).

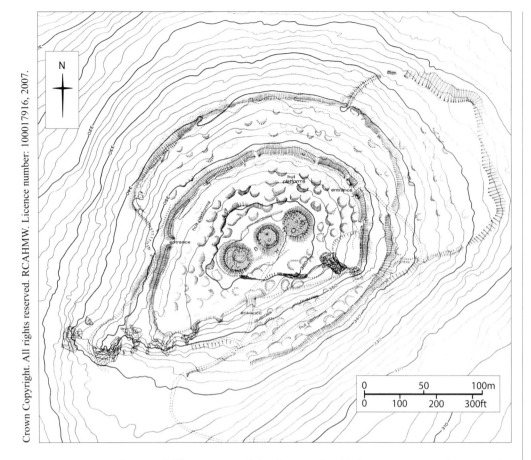

Figure 199. Foel Trigarn hillfort. Survey by RCAHMW and the University of Portsmouth. The colours show Iron Age ramparts in light brown, the massive central cairns in grey, and in green the house platforms, of which there are at least 227 (Survey by David Browne and Dr Alastair Pearson. RCAHMW/courtesy of Dr Alastair Pearson and the Department of Geography, University of Portsmouth; DI2006-0507).

of the first, and a third outer annex to the east. The most striking characteristic of Foel Trigarn is its pock-marked interior, the sites of at least 227 levelled house platforms where Iron Age houses once stood. There are also fainter traces of a further 42 uncertain platforms bringing the total closer to 270 house sites. It is highly unlikely that all these house sites were occupied at the same time. The entire hillfort was probably occupied and expanded over many centuries, rather than being used by a single leader or group of people. We are effectively seeing the remains of a complex and long-lasting prehistoric village, with all its phases of occupation on show. Early excavations in 1899 by S. Baring Gould unearthed Iron Age and Roman pottery and artefacts which included spindle-whorls, fine glass beads and a jet ring from some of the house platforms. Sling stones were also found in '…great numbers…some in piles...' (Baring Gould *et al.,* 1900, 210). A new survey by the Royal Commission and researchers from Portsmouth Polytechnic (in 1988) provided the first detailed plan.

On the summit stand three massive stone cairns after which the hill is named. These are interpreted as Bronze Age burial cairns, massive communal monuments covering the bones, or ashes, of one or several special individuals. Similar examples of pre-existing cairns surviving within later stone forts can be seen at Carn Goch in Carmarthenshire, Pen Dinas, Aberystwyth in Ceredigion and at Tre'r Ceiri on the Llŷn Peninsula, Gwynedd. As these cairns were never plundered for their stone, despite being surrounded by hundreds of houses, we must conclude that the occupants venerated their distant ancestors, while at the same time deriving power and social status from the acquisition of such a prominent, and sacred, hilltop.

The size and complexity of Foel Trigarn, one of the largest north Pembrokeshire hillforts along with Carn-ingli, Garn Fawr and St David's Head, suggests a role and function distinct from the numerous smaller hillforts like Castell Henllys. It is likely that this was a significant centre of population in its time, its design and construction initiated and overseen by a powerful regional leader. If, as one interpretation of the place mentioned by Ptolemy indicates, the Octapitai tribe occupied St David's Head, perhaps a similar group whose name was never recorded by the Romans sited their 'tribal capital' here, commanding the Iron Age lands hereabouts.

CARN ALW AND ITS IRON AGE DEFENCES

Figure 200. Carn Alw. Missed by generations of archaeologists and antiquarians, the fort was first documented by Chris Houlder and Richard Atkinson of RCAHMW in 1960. It was photographed from the air by Cambridge University in January 1970, revealing the richness of the surrounding upland archaeology. It was subsequently published by Terry James in his 1980 book with Doug Simpson, Ancient West Wales from the Air *(RCAHMW 905548-12).*

Low down on the northern side of Mynydd Preseli, due north of Carn Meini, is the shattered rhyolite outcrop of Carn Alw. Clinging to the west side of the outcrop is a small fort, occupying a restricted plateau and defended by a tumbled rampart of scree and larger boulders. Below this is a rare defensive survival from the Iron Age which makes Carn Alw extraordinary. The immediate approaches to the fort are protected by one of the few *chevaux-de-frise* visible around an Iron Age fort in the British Isles, a wide curtain of upright pointed rocks and boulders which originally made an attack on foot or horseback difficult and dangerous. Many of the rocks which make up the *chevaux-de-frise* are naturally occurring boulders, but many more, smaller, pointed stones have been set up within the spread to complete the defence. Mytum and Webster, who surveyed Carn Alw and published their results in 1989, note that the rock spread is at its most dense along its outer edge, where a 5-metre wide band of close-packed stones would have ensured a grisly end to anyone attacking the fort at speed. Beyond this the moorland is almost picked clean of usable stones, encouraging archaeologists to think that rocks were gathered up from all around to form the defence. Two well-marked paths exist through the stones, a main gateway with side-annexes on the west side, and a more hidden path approaching on the south side. *Chevaux-de-frise* are known from a handful of other Welsh hillforts, including Pen-y-gaer in the Conwy valley in north Wales, but the example from nearby Castell Henllys shows that many more may await discovery at unexcavated hillforts in Pembrokeshire. Coastal erosion has recently exposed one example at Black Scar Camp promontory fort, Broadhaven, and one

Figure 201. Carn Alw. An extraordinarily clear view of the many old trackways which cross the uplands of Mynydd Preseli and pass by Carn Alw. Although widened and deepened by historic traffic and drovers, they undoubtedly have their origins in prehistory (RCAHMW, 90-cs-0607).

may also defend Clawdd y Milwyr fort on St David's Head.

The lack of house platforms within Carn Alw, in contrast to Carn-ingli hillfort and Foel Trigarn, together with the very small enclosed space, made Mytum and Webster conclude that this may have been a summer grazing retreat or a refuge in times of strife, linked to the lowlands by a well-marked roadway. The immediate surroundings are famous among archaeologists for the density of well-preserved fields and settlements which probably date from prehistoric and medieval times. Certainly these now inhospitable uplands once proved good ground for permanent settlement and even, it seems, the clearance of small fields for the cultivation of crops. New survey work by SPACES discovered a chambered tomb nearby.

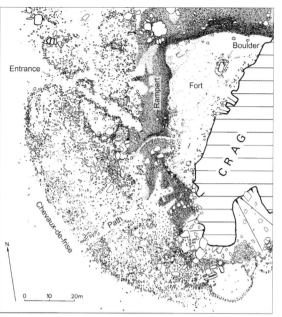

Figure 202. Detailed survey of the fort and chevaux-de-frise at Carn Alw by Mytum and Webster. The main entrance approaches through the curtain of stones on the north-west side. The only recognisable internal feature at Carn Alw is a mysterious natural boulder (top right), arguably dug out all around its base (after Mytum and Webster 1989, Figure 2; by kind permission of Harold Mytum; DI2006-0518).

Figure 203. Carn Alw. The well preserved boulder-lined entrance passage through the chevaux-de-frise on the north-west side, attesting to the skills of prehistoric builders (RCAHMW, 2006-cs-0023).

Figure 204. Faint traces of curving field boundaries, circular animal pounds and smaller round houses survive on Bernard's Well Mountain to the south of Mynydd Preseli near Rosebush reservoir. The main road in the background crosses Mynydd Preseli, linking Eglwyswrw to New Inn and Tufton. Surviving landscapes like these are among the earliest farming settlements in the British Isles (RCAHMW, 96-cs-1014).

One of the most remarkable features of the southern slopes of Mynydd Preseli is the great extent of historic desertion visible in the many abandoned farms, relict fields and old stone quarries which expanded into these upland commons from the seventeenth century onwards. New field patterns and planned farms took in open moorland, while stone quarries exploited the excellent rocks, with accompanying settlements springing up, later connected by railways. Sadly, many of these industries vanished as quickly as they had come, and farms built in a spirit of optimism were abandoned.

The western foothills of Mynydd Preseli, including Mynydd Morvil, Mynydd Castleblythe, Mynydd Cilciffeth and Bernard's Well Mountain, preserve an extensive abandoned landscape from prehistoric and historic times. Remains include villages of round houses and substantial terraced fields thought to date from Romano-British times, and earlier more sinuous fields and huts believed to date from the Bronze or Iron Ages. Elsewhere, tracts of ridge and furrow are well preserved from Norman times. Some sites lie well away from footpaths and the better-visited heritage sites of Pembrokeshire with their car parks and interpretative panels. Only from the air can their remarkable survival and original extent once again be recognised.

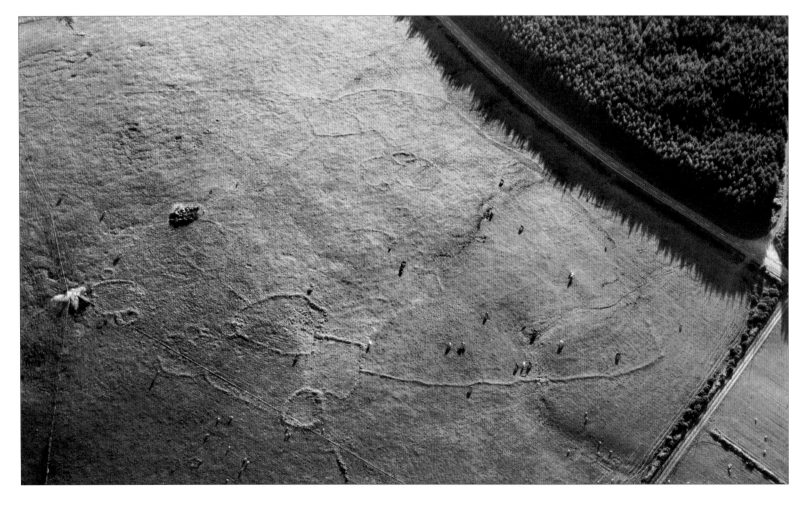

Figure 205. Deserted farmsteads at Tafarn y Bwlch, with rectangular long huts visible within the larger fields. Although undated by excavation, these abandoned farms are thought to have medieval origins and are now protected as Scheduled Ancient Monuments (RCAHMW, 96-cs-1005).

Figure 206. The historic farm on the slopes below Waun Clyn-coch was laid out with complete disregard for the local terrain and now lies abandoned. This view in fading light from winter 1990 shows plough-ridges in some of the fields (RCAHMW, 90-cs-1007).

Figure 207. Earthworks of a prehistoric defended farm and associated fields and pounds at Waun Clyn-coch on the southern flanks of Mynydd Preseli (RCAHMW, 90-cs-1009).

Figure 208. Fagwyr Fran, south-west of Mynydd Cilciffeth to the north of Puncheston/Cas-Mael. A deserted hamlet of round huts set within a wide-spreading system of rectangular fields, some terraced through years of ploughing, is believed to be of prehistoric or Romano-British date (RCAHMW, 905549.8).

Figure 209. A well preserved settlement on Mynydd Morvil, west of New Inn. The earthworks show two field enclosures with a single round hut on the near side, and with contemporary and later ridge-and-furrow surviving all round. Like so many Welsh upland settlements this site is undated by excavation but would appear to be a farmstead of the later prehistoric or Romano-British period (RCAHMW, 2002-cs-1736).

Figure 210. Before excavations began. Castell Henllys seen from the west on 6 July 1955, a partly tree-grown promontory fort among hundreds of similar sites in the Pembrokeshire countryside. The site was visited by Royal Commission surveyors on 8 July 1914 during compilation of their 1925 Pembrokeshire Inventory. They noted it was '... a fine promontory fort situated some 300 yards north-west of Meline parish church' and that the promontory was cut off by a '...formidable rampart' (RCAHMW, 1925, No. 770, p 259). However, the main north gateway appears to have been entirely obscured and is not described. Instead, the minor east gateway was considered to have been the main entrance (Original photography held at Cambridge University Collection of Air Photographs, Unit for Landscape Modelling, QP27, DI2006-0034).

Castell Henllys is a rare site in Welsh archaeology. It has been the focus of scientific excavations since 1980 which have provided an unparalleled understanding of a small promontory fort occupied from Iron Age to Roman times. These excavations have also informed a long-term exercise in 'experimental archaeology', in which Iron Age houses and other buildings have been reconstructed on their original foundations using prehistoric building materials and techniques.

Remains of Iron Age settlements, including smaller hillforts, promontory forts and defended farmsteads, are plentiful in northern Pembrokeshire. These settlements represent the homes of countless families and dynasties which came and went in the centuries following the Bronze Age and lasted often

Figure 211. Castell Henllys from the south-west on a summer's evening in 1990. Excavations were in their tenth year, and postholes and other features can be seen exposed outside the north gate on the left-hand side (RCAHMW 905513-17).

Figure 212. The hillfort in July 1996 at the height of the excavation season. Excavations on the main gate have exposed the massive pairs of postholes which once supported the gateway tower (parallel holes, centre right). Paths, steps and viewing platforms have been laid to accommodate the growing numbers of visitors (RCAHMW, 96-cs-1117).

Figure 213. By 2003 four reconstructed round houses together with a four-post food store dominate the interior of the hillfort. Excavations on the main gateway (centre right), now finished, have been backfilled and the original plan of the Iron Age gateway passage, with recessed guard chambers, will be restored. In 2001 the fort was the setting of the BBC reality show 'Surviving the Iron Age' (RCAHMW, 2003-cs-0867).

into the Roman period. Very few have been excavated and most will probably remain unexplored beneath a covering of trees and scrub for centuries to come. Excavation, properly conducted, is a time-consuming and very costly exercise. For anything more than a small trench across a site a team of diggers, supervisors and a director is required. Excavations are best planned to last several years so that a large enough area, or areas, can be explored to understand fully the buried remains. Meticulous notes are kept during the dig, and when the last hole is backfilled the lengthy process of post-excavation analysis commences. During this second stage potsherds and other finds are drawn and catalogued, soil samples analysed, and complicated sequences of building and remodelling are interpreted. It can take years to produce a final report, but only in such a careful way can we begin to approach an understanding of these ancient sites.

Castell Henllys (the name implies an 'old palace' or early medieval court) was originally purchased privately with the intention of turning the fort into a tourist attraction as work progressed. In time the site was bought by the Pembrokeshire Coast National Park Authority and now functions as an exemplary centre for education, interpretation and archaeological training in west Wales, with annual projects run by Cambria Archaeology and the University of York. Despite its relatively small size, the history of Castell Henllys has proved to be anything but simple. The main gateway was begun in the fifth century BC and started as a long stone-walled passageway flanked by pairs of massive timber posts supporting a large gate and, probably, a bridge or tower over the entrance. Two pairs of guard chambers, semi-circular rooms where the gatekeepers could shelter and inspect visitors, were recessed into the sides of the passage. The excavators felt that this specialised gateway was built not by the inhabitants of the fort, but by visiting artisans who had the knowledge and expertise to undertake such a complicated piece of building. The gateway was rebuilt several times during the occupation of the fort, and there were episodes when it was on the point of collapse, or even burnt down. Outside the main fort was a further set of defences. Early on these included a *chevaux-de-frise,* a curtain of sharp, upright stones similar to that at nearby Carn Alw in Mynydd Preseli. It may originally have been far more extensive, but later, around 300 BC, the *chevaux-de-frise* was replaced by a substantial bank and ditch and only survives today where this later bank covered it. Excavations at Castell Henllys also uncovered a cache of several thousand sling stones stored behind the rampart. These were a common weapon on Iron Age hillforts, and an experienced slinger could kill or injure a victim at a distance of 60 metres or more.

Inside Castell Henllys stand reconstructed round houses in their original positions. These conical thatched buildings represent carefully-considered experiments in archaeology, rebuilt from the patterns

of postholes and wall-trenches discovered on site. Such substantial buildings required large quantities of raw material. Phil Bennett (in Frodsham 2004) has documented the 30 coppiced oak trees, 90 coppiced hazel bushes, two thousand bundles of water reed and two miles of hemp rope and twine consumed in the construction of the largest round house alone, forming its rafters, posts, ring-beams and wattle walls. The houses stand around an open area within which were found the remains of hearths, perhaps used for feasts. Some of the hearths were carefully made of stone and were surrounded by postholes to support cauldrons over the fires. Blacksmiths also plied their trade using metal-working hearths dug into the back of the ramparts. Castell Henllys probably supported a wealthy farming community of several families under a local aristocratic leader. Crops, cereals and perhaps beans, were no doubt grown nearby, with livestock grazed on surrounding fields. However, the lack of evidence for threshing and primary processing of grain on site has led archaeologists to think that food may have been brought to the fort by the surrounding populace, as tribute payments for a local leader. After the fort was abandoned in the late Iron Age, a small but well-off Romano-British farmstead was established just outside. A later refortification of the fort may suggest occupation by Irish settlers in the post-Roman period, but after this Castell Henllys became lost and overgrown until it was surveyed and named on a late-eighteenth-century estate map.

Today one could think of Castell Henllys as something of a special site, given the range of extraordinary finds, the complexity of its settlement history and the special defensive features discovered, including the guard chambers at the gateway and a *chevaux-de-frise.* However, this small promontory fort is one of hundreds of similar sites in the south-west of Wales. At each one we may expect similar revelations and surprises. Such long-term excavations can only serve to increase our understanding of, and respect for, the achievements of the pre-Roman population of Wales.

Figure 214. Excavations in progress in 1996 on the Penpedwast enclosure, a rectangular prehistoric site discovered from the air as a cropmark on a hill to the east of Castell Henllys. The campsite for the excavation team at Castell Henllys can be seen to the left (RCAHMW, 96-cs-1413).

Figure 215. Newport medieval borough: high view from around 6,000 feet showing the grid-like pattern of the medieval streets stretching from the edge of Newport Bay in the north to the edge of the moorland bordering Mynydd Carningli, with the castle at the centre of the frame (RCAHMW, 2000-cs-0496).

Figure 216. Newport Castle, sited at the southern edge of the medieval borough with farmland beyond, July 1990 (RCAHMW, 90-cs-0462).

The town of Newport/Trefdraeth occupies an advantageous position at the mouth of the Afon Nyfer, looking out across Newport Sands to Cardigan Bay and backed by the higher slopes and hillgrazing on Mynydd Carn-ingli. The earliest human activity dates from the Mesolithic period, with a flint-working site uncovered during the Dyfed Archaeological Trust's excavations near the coast in the early 1990s. An elegant Neolithic chambered tomb, Carreg Coetan Arthur, also survives in the eastern part of the town, now sadly encroached upon by modern housing. It serves as a reminder of a very different way of life along this coastal plain 5-6,000 years ago.

The town as we see it today is a Norman foundation of the Fitzmartins, lords of Cemais from c.1197. Robert Fitzmartin's castle was originally sited nearly 3 kilometres to the east at Nevern, presumably taking advantage of the settlement's pre-Norman ecclesiastical status. Following a brief seizure of the castle by Rhys ap Gruffudd in 1191, the Fitzmartins established a new castle and town downriver at Newport. The town was formally laid out as a rectangle of narrow burgage plots between the two main north-south roads of Long Street and St Mary's Street. Newport Castle was twice destroyed by the Welsh in the early and mid-thirteenth century, causing

Figure 217. Revealing Newport's medieval past. Excavations by Ken Murphy for the Dyfed Archaeological Trust on the site of Newport's new primary school in 1991, close to the sea, revealed three medieval burgage plots. These two views show (upper) the cross-shaped evaluation trenches in March 1991, dug to assess the extent of the buried archaeology, followed by a full scale excavation (lower), in July 1991, with the foundations of medieval buildings visible. These discrete parcels of land, owned by individual householders, contained at least five phases of building and replanning. Medieval houses were discovered within the plots, remains of the first settlement established when Fitzmartin's castle was moved from Nevern to Newport in about 1197. The buildings were not grand stone structures; excavations suggested that they had thick clay or 'clom' walls, sunken floors with hearths and thatched roofs. The plots were abandoned when the new stone castle was established away from the coast to the south of the town (RCAHMW, Evaluation 91-cs-0217; Excavation 91-cs-0428).

Figure 218. Nevern is dominated by the remains of Castell Nanhyfer (foreground). This wooded motte-and-bailey castle, which began life as an Iron Age promontory fort, was built by the Fitzmartins, the Norman lords of Cemais, in 1191. It was seized by Rhys ap Gruffudd, who was later imprisoned by his sons in the tower which he built (RCAHMW, 96-cs-0678).

considerable disruption to the town and its populace. Ken Murphy considers the circular earthwork, Old Castle, on the coast at the north end of Long Street to be the original site of William Fitzmartin's first castle. Later the present stone castle was established on higher ground to the south. Excavations by the Dyfed Archaeological Trust of former medieval burgage plots in the north of the town suggest that these were abandoned following the Welsh attacks on the old castle. The focus of the town subsequently shifted to the south around the new castle.

Despite periods of decline, Newport's prosperity has always been based chiefly on the agricultural wealth of its hinterland and its excellent coastal position for trading and fishing. During the sixteenth century it began to export cloth and wool from its port, and a new quay was later built to the west at The Parrog in response to silting of the estuary; the port thrived into the nineteenth century.

Figure 219. Dinas Island and Cwm-yr-egwlys. Cwm-yr-egwlys, a secluded former fishing village, occupies the eastern side of the low-lying isthmus of dry ground which separates Dinas Island from the mainland. The precarious nature of the position is demonstrated by the remains of St Brynach's church, of which only the west wall survives at the far end of the graveyard adjacent to the beach (centre left). This was largely destroyed in the great October storm of 1859, and a sea wall now protects the remaining parts of the church and churchyard from further erosion (RCAHMW; landscape, 2002-cs-1479; detail, 2002-cs-1480).

Figure 220. The landscape of northern Pembrokeshire, looking north-east over Foel Trigarn hillfort (foreground) towards Llanfair Nant-gwyn (left, background; RCAHMW, 905513-9).

Figure 221. St Dogmaels Abbey. At St Dogmaels/Llandudoch, on the southern banks of the Teifi (upper view), stand the abbey ruins which were once home to a group of monks belonging to the austere Order of Tiron. A priory was founded here in 1115 by Robert Fitzmartin, the Norman lord of Cemais. In 1120 St Dogmaels became an abbey and the mother house of three priories at Caldey, Pill (Milford) and at Glascarreg in southern Ireland. The abbey and church had a mixed history of construction, remodelling and reduction, in part due to the changing fortunes of the local Norman lords, but also reflecting later troubles, including the impact of the Black Death in 1349. This view (lower) from the south-east looks across the abbey ruins, with the open square of the cloister clear at centre-left, the ruins of the roofless infirmary at bottom right casting a long shadow, and the main ruins of the church and tall stonework of the north transept at centre. Beyond can be seen St Thomas's Church, the main building dating to the early eighteenth century. (RCAHMW, wide view, 94-cs-1286; detail 94-cs-1285).

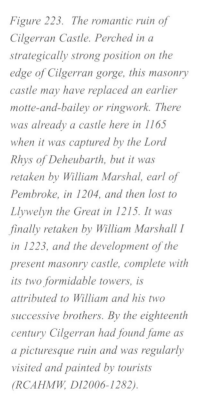

Figure 222. Cilgerran, from the east-north-east, with its castle perched on the edge of the Teifi gorge and the church of St Llawddog beyond, whose churchyard is home to a fifth- or sixth-century inscribed stone (RCAHMW, AP-2006-1087).

Figure 223. The romantic ruin of Cilgerran Castle. Perched in a strategically strong position on the edge of Cilgerran gorge, this masonry castle may have replaced an earlier motte-and-bailey or ringwork. There was already a castle here in 1165 when it was captured by the Lord Rhys of Deheubarth, but it was retaken by William Marshal, earl of Pembroke, in 1204, and then lost to Llywelyn the Great in 1215. It was finally retaken by William Marshall I in 1223, and the development of the present masonry castle, complete with its two formidable towers, is attributed to William and his two successive brothers. By the eighteenth century Cilgerran had found fame as a picturesque ruin and was regularly visited and painted by tourists (RCAHMW, DI2006-1282).

Figure 224. Two views of the simple Calvinistic Methodist chapel at Bwlchygroes, originally built in 1832, which nestles on the crossroads of this small village in hills to the east of Crymych (RCAHMW, 2002-cs-1424 & 1426).

CHAPTER SIX

CENTRAL PEMBROKESHIRE: FROM HAVERFORDWEST TO NARBERTH

The heartlands of Pembrokeshire, extending from Llanddewi Velfrey and Narberth in the east, across Haverfordwest to St Brides Bay, encompass some of the most productive farmland in the county. Great systems of Norman strip fields, most clearly revealed from the air, remain fossilised in the landscape north of Haverfordwest and to the south of Narberth. The two major rivers of Pembrokeshire, the Western and Eastern Cleddau, cut across these central lowlands like a great 'Y', linking distant villages and hills along a common waterway. They meet to form the Daugleddau in the south to flow into Milford Haven, and ultimately the Atlantic Ocean.

The Western Cleddau rises near Square and Compass, not far from the northern coastal cliffs of Pembrokeshire and Pen-caer/Strumble Head. Gathering pace, and combining with numerous streams including the Afon Cleddau and Afon Anghof, it cuts a rocky gorge between Wolf's Castle and Treffgarne, overlooked by Iron Age forts and the shattered crags of Maiden Castle. The Western Cleddau then runs south through Haverfordwest town, a once navigable artery for trade and communication. The Eastern Cleddau rises from a series of springs near Waun Cleddau, amidst burial chambers and standing stones, in the shadow of the eastern arm of Mynydd Preseli. From there it winds its way south, through Mynachlog-ddu, to form the eastern county boundary with Carmarthenshire. Entering central Pembrokeshire it is overlooked by the medieval castle at Llawhaden and an older community of Iron Age hillforts on the rounded hills just above the village. The course begins to widen into the broader, muddier tidal estuary near the great houses and estates of Slebech Park and Picton Park, before joining with the Western Cleddau at Landshipping to form the Daugleddau.

Despite considerable improvement of the farming land in this part of Pembrokeshire during the twentieth century and before, prehistoric settlements abound. These take the form of Iron Age defended farmsteads and hillforts, variously labelled 'rath', 'settlement', 'fort' or 'homestead' on tourist maps. Whilst some can be visited or seen from the road, many more have long since been levelled by the plough, only to be re-discovered by aerial photographers during dry summers. This part of central Pembrokeshire is also traversed by the Roman road west of Carmarthen, whose ultimate destination is still unknown. Its incomplete line shows as a paved roadway or *agger*, variously flanked by ditches and quarry pits, where gravel was dug for re-surfacing. So far, the road has been traced from the air passing just to the north of Whitland, St Clears and Llawhaden and is last seen near Wiston. Archaeologists and historians now have the task of rediscovering its course, if one exists, further west, and may one day find its original destination.

Figure 225. Wiston Castle, one of the best preserved motte-and-baileys in Wales (Rees, 1992). It was abandoned after 1220 in the process of being transformed from an older earthwork castle to one of stone. The stone keep survives on top of the earthen motte (left of centre), having replaced its timber predecessor. Low January sunlight in 2006 highlights the surrounding earthworks, which have been cleared in recent years to present the castle to the public (RCAHMW, AP-2006-0015).

Figure 226. Narberth from the south-west, under fog on a cold spring morning in 2002. One of the few discernible features is St Andrew's Church, bottom left, with the Market Square just above and the curving line of St James's Street beyond. The mist-shrouded woodland around Blackaldern can be seen on the right (RCAHMW, DI2006-0372).

Figure 227. Castle Bucket Iron Age fort, Trecwn: looking south-west with mayflower in the hedgerows. The fort occupies a good promontory position, with traces of a once elaborate 'antenna' entrance-way on the far side. The bend of the field boundary on the left might fossilise an original outer enclosure or annexe (RCAHMW, 96-cs-0570).

Figure 228. New monuments to tourism. The towering 24-metre-high (80ft-) wooden rollercoaster, Megafobia, *the centrepiece of Oakwood leisure park west of Narberth, is seen casting long winter shadows in January 2006. Oakwood is one of the biggest tourist attractions in Wales, attracting 400,000 visitors a year, and represents a new type of industry for the Daugleddau region, historically dominated by limestone quarries and coal workings (RCAHMW, AP-2006-0036).*

Figure 229. Withybush circle, near Haverfordwest. Cropmarks of about thirty pits, highlighted by the setting summer sun, show us the original location of what was probably a late Neolithic timber circle. Such a monument may have contained special burials at its centre and a designated gateway somewhere on the perimeter for onlookers to enter and observe or take part in rituals (RCAHMW, 90-cs-0616).

During the dry summer of 1990, barely 500 metres from Haverfordwest airport, a very rare type of prehistoric ritual monument was discovered by Chris Musson, then of the Royal Commission. Perfect seasonal conditions for cropmark formation, combined with perfect evening summer sunshine striking low across a ripened arable crop, combined to reveal the position of about thirty pits in a perfect circle. This cropmark represents the buried remains of a prehistoric circular temple, long since erased as a standing monument. The cropmarks, which have not

been excavated, appear to show the site of a timber circle, a particular type of later Neolithic or early Bronze Age ritual monument comprising a circle of upright timbers, most commonly built around 3,000 BC. A complex late Neolithic timber circle was excavated near Welshpool in 1990-2 at Sarn y Bryn Caled, and its subsequent reconstruction gives us some idea of how impressive the Withybush monument may have appeared to the rest of prehistoric Pembrokeshire. Alternatively, the cropmarks may represent a Bronze Age pit circle, where, instead of standing timbers, the holes would have contained special offerings and perhaps cremated remains, or even a stone circle whose stones have been removed. Without excavation its interpretation as a timber circle is the most likely, and

as such its discovery reminds us of what else may be awaiting discovery in Pembrokeshire. The chances of similar monuments existing elsewhere are high, but if they lie under woodland, under towns, or in damper ground where cropmarks never form it is unlikely we will ever rediscover them. We can only say with some certainty that the present-day distribution of Bronze Age burial cairns and stone circles on the hill tops and upland fringes of Pembrokeshire is not representative of the original distribution of prehistoric temples. While the Gors Fawr stone circle (Fig. 182) sits in splendid, rugged, isolation at the foot of Mynydd Preseli, it is entirely plausible that similar monuments, now lost or ploughed away, once dotted the productive Pembrokeshire lowlands or overlooked the wide vistas of the Daugleddau estuary.

Figure 230. Reconstruction of the late Neolithic timber circle at Sarn y Bryn Caled near Welshpool, first discovered from the air and excavated by the Clwyd-Powys Archaeological Trust. The appearance of the timber monument was enhanced when lintels were added to the upright posts. Although this in-situ reconstruction was later dismantled, a permanent version exists at the National History Museum at St Fagan's, Cardiff. It gives some idea of how the Withybush monument may have appeared, 5,000 years ago (RCAHMW, 91-cs-0075).

Figure 231. Landscape change at West Ford Rings, a small hillfort south-west of Wolf's Castle. This Cambridge University view from the south-east, taken in 1960, shows a rural landscape of partly improved small fields, some put down to pasture, others still rough with scrub vegetation. The circular defences of West Ford Rings can be seen centre-left, passed by two footpaths, but the form of the fort is partly obscured by the covering of thick vegetation (Copyright reserved Cambridge University Collection of Air Photographs, ABT 75; Friday 1 July 1960, DI2006-0042).

Figure 232. West Ford Rings today: the same view in January 2006 showing a very different scene. The basic structure of the 1960s landscape is still recognisable, but most of the smaller subdivisions have been swept away to create larger fields. The grassland is improved and closely grazed, appearing far 'smoother' from the air than in 1960. The greatest changes have occurred around the fort itself. Bushes still remain growing on the circular rampart, but all around the fields have been cleared of scrub vegetation and stones. Vestigial earthworks of the footpaths seen in the 1960s view can still be made out (RCAHMW, AP-2006-0005).

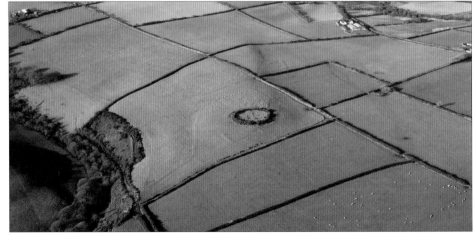

Figure 233. West Ford Rings. As if to remind us that the archaeology of Iron Age hillforts does not stop at the edge of their outer ramparts, the improvement of the fields around West Ford Rings has helped to reveal low banks of a formerly extensive system of prehistoric fields. These rare survivals, extremely fragile in the face of modern farming techniques, give some sense of a more organic patchwork of smaller fields which may have characterised the later prehistoric landscape in this part of Pembrokeshire prior to Norman reorganisation (RCAHMW 2004-cs-205).

Figure 234. A glimpse of lowland Pembrokeshire in 3,500 BC: amidst the improved pasture and fields of lowland central Pembrokeshire, not far from Wolf's Castle, stands the impressive slumped burial chamber of Carn Turne, surrounded by uncleared rocks. At one time most of Pembrokeshire would have been rock-strewn from the last glaciation, but centuries of field clearance have left Carn Turne as a rare survivor. The massive capstone of the burial chamber has collapsed backwards, but the remains of a V-shaped forecourt of upright stones can still be seen. The setting of the tomb below the outcrop is striking. It may be that the builders considered the natural rock to have sacred or symbolic properties, or perhaps it simply proved to be a convenient source of suitable slabs and boulders. Not far from the tomb is a standing stone, perhaps contemporary but possibly erected during the Bronze Age (RCAHMW, 2004-cs-0215).

However untouched the rural landscape of Pembrokeshire may seem to us today, we must remember the considerable changes it has witnessed over past centuries. The lowlands have always been productive for farming, ever since Neolithic farmers first broke the ground with their wooden or stone-tipped ploughs. Since that time agricultural intensification and clearance have barely ceased, presenting us with the heavily improved, managed, sub-divided farmland we see today. The pace of change in agriculture since the end of the Second World War has been particularly relentless. Although periods of economic instability have seen down-turns in farming revenues during recent decades, the general picture is one of clearance, improvement and intensification. Within this arena of change certain prehistoric monuments have survived to the present day, seemingly against all odds.

Figure 235. The Brechfa concentric antenna enclosure, probably a specialised Iron Age/Roman corral. A long 'smudge' entering the enclosure from the bottom left shows the former position of a muddy, prehistoric trackway, now preserved as a cropmark (RCAHMW, AP-2006-3281).

Rediscovering the hidden Iron Age landscape, aerial discoveries made during the 1980s by Terry James and Chris Musson have steadily revealed the original scale of late prehistoric farming in Pembrokeshire. Terry James (1990) named these types of prehistoric farmstead 'concentric antenna enclosures'. The great enclosures have three elements: an inner ditched enclosure thought to have been used for settlement, a wide-spaced concentric outer enclosure thought to be a corral for livestock, and a corridor entrance, the 'antenna', linking the outer to the inner and creating a very impressive front door to the farm.

The land covered by these prehistoric farms is considerable: the Brechfa enclosure is approximately 227 metres in diameter, enclosing 0.4 hectares; the Glancleddau enclosure is approximately 200 metres in diameter, enclosing 0.3 hectares. They appear to be specialised corral sites, given their wide outer enclosures, ideal for penning

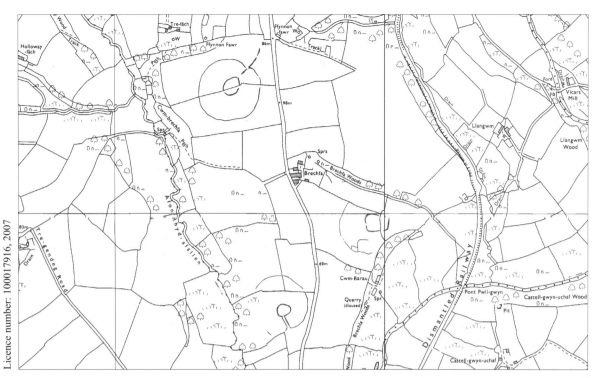

Figure 236. An Iron Age farming landscape, centred on Brechfa, west of Llandissilio at SN 096 221, dwarfs present-day farms. This air-photo map shows the concentric antenna enclosures of Brechfa (top), Brechfa II (centre, right) and Glancleddau (bottom). Note the relationship of the enclosures to the high ground of the ridge, bounded on both sides by rivers, and the way the antenna entrances to Brechfa and Glancleddau give access to the respective enclosures to visitors from north and south (1km squares, north to top; RCAHMW).

or managing stock. Alternatively, the outer enclosures may have been planted with arable crops, with stock left to graze beyond the perimeter, in an early infield/outfield system. Round houses and other farm buildings doubtless occupied the central enclosure.

These aerial discoveries have other implications; they are evidence for the existence of open ground in prehistoric Pembrokeshire, clear of trees, sufficient for the planning and construction of great, wide-spaced enclosures. They represent a considerable imposition on the prehistoric landscape, penning large areas with only one main way in. The ditches of both the Brechfa and Glancleddau enclosures are deeper and wider where they flank the main entrance, suggesting that the builders were keen to construct a grand, impressive gateway. They are also all built slightly differently, suggesting either differing periods of construction and use, or individual landowners keen to build in a distinctive way. Similar contemporary corrals in parts of Africa could provide valuable parallels to show how stock was managed in prehistoric Wales.

Figure 237. The Glancleddau enclosure: the cropmark has grown taller and thicker over the buried ditches of a prehistoric or Roman period farm than over the surrounding subsoil. The cropmark thus shows up as a 'shadow site' in low sunlight (RCAHMW, 905528-18).

Figure 238. Llawhaden: the castle and village on a summer's afternoon in 2005, seen from the east (RCAHMW, AP-2005-0884).

The present-day village of Llawhaden is dominated by its Norman castle, which commands a bluff at the end of a long eastward ridge. The earlier origins of the village are to be found just to the north in a close-knit group of Iron Age hillforts. On undulating high ground between Llawhaden and Gelli, overlooking the Eastern Cleddau, are eight prehistoric defended settlements, some with activity during the Bronze Age, others prospering before and during the Roman period into elaborately defended farms and forts. Excavations were carried out by George Williams of the Dyfed Archaeological Trust during 1980-4, and the work is still considered to be some of the most important research into a group of Welsh Iron Age forts in recent decades. At Woodside and Dan y Coed forts,

where the main excavations were focused, massive entrance works were uncovered, including surfaced roadways forming long 'antenna' banks and ditches which funnelled visitors into the main gates. The approach to Woodside camp was further protected with two gate towers at the outer and inner gates. The posts of the outer gate tower were doubled up suggesting a further storey or display platform above. At Drim camp nearby the four-post foundations for the gateway tower were substantial enough to suggest double gates, a first-floor platform and perhaps another storey above that. To find such complexity at these small hillforts, of which there are hundreds of unexcavated examples in the country, has taught us a great deal about Iron Age life in west Wales.

Figure 239. Reconstruction, based on excavation, of the two Iron Age defended enclosures at Woodside (left) and Dan-y-Coed (right), Llawhaden. At Woodside an elaborate timber-lined entrance guided visitors through outer and inner gateways. This scene gives us a good idea of how many of the plough-levelled prehistoric farms in the Pembrokeshire landscape may once have appeared (drawing by R Vickery, 1984. © Cambria Archaeology).

Figure 240. A view of the Llawhaden defended enclosures from the west, matching the reconstruction above. The partly excavated ditches of Woodside (left) and Dan-y-Coed (right) show as cropmarks in dry grassland in summer 1989. Traces of the outer gateway ditches are also visible (RCAHMW, DI2006-1506).

Figure 241. The Rath, Crundale: a familiar landmark for aerial archaeologists returning to Haverfordwest Airport from reconnaissance work to the east. Two iron rings, possibly torcs, and an iron model of a hand, possibly a votive deposit, were found here in or before 1865 and are now in the British Museum. This view from December 1999 looks south-east across The Rath to the low, curving earthworks of Little Hare's Head defended enclosure on the hillslope beyond (RCAHMW, 99-cs-2373).

Figure 242. The Rath, Crundale: looking down into the fort during the dry summer of 1995, cropmarks show the small, semi-circular inner enclosure built against the south-west rampart. Although The Rath is certainly an Iron Age hillfort, it is thought that it was remodelled to form a medieval motte and bailey. As such it is a good example of medieval and prehistoric tacticians seeking out the same defensible positions in central Pembrokeshire (RCAHMW, 95-cs-1716).

Figure 243. The wide-spaced concentric earthworks of Keeston Castle, or The Castle, between Keeston and Simpson Cross north-west of Haverfordwest, looking south. The curving ramparts are inconspicuous in the modern landscape but would once have formed a complicated and formidable prehistoric defended farm. Centuries of ploughing on the far (south) side have reduced the surviving earthworks to a point where they are best visible in low winter light; this view is from January 1994. Conversely, on the near (north) side the ramparts have been 'fossilised' and preserved in present-day field boundaries. The small circular enclosure on the far side may have been an earlier site, absorbed in the later concentric earthworks (RCAHMW, 94-cs-0077).

Figure 244. A rath revealed by parching. Pelcombe Rath Iron Age fort appears as an inconspicuous curving bank in spring grassland (upper right), looking as if it has almost been ploughed away. Photographed in parched conditions in late July 1989 (right) the field acquires the qualities of an 'x-ray', and the full circuit of the rath can be seen. A complete encircling ditch survives with a main gate on the south-east (left) side, while the inner bank has been partly ploughed away. Former stream-channels, now dry, appear as darker, damper sinuous lines in the dry pasture (upper: RCAHMW, 89-cs-197; lower: © Cambria Archaeology AP89-207.25).

Figure 245. A previously unknown concentric Iron Age fort emerges in a strip of 'responsive' crop in 1996, with the remainder of the enclosure remaining invisible. This large prehistoric defended farm lies to the north-east of South Hills Farm, Merryborough, just east of Haverfordwest. Compare with Figure 373 (RCAHMW, 96-cs-1472).

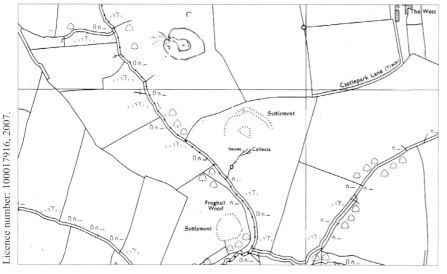

Figure 246. Filling in the gaps in the Iron Age landscape: three prehistoric enclosures, one revealed by aerial photography, the others mapped decades ago by the Ordnance Survey, overlooking Cartlett Brook just west of Walton East. The map shows Plenty Park Rath (bottom), West Rath (centre) and the West Rath II enclosure (top). New mapping of West Rath II revealed a complex entrance on the north-west side, flanked by ditches and two lines of pits (RCAHMW).

Figure 247. The striking concentric farmstead at West Rath II, Walton East, discovered as a cropmark by Terry James in the summer of 1989. A central dark circle may be a massive pit in the centre of the farmstead, or the site of a particularly large or important round house. The curving outer boundary is remarkably straight for part of its length on the far, south, side, suggesting it was laid out to respect a pre-existing boundary (© Cambria Archaeology, 28/07/1989).

TRACING THE ROMAN ROAD WEST OF CARMARTHEN

Figure 248. Castell Flemish or Castell Fleming defended enclosure from the north-east. This is the fabled site of Ad Vicessimum, thought by antiquarians to be a Roman station between Carmarthen and St Davids. It is now understood to be a prehistoric or Romano-British defended farmstead (RCAHMW, 97-cs-0214).

Following the conquest of Wales in the late AD 70s, the Romans moved quickly to establish a network of military rule across the country. Well-engineered roads were central to this control and allowed troops and supplies to be moved rapidly between forts. A Roman road linking Carmarthen to St Davids has long been a part of local Pembrokeshire folklore, largely thanks to an unfortunate forgery dating back to the eighteenth century whose history has been discussed by Heather James in the *Carmarthenshire Antiquary* (2000).

In 1755 Charles Bertram of the Marine Academy, Copenhagen, passed a map of Roman Britain to the eminent antiquarian, William Stukeley (famous for his renderings of Avebury in Wiltshire); it was said to have been copied by a fourteenth-century monk, Richard of Cirencester (a genuine historical figure), from a hitherto lost Roman Itinerary. This forgery spoke of a road west of Carmarthen, the *Via Julia*, which passed through a station called *Ad Vicessimum* to *Menapia* near the present St Davids. *Menapia*, although concocted by Bertram, sounded very like the medieval Latin name for St Davids (Menevia), and a number of antiquarians, among them Richard Fenton, became firm believers in this forged map. Finds of

Figure 249. The unmistakable line of the Roman road west of Carmarthen, here running east of Whitland below Moor Farm (SN 232 169) in the left distance, approaching the railway embankment. The Roman road shows up in the centre of the frame as a parched line of the buried road surface or agger. This is flanked by intermittent quarry pits visible as dark green hollows of lush grass growth, where forced labour supervised by Roman soldiers dug stone for surfacing (RCAHMW, 95-cs-1703).

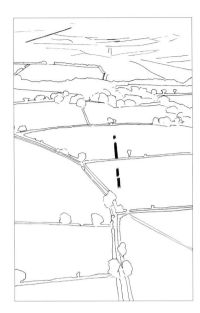

Figure 250. To the east of Clunderwen a minor road fossilises the line of the Roman road before it turns away north, and the parched Roman road surface can once again be traced in the pasture. This view looks east towards Glan-rhyd (SN 146 185; in trees, middle distance) with the intermittent parchmark of the Roman road just visible. The 'rhyd' element of the place name records the fording point of a river (RCAHMW, 92-cs-0350).

Roman material at Castell Flemish, an enclosure near Woodstock, made by Fenton in 1805, convinced him that this was *Ad Vicessimum*. A Roman site was also located beneath the dunes bordering Whitesands Bay. Subsequent exposure of the forged map discredited much of this early antiquarian work and it was slowly excluded from historical research.

The rediscovery of a genuine Roman road west of Carmarthen has proved a curious twist in this long tale. In 1989 Terry James discovered an engineered Roman road running west of Carmarthen, identified from aerial photography, and this line was extended as far west as Wiston by Chris Musson flying for the Royal Commission during the hot summers of 1992 and 1995. The road was confirmed by excavation in advance of the Whitland bypass in 1995 (Fig. 77), which showed it was here fitted with timber culverts to drain water across the cambered surface. West of Wiston the trail goes cold at a crucial junction where the road could have continued in any direction: south-west to Haverfordwest or the natural harbourage of Milford Haven, due west to St Brides Bay or north-west to St Davids. Recent research by Dr Mark Merrony, linked to excavations of a possible

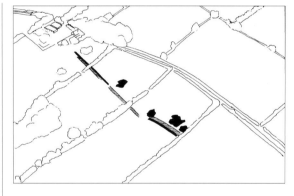

Roman villa at Ford, near Wolf's Castle, suggests further extensions of the road based on place-name and field-name evidence. Each summer likely cropmarks of Roman roads or military installations are searched for from the air. The Roman road must link forts west of Carmarthen, so we should expect future discoveries of a fort or forts, or even a port and town on the coast. Such findings are not impossible, as was seen with the discovery of an entirely new, but long suspected, buried Roman fort in Dinefwr Park, Llandeilo, in Carmarthenshire in 2003. Roman forts are expected in the vicinities of Whitland (Carms.) and Haverfordwest (Fig. 78).

Figure 251. Characteristic but faint traces of the Roman road agger, flanked by quarry pits, recorded at Longlands Farm, Wiston. Just west of this section the road line is lost (RCAHMW, 96-cs-1467).

FROM *HAVERFORD* TO HAVERFORDWEST

Haverfordwest has its origins in the medieval town of Haverford, founded around the prominent castle and sited close to the navigable reaches of the Western Cleddau. It is believed that the castle was first founded about 1110 by a Fleming, Tancred (or Tancard), and in its early years Flemish settlers completely transformed the local landscape, all but replacing the native population. The rise of similar boroughs in southern Pembrokeshire hastened the decline of the Welsh language, a pattern which persists in the modern landscape of the south. By the thirteenth century Haverford was a thriving town with the defended borough of Castleton extending to the west and north of the castle. Haverford developed quickly in the early fourteenth century, expanding beyond the walled Castleton area, but began to decline following the Black Death of 1349. Even so, by the outbreak of Civil War nearly 300 years later (1642-8), Haverfordwest was considered to have been the third-largest town in Wales. Following that war the town became crippled by debt, particularly when the demolition of the castle was ordered by Oliver Cromwell and had to be paid for by the town. Parliamentary troops were quartered there, and heavy taxes began to drive out some of the inhabitants. During an outbreak of the plague, in 1651-3, some 500 people died and over 900 poor faced starvation in Haverfordwest, and it was some time before the town regained a measure of its former success. Today Haverfordwest's town plan is still dominated by its castle and three parish churches, St Martin's, St Mary's and St Thomas's.

Figure 252. Haverfordwest in 1948. By examining the surviving topography of the town and contemporary records of land ownership and valuation, James (1999) reconstructed a map of medieval Haverford. This saw the survival of the medieval market square within Castleton in the present-day Queen's Square (A) near St Martin's Church (B), and the fossilisation of medieval S-curved open field strips in the present housing and property boundaries to both sides of Dew Street (C). James also concluded that in its day the prominent church of St Thomas á Becket (D) may have stood among common pasture or fields to the south of the castle and borough. These patterns can still be seen particularly well in the aerial photographs reproduced here (Crown Copyright MoD/1948, CPE/UK/2500 frame 4068, 12 March 1948).

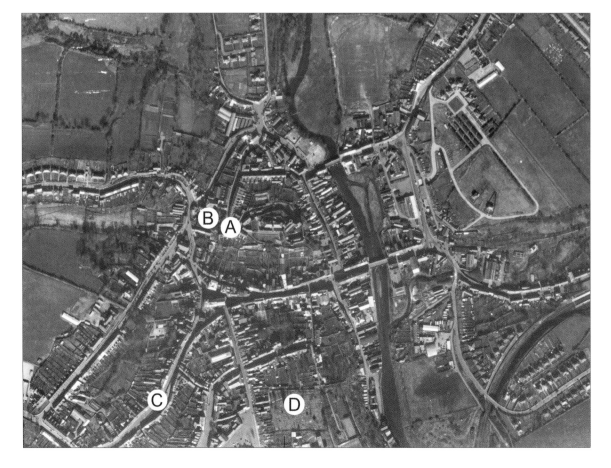

Figure 253. Haverfordwest castle and town centre from the south-east in May 2000. Compare with the LIDAR image taken from the same direction (RCAHMW, 2000-cs-0412).

Figure 254. LIDAR image of Haverfordwest castle and town centre from the south-east, captured by an airborne scanning laser in February 2004. LIDAR creates a digital height model for the town with all features – buildings, trees (here leafless), cars and people in the street – presented as a virtual landscape (© Environment Agency copyright, D0031908. All rights reserved. View generated by RCAHMW)

Figure 255. LIDAR image of Haverfordwest Castle from the north-west, clearly showing the survival of the curving defences of the 'castle borough' of Castleton within the modern town. The spire of St Martin's Church can be seen at lower right, with the Western Cleddau beyond (© Environment Agency copyright, D0031908. All rights reserved. View generated by RCAHMW).

Figure 256. On the south-east side of Haverfordwest is the Augustinian Priory, founded at the start of the thirteenth century by Robert FitzTancred. This view from the north-east shows the north and south transepts in the centre, with the ruinous white-floored presbytery and body of the main church crossing left to right. The cloister lies to the right. Excavations by Siân Rees (Rees 1999) revealed the medieval gardens with a series of raised beds divided by pathways (RCAHMW, 2002-cs-0790).

Figure 257. The ruins of Haroldston, showing scrub clearance between 1993 and 2005. On the south side of Haverfordwest, once occupying an elevated and delightful spot but now bounded on the north by a bypass, railway and modern sewage works, are the ruinous remains of one of Pembrokeshire's oldest houses. Haroldston was the home of the important Perrot family from 1370 to the early eighteenth century. Sir John Perrot was born here in 1530 and went on to remodel the castles at Carew and Laugharne. The ruins of the house, parts of which date back to the medieval period, include the remains of the Steward's Tower, an expansive courtyard and a vaulted range to the west. Haroldston has well preserved garden earthworks which include an L-shaped raised walkway just to the south of Steward's Tower, garden terraces and a sunken garden extending to the north. These formal gardens are believed to date back to the late sixteenth century. From the air the formal gardens show up well, particularly in low, raking winter light. A new survey was made of the gardens by the Royal Commission in 2005/6 (RCAHMW, 93-cs-0002; AP-2005-2765).

Figure 258. Looking down on Narberth. View from the south in 1990, showing the wooded castle in the foreground and the 'Y' of the two main streets diverging from the Market Square in the background (RCAHMW, 90-cs-0563).

Narberth's market town is dominated by its ruined Norman castle, which overlooks the settlement from a hill on the south side. Once a forgotten and tree-grown ruin, it has now been opened to the public after several years of restoration and some £400,000 funding, assembled by Pembrokeshire County Council and Cadw. The castle has been historically under-researched, but it has been suggested that the first building on the site was a pre-Norman Welsh *llys*, associated with the Mabinogion. Neil Ludlow, an archaeologist with Cambria Archaeology, considers that the small motte and bailey of Sentence Castle to the south at Templeton may have been the first Norman castle in the area, later superseded by a new timber castle at Narberth. Narberth is first mentioned in 1116 when it was burnt following a Welsh attack, an event repeated in its history. It became a truly impregnable and imposing stone fortress when rebuilt by the Marcher lord Roger Mortimer sometime after an attack by Llywelyn the Last in 1257. A triangular ravelin on-site suggests refortification during the Civil War (1642-48), and the castle was last inhabited in 1677 (Iorwerth 2005).

Figure 259. Narberth Castle, cleared of vegetation and open to the public, winter 2006 (RCAHMW, 4P-2006-0041)

Figure 260. A virtually intact Norman landscape: Templeton from the south-west, with the planned village and its burgage plots in the centre, looking out to Woods Cross (left) and Cold Blow (background) across medieval open field strips preserved by hedge lines in the more recently enclosed farmland (RCAHMW, 90-cs-0564).

Figure 261. New Moat, east of Llys y Fran reservoir (left). A general view of the village from the east, with its Norman motte well-preserved under trees (centre). (Right) looking down on the late medieval church of St Nicholas, undergoing restoration in 2003, which lies to the south-west of the castle mound (RCAHMW. village, 97-cs-0209; church, 2003-cs-1036).

Figure 262. Maenclochog village in the north of the area, with its strip of houses, central village green and St Mary's Church. View from the south-east in 1997 (RCAHMW, 97-cs-0205).

Figure 263. Panorama over the Western Cleddau, looking south-east over Boulston, towards its confluence with the Eastern Cleddau (left, background) below Picton Point, with the Daugleddau flowing to the south (right, background; RCAHMW, AP-2005-1804).

Pembrokeshire is famed for its historic houses and gardens, a number of which, like Picton, are regularly open for the public to enjoy. Many more remain in private possession but have been researched by generations of family historians and, more recently, garden archaeologists. Aerial photography remains a particularly effective method of recording historic gardens and estates, because it is able to illustrate not only the main houses and stables, together with other ancillary buildings usually hidden from view, but the wider context of landscaped grounds and planting schemes with broader views to the world beyond. Historic air photographs capture the great estates of Wales in working order, before post-war dereliction and demolitions altered them forever.

The wooded reaches and gentle contours of the Daugleddau estuary are home to a number of historic houses and gardens. Picton and Slebech to the north of the Daugleddau are the most visible from the air and dominate truly enormous areas of parkland. Further south a garden survives at Lawrenny, even though its main house, the mid-nineteenth-century

Figure 264. Lost gardens at Coedcanlas. On gently sloping ground west of Martletwy, overlooking Beggar's Reach on the Daugleddau, is the great house and garden at Coedcanlas. In 1362 it was in the ownership of Sir John Carew, and down the ages it passed to several different owners, including the Owens of Orielton in the mid-seventeenth century. Here, as at Landshipping, historical research and follow-up aerial photography have revealed the extensive earthworks of lost formal gardens, thought to have been established by the late seventeenth century. To the north of the house, in an area known as the 'Old Garden', earthworks of a former water garden survive, partly wooded. More extensive earthworks to the south, seen in this view from the north, survive in a field known as the 'Hop Garden'. Although at first glance the field would appear to be open pasture bisected by a stream and an oval pond, faint grids and squares can also be made out. A larger, square enclosure on the east side (here, left) of the central stream is flanked on the west side (right) by a series of six box-like enclosures along the edge of the field. These appear to be the footings of former walled gardens, surrounded by moats or ditches and once containing paths, plants and trees. Although we have no direct record of the construction of these elaborate formal gardens, they are stylistically very similar to those at nearby Landshipping and may have been constructed by the same designer (RCAHMW, 94-cs-226).

Lawrenny Castle, was demolished in 1954. Closer to Pembroke Dock, between the Daugleddau and the River Carew, are the ornamental gardens at Cosheston Hall and the famous grounds and planting schemes of Upton Castle.

Two very old gardens, long lost to local knowledge, were rediscovered through a combination of historical research and aerial photography. At Coedcanlas and Landshipping documentary research by Thomas Lloyd in the early 1990s, followed by aerial photography in low light by Chris Musson of the Royal Commission, revealed low earthworks of two lost gardens thought to date from the late seventeenth century. These early formal pleasure grounds, once attached to great houses, represent extremely important finds for the study of the garden history of the county and, indeed, of Wales as a whole. Both sites are now protected as Scheduled Ancient Monuments to ensure their safekeeping in the future.

Amongst country lanes on the south-eastern approaches to Landshipping, overlooking the Eastern Cleddau, can be found Landshipping Farm, the site of the lost mansion of Old Landshipping house recorded by Fenton in 1811. With origins in the sixteenth century, Landshipping was acquired by the Owens of Orielton in the seventeenth century, and it would appear that new and impressive formal gardens were constructed during their ownership. The construction of the gardens is recorded in a letter of about 1696-7 from Sir Hugh Owen to Sir John Philipps, noted by Francis Jones in 1996, which describes the 'new modelling and a water folly at Landshipping'. Now famous among garden archaeologists and historians and a protected ancient monument, the remains were rediscovered in the same manner as Coedcanlas and unknown before 1990. The garden historian Elizabeth Whittle (2002) writes: 'The five areas that make up this great garden have an unmistakable feel of a formal garden created and planned to provide walks and vistas.' Today we must use our imagination to rebuild the wonders which must once have graced this corner of the Daugleddau region.

Figure 265. A wide view over the Landshipping garden earthworks in January 2006. This shows the complex earthworks which originally formed a garden with three main terraces, subdivided by raised beds and wide paths or walks. At the centre is the rectangular depression of a former pond, flanked on the right-hand side by chevrons of raised beds and on the left by rows of circular mounds showing the remarkable vestiges of rows of trees, once forming an orchard or a formal tree-planting scheme. All around are cultivation ridges and low banks which may represent the footings of more substantial garden walls. Compare with Figure 30 (RCAHMW, AP-2006-0437).

Figure 266. Picton Castle from the south in 2006. Picton began life as a medieval castle, thought to have been originally built by Sir John Wogan about 1300, in a strong position overlooking the confluence of the Western and Eastern Cleddau, and possibly pre-dated by an earthen motte which survives to the east. However, the building was heavily redeveloped in the latter half of the eighteenth century, and some older elements of the parkland were remodelled to present us with the grand house and estate we see today (RCAHMW, AP-2006-1208).

Figure 267. Picton Castle gardens, from the air in July 2004. A formal maze peeps out from the shrubs and trees of the main garden, revealing visitors exploring its concentric paths (RCAHMW, 2004-cs-0974).

Figure 268. Slebech Park from the east in 1997. The main house was constructed around 1776 with an ornate stable block just to the north-east. Originally both were castellated, but today only the stable block retains such features. The main ornamental terraced gardens at Slebech were built slightly to the west of the house in an outstanding south-facing position overlooking the Eastern Cleddau (RCAHMW, 97-cs-0030).

Figure 269. Slebech Park from the east. The site of this house and park, impressively situated on the edge of the Eastern Cleddau, was first occupied by the Order of the Knights Hospitallers when it functioned as the headquarters of the order in Wales. The shell of their medieval church survives. This view shows the main house and castellated stable block in 2006, with the ruined medieval church in trees close to the water's edge (RCAHMW, AP-2006-1210).

Figure 270. Slebech Park. Over a kilometre to the east of the main house stands the Temple of the Four Winds, a ruinous tower originally rising to two storeys. It was probably a folly of the main park, designed as an eye-catching focal point and a place of retreat on long walks (RCAHMW, 2004-cs-0963).

Figure 271. Upton Castle, Cosheston, from the south-east in 2006. Occupying an undulating peninsula bordered by the Daugleddau to the west and Carew river to the east, Upton Castle and its neighbouring chapel both have their origins in the medieval period, although they have been much altered since. The fine gardens and arboretum, for which Upton is famed today, were mostly established by the Neale family after their arrival in 1927 (RCAHMW, AP-2006-1198).

CHAPTER SEVEN

THE SOUTH-WEST: MILFORD HAVEN TO CASTLEMARTIN

Milford Haven/Aberdaugleddy, the industrial and urban heart of Pembrokeshire, is dominated by the relatively recent structures of the oil and gas industries. To some extent these mask the great antiquity of the Haven and its outlying settlements, which demonstrate human settlement around this inland waterway for thousands of years. Milford Haven is a great ria or drowned valley, partly submerged by glacial melt-waters after the last Ice Age, and forms a divide in the south Pembrokeshire landscape. Much of the waterway cuts through the strata of the Old Red Sandstone, visible in the vibrant pinkish reds of the coastal cliffs and the ploughed fields inland. Access to the Haven for large tankers is through a narrow passage, passing beneath the lighthouse on St Ann's Head, although the opposing headlands stand over two kilometres apart at their narrowest point. Milford Haven is one of the few deep-water natural harbours in the British Isles capable of being entered in all weathers and at any stage of the tide. It is a classic 'harbour of refuge', and for this reason it has been home to the Royal Navy and is now an integral part of Britain's oil and gas infrastructure. Currently the Milford Haven waterway is the fourth busiest port in the British Isles, with freight tonnage expected to increase in the coming years. The waterway extends some 16 kilometres from Dale in the west to Neyland in the east, and a further 10 kilometres inland along the muddy, wooded reaches of the Daugleddau. To the south the great Carboniferous Limestone plateau of the Castlemartin range is renowned for its archaeology, geology and wildlife. The climate is also benevolent here, the south-west extents of the Pembrokeshire coast from Castlemartin, west to St Ann's Head, Dale and Marloes, being the sunniest region of Wales during the month of July, with an average 7.5 hours of bright sunshine a day (Carter (ed.) 1989).

Strong Iron Age promontory forts fringe the Haven and the south coast, using the cliffs to defensive advantage in positions often redefended by later tacticians. As in most of the county, hard evidence of Roman occupation or military installations eludes us at present, although it is difficult to believe that such an efficient conquering force would not have exploited the maritime potential of the Haven. Tantalising stray finds, like three Roman coins dug up in 1922 on Military Road, Pennar, Pembroke Dock (Nash-Williams, 1931), may be the chance losses of a Roman detachment, but are equally likely to be coins used by local leaders in an economy dominated by the regional urban centre of Carmarthen/Moridunum. The Norman Conquest exploited the strategic potential of the waterway, and new castles were set close to the navigable rivers leading from it, while new boroughs and open field systems reshaped the rural hinterland. English, French and Flemish colonists were apportioned land across south Pembrokeshire, leading to the virtual elimination of the Welsh language. During the Civil War Pembroke proved to be a long-standing stronghold for parliamentarian resistance in western Britain, warding off several royalist advances.

The history of the Haven over recent centuries is inexorably linked to the changing fortunes of the fishing and shipping industries, while the skyline became dominated by ever evolving coastal defences developed by successive kings and governments. In time Milford Haven became one of the most heavily defended waterways in the British Isles, although many of the defences were only truly tested by air raids in the Second World War. Although oil was

Figure 272. Scoveston Fort. Palmerston's defences haunt the coastline of Milford Haven. These impressive, complex, majestic stone-built forts, constructed to counter the threat of a French invasion of the Royal Navy dockyards at Pembroke Dock from the middle of the nineteenth century onwards, never saw active service and were often obsolete soon after completion. Their geometry and scale can be appreciated from the air, but their size often defies modern reuse. Long field strips first laid out by Norman colonists can be seen in the background near Neyland; those closer to the fort were cleared to enable an open field of fire for its defenders (RCAHMW, 905545-2).

stored at Pembroke Dock during the war, the industry more fully developed during the 1950s, with Esso building the first refinery in 1957 on the north side of the waterway. This was closed and dismantled in 1983, but three further refineries had been built between 1964 and 1973 to the north and south. An integral development was the oil-fired Pembroke Power Station, which closed in 1996. Development continues apace with the construction of two Liquified Natural Gas (LNG) terminals on the north side of the Haven. Such a level of industrialisation in the heart of a coastal national park has not been without its disadvantages, not least the Sea Empress disaster of 1996.

Figure 273. The dramatic Carboniferous Limestone coastal scenery of the southern Castlemartin peninsula, looking west across Flimston Bay with Elegug Stacks in the foreground and beyond to the natural arch of the Green Bridge of Wales. This coastline is one of the finest stretches of limestone cliff scenery in Britain and ranks as a Site of Special Scientific Interest (SSSI), a Special Protected Area (SPA), and a Special Area of Conservation (SAC) for its geological and fossil record. The freestanding former arches of Elegug Stacks or Stack Rocks are named after the guillemots ('elegug' in Welsh) which nest here along with razorbills, fulmars and cormorants (RCAHMW, AP-2005-2627).

Figure 274. Orielton. Overlooking the Castlemartin peninsula from the north is the great country house and estate of Orielton. The present building, with its austere plain façade, dates from around 1810 and is a remodelling of an eighteenth-century house. Parts of the estate are overgrown, but walled gardens and other planned elements can still be made out from the air. The early-nineteenth-century stable court is elegant in its simplicity (RCAHMW, 2004-cs-1633; 2004-cs-1635)

Figure 277. Oil tankers tied up in Milford Haven (RCAHMW, 2000/5507-5; DI2006-0523).

Figure 275 (above). Before heavy industry arrived. A panoramic view of Milford Haven from the east, taken on 13 June 1958 by Terrence Soames, from about 3,000 metres (10,000 feet) on a very clear day. The view shows Pembroke Castle and town (left foreground) on its tidal creek, Pembroke Dock (right centre), and the future site of the power station and refinery at Rhoscrowther (left background). In the distance, beyond the Dale peninsula and St Ann's Head, can be seen Skokholm (left) and Skomer (centre) Islands (© Copyright, Mike Woodward Photography, ref. 2258/8).

Figure 276 (right). Coming home: the Irish Ferries' Isle of Inishmore cruises along the narrowing waters of the Haven towards Pembroke Dock, passing the former Gulf refinery at Waterston. Returning to Wales from Rosslare, the ferries continue a maritime tradition spanning thousands of years. The Vikings may have been drawn to the sheltered waters of the Haven on their coastal raids and over-wintered there. Their distinctive language survives in the name Milford, 'sandbank', showing their understanding of the local terrain and their naming of key features to aid coastal navigation (RCAHMW, 2002-cs-0520).

THE PREHISTORY OF SOUTH-WEST PEMBROKESHIRE

Our perception of large parts of contemporary south-west Pembrokeshire is one of industrialisation and urbanisation, particularly fringing the Milford Haven waterway, but aerial photography from as recently as fifty years ago shows a much more open, farmed landscape than exists today. Within this agricultural setting, dramatically reshaped by Norman and Flemish colonists, remnants of Pembrokeshire's prehistoric past survive either as visible, upstanding monuments or as buried remains.

Programmes of excavation and survey, particularly since the 1970s, have taught us more about the development of south-western Pembrokeshire in prehistory. Stackpole Warren is a low-lying area of windblown sand and dunes framed between the spectacular coastal headlands of St Govans Head and Stackpole Head. The Warren is home to some well preserved, visible prehistoric monuments, including The Devil's Quoit standing stone and a small prehistoric farmstead. Excavations from 1977 to 1979 and later in 1985 revealed unexpectedly rich remains beneath the sand dunes, providing a snapshot of rural Pembrokeshire life between the Beaker period and early Roman times

Figure 278. '...Dry Burrows, a furzy moor covered with tumuli, the largest group I ever recollect to have seen in this county, as the spot never seems to have undergone cultivation since those sepulchral mounds were raised over the ashes of the heroes they cover.' So wrote Richard Fenton in 1811. His son John Fenton excavated some of the Bronze Age burial mounds in the same year (RCAHMW, 97-cs-0576).

Figure 279. Stackpole Warren, from the south-east. Excavations by the Dyfed Archaeological Trust in the late 1970s and 1980s revealed settlement evidence from the Early Bronze Age to the Roman period. An ancient field system was also investigated and found to have been first laid out during the Iron Age in about 400 BC, before being replanned as a set of rectangular stone-walled fields in about 90 BC. The preservation of buried land surfaces at Stackpole was so exceptional that prehistoric plough-marks were excavated in some trenches, showing which fields had been used for cultivation and which for keeping cattle (RCAHMW, 2000-cs-0897).

Figure 280. Devil's Quoit: ground view with stone fan. Standing stones are a common Bronze Age monument in Wales, but very little is known about how they were used or why they were erected. Excavation around the Devil's Quoit revealed a truly remarkable ritual setting of 2000 small stones, placed in a trapezoidal 'fan' of flat and upright stones encircling the standing stone (© Cambria Archaeology).

Figure 281. Well-preserved Iron Age promontory fort at Woodlands, or Strawberry Hill, south of Little Haven, containing substantial circular sunken footings of former prehistoric round houses, and an inturned gateway at top left. The fort was partly excavated by W. F. Grimes in the mid-1960s before he worked on Dale fort (RCAHMW, 96-cs-0219).

Figure 282. Dale Promontory fort from the north-west. Among the earliest dated promontory forts on the Haven is that at Dale (main prehistoric rampart, far right), partly hidden today beneath a nineteenth-century coastal fort. Excavations revealed that this rocky promontory was first fortified in the later Bronze Age and subsequently developed into a formidable Iron Age stronghold. The buildings at Dale Fort have been a Field Study Centre since 1947 (RCAHMW, 96-cs-0271).

(Benson *et al.* 1990). Ritual activity surrounding the Devil's Quoit had been preceded by an Early Bronze Age round house at one end and was superseded by Iron Age or Roman crouched adult burials and three child burials. This site hints at the complex features which could be buried close to other standing stones in Pembrokeshire, where they have not been disturbed or destroyed by later ploughing.

Continuing aerial reconnaissance and excavations in the south-west yield results each year. Most recently, in 2003, survey and excavation at Newton Farm, south of Waterston, in advance of an extension to the Petroplus gas storage facility, discovered the remains of a Bronze Age house. This was a post-built round house, five metres in diameter, with a two-metre-wide doorway which faced south-east. Bronze Age pottery was also found with the house structure, and radiocarbon dating suggests that the house belonged to the Middle-Late Bronze Age (Crane 2004). It was similar in size to the Bronze Age round house excavated at Stackpole Warren, but such domestic sites are still extremely rare in south-west Wales.

Figure 283. Great Castle Head, Dale, in 1993. Weather and waves have taken their toll on Great Castle Head for over two millennia. The site has some of the most massive promontory defences of all the Pembrokeshire coastal forts. In the late 1990s, with a serious danger that the remainder of the fort might be lost to coastal erosion without record, an excavation was mounted by Cambria Archaeology, funded by Cadw. Postholes, a spindle-whorl and sherds of pottery confirmed Iron Age and Roman occupation; medieval pottery also suggested that this may have been the first Dale Castle. A further find of a First World War cap badge dates from when the fort was used as a look-out post for coastal defence (RCAHMW, 93-cs-0111).

Figure 284 (right). The elegant church of St James the Great at Walwyn's Castle is dwarfed in this view by the earthworks beyond, thought to be a medieval castle with two wards adapting a pre-existing Iron Age promontory fort (RCAHMW, 2002-cs-0437).

Figure 285 (far right). West Pickard Camp, south of Angle. Picked out in low winter sunlight, the Old Red Sandstone cliffs glow red and yellow below the single rampart of the Iron Age fort. The site was later used during the Second World War, with weapons pits for light anti-aircraft machine guns and a searchlight battery sited close by (RCAHMW, 97-CS-0557).

200

Figure 286. Rosemarket, near Neyland: the planned village lies to the north of the circular Iron Age fort of Rosemarket Rath (foreground), which is thought to have been refortified in the medieval period (RCAHMW, 89-cs-0191)

The early medieval kingdom of Deuheubarth, approximating to modern-day Pembrokeshire and Carmarthenshire, contained two *cantrefi* which encompassed the waterway: Rhos to the north-west, running from Roch to Haverfordwest, and Penfro, taking in the entire southern part of Pembrokeshire from Angle to Carmarthen Bay. Deuheubarth finally fell to Norman control after 1093, following the death of the Welsh prince Rhys ap Tewdwr, whose authority William the Conqueror had respected during his reign. Incursions were then led by the Norman lords William fitz Baldwin of Devon and Roger de Montgomery of Shrewsbury, the latter marching south to found Pembroke Castle in 1093. Pembroke was granted to Roger's son, Arnulf de Montgomery, under whose subsequent rule the cantref of Penfro became the earldom of Pembroke, and the conquest of southern Pembrokeshire was consolidated through a series of new lordships granted in the region. Each lord founded a castle, and these stood as major symbolic and administrative bases from which they could exercise their own brand of government and territorial control. The early castles were rapidly constructed in earth, with a towering castle mound or *motte* presiding over a defended lower enclosure or *bailey*. Many mottes, which survive today as earthworks, were superseded in the later consolidation of power and fell into disuse; some sites were retained and rebuilt in stone.

The latter castles became focal points in the landscape for the growth of trading settlements, and it was not long before early towns were established in the shadow of key castles. These were granted borough status, formalising early urban settlements such as Haverfordwest, Pembroke and Tenby, which

Figure 287. The whitewashed walls of the restored Benton Castle, overlooking Castle Reach on the southern reaches of the Daugleddau; the medieval origins of this site are obscure. In recent years an elaborate stone labyrinth has been constructed in its grounds (RCAHMW, DI2006-0379).

Figure 288. Castlemartin Castle: a ringwork and bailey surviving at the centre of the village and impinged upon by housing. The radiating field boundaries are thought by Kissock (1997) to imply a pre-conquest origin to this settlement. This early view was probably taken in 1938 by the 210 Squadron based at nearby Pembroke Dock, but the print is unlabelled (Crown Copyright MoD/1938; from the Grimes archive, Grimes 77, DI2006-0420).

were later augmented with impressive town defences. Murphy (1997) reminds us of the peculiar conditions which prevailed during Anglo-Norman settlement in south-west Wales, particularly in the sheer number of lordships which were initially established, leading to a multitude of closely-spaced small boroughs and towns. He also notes that some small towns may even have been founded to attract settlers and increase revenues for individual lords, who had no long-term plan for their development into boroughs.

After the exile of Arnulf de Montgomery in the early part of the twelfth century, the Crown under Henry I took over the earldom of Pembroke. Some historians, such as Kissock (1997), believe that the widespread influx of Flemish settlers into the region at the same time may have been a deliberate attempt to wipe out both Welsh communities *and* sympathetic followers of de Montgomery. Most scholars agree that the combination of the Norman conquest of the region and Flemish settlement forever altered the

Figure 289 (above). Angle. The name means 'nook' or 'corner' in Middle English, and at Angle we have a well-preserved example of a planned Norman village, its single main street focussed on the sheltered anchorage of East Angle Bay. Key elements of the Norman village survive intact, including the late medieval church of St Mary, the medieval, fortified tower house of the Old Rectory, the dovecote and, most visible from the air, the planned rows of open field strips to the north and south. Recent work by archaeologists from the National Park and Cambria Archaeology has confirmed early medieval activity, including burials at West Angle Bay at the opposite end of the peninsula. The aerial view (right) shows these excavations in progress in the summer of 2006 (RCAHMW; wide view, 97-cs-0550; West Angle excavation, AP-2006-3303).

Figure 290. Pill Priory, Milford Haven. A ground view of the priory showing the fragments of surviving masonry, principally here the wall of the chancel arch. Pill was founded around 1200 and was a dependent priory of St Dogmael's Abbey (RCAHMW, DI2005-0205).

Figure 291. The ruins of Lamphey Bishop's Palace, set along a quiet valley east of Pembroke, once stood at the heart of a productive country estate owned by the bishops of St Davids. The arcaded parapet of the roofless de Gower's Hall in the right foreground, built after 1328, echoes similar ornamentation found at St Davids Bishop's Palace to the north-west (RCAHMW, 93-cs-0155).

structure of the landscape from the cantref of Rhos southwards. New villages were established along Norman lines, with a main street, a prominent church, a village green and strips of open fields striking out from the village core. Around the Haven we have excellent surviving examples of planned villages with their field systems, as at Angle, and of farms of medieval origin across the Castlemartin peninsula. The Normans controlled all aspects of commerce, town and village life, farming and religion. New churches were founded; bishops fulfilled parallel roles as their own Marcher lords, administering revenue, justice and managing farming lands within their lordships. Bishops' palaces, like Lamphey, reflected the enormous prosperity and ostentation of the medieval church. Pre-existing Celtic monastic communities in which the region was so rich were no longer tolerated and were brought under the control of new monasteries founded by the Norman lords. Priories like that at Pill to the north of Milford Haven represent more modest religious houses in the medieval landscape and they stood until their eventual slighting during the Reformation.

Figure 292. Pembroke from the air on a glorious, clear July day in 1946, recorded by Royal Air Force photographers. This view captures the castle and medieval walled town of Pembroke prior to the expansion of post-war development and housing. The strategic position of the castle, surrounded by tidal flats on almost three sides, is most obvious in this view, commanding the head of a long, rising promontory, looking north-west towards the wider waters of the Haven. Behind the castle the plan of the medieval town is striking in its completeness. Pembroke is characterised by an exceptionally long central street, off which run narrow burgage plots downhill to the encircling town walls (Crown Copyright MoD /1946, 106G/UK/1625-4355, 7 July 1946).

Pembroke Castle is among the great surviving medieval fortresses of Wales, and its importance is matched by the survival of a virtually complete Norman planned town. From the air the strategic might of its position can be easily appreciated, on the edge of a long promontory bordered to north and south by tidal waters. The position was so strong that Pembroke Castle famously never surrendered to a Welsh attack, and it also proved a valued stronghold for the parliamentarians during the Civil War. Pembroke was founded by Roger de Montgomery in 1093, early in the Norman conquest of south-west Wales, and the strength of the position was obvious to the Anglo-Norman lords. The early timber castle was superseded and rebuilt in stone following William Marshal's acquisition of the site in 1204, when the castle familiar to us today was largely constructed. The earliest part of this new castle was the semi-circular Inner Ward sited on the north-west tip of the promontory and backed by the enormous tower of the circular keep, one of the earliest of its kind built in Britain. The oval Outer Ward engulfs the Inner and encloses a large open area fringed by a high curtain wall, round towers and a strong gatehouse on the south-east (town) side. The Henry VII Tower immediately south of the gatehouse is reputedly the king's birthplace.

Figure 293. Pembroke Main Street from the south-east in 2002, showing, in the centre, the boldly placed former Wesleyan Chapel, with its classical façade, on an island between Main Street and East Back and St Michael's Church on the right-hand side (RCAHMW, CD2005-601-015).

Figure 294. Pembroke Castle in 1990: a panoramic view of the castle and town from the north-west, showing the great expanse enclosed by the castle walls and the restricted area of the Inner Ward in the foreground backed by the great circular keep. On the left-hand side of the town Dark Lane leads down to the mill bridge, the site of a mill since medieval times (RCAHMW 905544.18).

The onset of Civil War (1642-8) saw Pembrokeshire's medieval castles pressed back into active service and placed at the centre of a prolonged struggle between the opposing forces of the royalists and parliamentarians. Pembroke remained a parliamentary stronghold until the end of the war, often against heavy odds. It frequently resisted attack from the successive royalist advances which saw surrounding castles at Haverfordwest, Picton, Carew and Tenby fall. The Haven remained a key strength in Pembroke's arsenal, allowing the parliamentarians to retain control over shipping and navigation in the Bristol Channel and the Irish Sea. Following the surrender of Pembroke to Oliver Cromwell in July 1648, orders were soon given for the standing castles in the region, which had functioned so well as Civil War strongholds, to be slighted. Pembroke Castle was only restored to its present condition in the latter years of the nineteenth century and early in the twentieth, providing us today with an image of a remarkably intact medieval fortress.

The Milford Haven waterway is one of the most comprehensively defended in Britain. The view from most points today is dominated by the remains of barracks, defended islands and elaborate stone forts, which are among the finest examples anywhere of the changing priorities of nineteenth- and twentieth-century naval defence. The proximity of this deep anchorage to the Irish Sea and southern shipping routes long made it both strategically vital to the Royal Navy and vulnerable to attack from overseas. Saunders (2001) noted that, prior to the rise of air power in the early twentieth century, the Royal Navy provided Britain's first line of defence, with Milford Haven providing anchorage between the naval bases of Plymouth and Cork and functioning as a base for operations into the Atlantic. Despite peripheral fortification of its shores by the Normans, whose castles included those at Pembroke, Dale, St Ishmael's, Carew, Benton and Cresswell, scholars agree that it was Thomas Cromwell in 1539 who first perceived the need to defend the Haven. Henry VIII established two stone blockhouses with guns to flank the entrance to the waterway. The Tudor West Blockhouse has been destroyed, but there is a

Figure 295. The fragmentary remains of Henry VIII's East Blockhouse, dating from the sixteenth century, overlooking the Haven mouth at the southern edge of West Angle Bay. It is protected as a Scheduled Ancient Monument (RCAHMW, AP-2006-1161).

Figure 296. The Defensible Barracks on Barrack Hill, Pembroke Dock, constructed between 1842 and 1845 to defend the developing naval dockyards. A striking building even today, the Pevsner Architectural Guide notes that it was 'extraordinarily old fashioned' in defensive terms even when built, following a seventeenth-century plan with angled bastions and musket-loops looking out over a dry moat. The enclosed yard remains notable for being the finest Georgian-style square in Wales. (RCAHMW, 915507-17)

replacement nineteenth-century fort between Dale Point and St Ann's Head; a fragment of East Blockhouse survives on a cliff edge, flanked by later gun emplacements. Later fortifications include those from the Civil War. One such was Pill Fort built in 1643 by Richard Steel, a royalist engineer, within the ramparts of an Iron Age fort on the eastern side of the present town of Milford Haven.

The majority of defences around the Haven date from the middle of the nineteenth century to the end of the Second World War. In the fifty years after the battle of Waterloo (1815), the threat of a French invasion was never far from politicians' minds. The impromptu French landing on the north coast of Pencaer/Strumble Head, near Fishguard, in 1797 during the Napoleonic wars, highlighted the vulnerability of the Pembrokeshire coast. The increasing pace of military and shipping development by the middle of the century, coupled with uncertainty about the French, meant that ever greater technological development and investment in coastal defences

were called for. Permanent coastal defences were required to defend not only naval dockyards, but also the ports and harbours used by merchantmen. Despite having the strongest navy in the world in the early nineteenth century, Britain was rocked by a series of damning reports into the condition of its coastal defences, which induced an atmosphere of political panic. Concerns raised by the Duke of Wellington in 1844, and then by Sir John Fox Burgoyne in 1846, prompted Lord Palmerston to petition the cabinet for a strengthening of the main dockyards.

The Haven defences were developed in two significant stages. Before 1858 several new defences were built to protect Pembroke Dock and its forward approaches from the west. The first was the Defensible Barracks on the hill above the town in 1842-5 to protect directly the new naval dockyards below. This was followed in 1848-51 by the construction of two off-shore Martello Towers, or gun towers, to flank the dockyard to the south-west and north-east. Both were considered redundant by

Figure 297. Stack Rock Fort. Perhaps the most striking of all the Haven forts, remote on a mid-channel rock (top left), Stack Rock was first developed in 1852 as a trefoil-plan battery similar to the north-east Martello Tower at Pembroke Dock. The view (top right) looking straight down at the fort illustrates the later extension added in 1870; an entirely new building enveloped the former tower within. In its day Stack Rock defended the middle part of the Haven with sixteen 18-ton Rifled Muzzle Loading (RML) guns, manned by 150 men (RCAHMW; general view 915507-8; detailed view, AP-2006-1165).

Figure 298. Inside Stack Rock. In 2002 Royal Commission photographer Iain Wright travelled out to Stack Rock to record its derelict interior with a Cadw field monument warden. Because of this rare opportunity a large quantity of camera and lighting gear was taken to cover every eventuality. The crossing proved tricky due to high winds and tides; an inflatable dingy was used to access the severely eroded steps and everything was off-loaded with considerable difficulty. Unfortunately, despite the hope of a long stay, the team was forced to abandon work after only 15 minutes. An urgent radio message was received from the inflatable with the news that a change in wind direction might make it impossible for a recovery to be attempted (RCAHMW, 2002.0209.3).

1882; the north-east tower was restored as a museum in 1994. Impressive island forts followed on Stack Rock in 1852 and Thorn Island in 1852-4, providing forward cover for the entrance to the Haven.

In 1852 Louis Napoleon was elected emperor of France and a fresh panic was set in train by Palmerston, who suggested that the French could mount a sizable invasion force to cross from Cherbourg in a single night. During the Crimean War (1854-6) new lessons were learnt about coastal artillery defences which would inform subsequent developments at Milford Haven. The strategy developed was to strengthen the defences at the entrance to the Haven to prevent enemy ships anchoring there. This led to the construction of two new forts, West Blockhouse and Dale Fort, between 1853 and 1857, to flank Thorn Island, along with the strengthening of Stack Rock. Even as these new forts were being constructed advances in weapons and warship technology were rapidly rendering them obsolete, necessitating some new strategic thinking. In 1859 a Royal Commission on the Defences of the United Kingdom was set up to inspect and report on all the main dockyards, including Pembroke, Portsmouth, Plymouth and Dover; it reported in 1860.

The result between 1859 and 1872 was one of the greatest episodes of fortress building in Britain.

Figure 299. Chapel Bay Fort. Although originally designed to complement the island forts at Stack Rock and Thorn Island, Chapel Bay was not completed until 1890. It is historically important in demonstrating the early use of shuttered concrete, rather than the masonry blocks used in the other Haven forts. Great circular gun emplacements looked out over the sea, while rooms below provided barracks and storerooms. These two views show the fort in 1993 (left) and 2006 (below), demonstrating the progress of a decade of clearance and renovation, with guns replaced in their concrete housings (RCAHMW, left; 93-cs-0132; below; AP-2006-1163)

Encircling the outer and middle approaches along the Haven, and defending the naval dockyards, new fortresses were erected on Popton Point, holding 31 guns, at Fort Hubberston with 26 guns and Scoveston Fort. Although the land was bought, Chapel Bay was not built until the 1890s. Stack Rock was also modernised and enlarged. These immense buildings, built at vast expense, were always meant to be 'state of the art', with the use of RML (Rifled Muzzle Loaded) weapons. However, the development of iron-clad warships rendered them redundant and ineffectual and most became obsolete once completed, seeing no military action. Some were barely used at all, never seeing a permanent garrison stationed. Although most were officially redundant at the start of the twentieth century, they saw brief reuse in the First and Second World Wars. They have come to be known collectively as 'Palmerston's follies' and stand as stark reminders of the fear that a seaborne invasion from France once engendered in military and political circles.

Figure 300. Scoveston Fort. Marooned in modern farmland and derelict and overgrown, this hexagonal fort was the only landward fort built in a proposed chain to defend Pembroke Dock. It was constructed during 1861-8 and manned and used as a depot during the First World War, but never saw action as originally intended (RCAHMW, 935501-3).

Figure 301. The Thorn Island battery was built during 1852-4 to provide the first forward defence for the Haven waterway, coupled with West Blockhouse, Dale and Stack Rock forts. Appearing like a film set for a spy thriller, it was converted into a hotel in 1932. This view looks north-west across from West Angle Bay on the mainland (RCAHMW, 2002-cs-0767).

A TALE OF TWO TOWNS: MILFORD HAVEN AND PEMBROKE DOCK

Milford was founded by Sir William Hamilton, who was granted permission by Act of Parliament in 1790 to 'provide Quays, Docks, Piers and other erections' and develop a new town. Several Quaker whaling families fleeing from the American War of Independence were encouraged to settle in the town in 1792, and in 1796 a new navy dockyard was built at the entrance to Hubberston Pill. While the whaling industry flourished for a time, it had declined by 1819, and a further severe blow was dealt to Milford in 1812 when the Admiralty decided to move the naval dockyards to a new site further east along the Haven at Pembroke Dock. For much of the nineteenth century various attempts were made to revitalise Milford's fortunes, and in 1888 a fully-functional floating dock was completed. Although planned to capitalise on transatlantic passenger trade, this also failed to prosper and the facilities reverted to use by the fishing industry.

The later town and royal dockyard of Pembroke Dock, sited some five kilometres eastwards up the Haven from Milford, developed rapidly during the nineteenth century and became a major Royal Dockyard. Like Milford, the town betrays its recent foundation in its gridiron street pattern and angular dock structures, so different to the more forgiving street plans of earlier historic towns. From its opening in 1814 as a naval facility and town, Pembroke Dock developed substantially through two further periods of extension in 1830-2 and again in 1844, constructing many of the Royal Navy's warships. Despite the decline and sudden closure of the once magnificent facilities

Figure 302. Milford Haven from the south-west in August 1950 and June 2006, looking over Hakin Point (right foreground) to Milford Docks beyond (Crown Copyright MoD/1950, 540/396-46; RCAHMW, AP-2006-1179).

Figure 303. The strict, planned layout of the naval dockyard town of Pembroke Dock, viewed from the north-west (RCAHMW, DI2006-1503).

in 1926, the town flourished again as preparations for the Second World War saw the establishment of a Royal Air Force flying boat base. The modern Irish Sea Ferries' terminal has been built over some of the ship-building slips that served the Royal Navy.

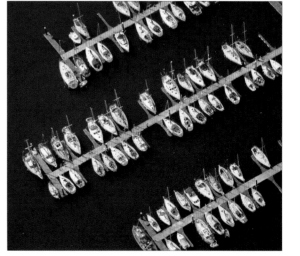

Figure 304. Changing prosperity: patterns of boats in Milford Marina (RCAHMW, AP-2006-1183)

Figure 305. Then and now: West Blockhouse Point, Dale, on 9 May 1941 (upper) and 27 February 1996 (lower). The Royal Air Force oblique aerial photograph taken in 1941 shows various wartime structures which are no longer extant. The visible remains include the curving concrete walls of gun casemates of the West Blockhouse Battery, left of centre, together with camouflaged barracks for accommodation at right rear. The nineteenth-century West Blockhouse Fort can be seen at the lower right, overlooking the entrance to Milford Haven. Its front wall has been modified to hold two concrete searchlight batteries, many more of which dot the neighbouring headlands. The more recent view from 1996 is significant in that it was taken twelve days after the Sea Empress disaster, close by in Mill Bay, St Ann's Head. The fort was converted to holiday accommodation by the Landmark Trust in the 1980s (Crown Copyright MoD/1941, Medmenham 2 TI3; RCAHMW, 96-cs-0268).

Figure 306. Dale Camp. The state of preservation of the wartime prefabricated buildings to the north of the main airfield is extremely good. These two views show, on the left, interlinked ranks of barrack blocks looking south-west and, on the right, further barrack buildings with the mess in the centre of the view, looking east (RCAHMW, left, 2003-cs-1005; right, 2003-cs-1106)

Figure 307. Dale camp. Second World War cartoons, or 'wall art', preserved within the airfield buildings (RCAHMW, DI2006-1303).

Despite its far westerly position in the British Isles, the Haven had a central role in the defence of southern Britain in the Second World War, particularly by providing strategic and radar cover across the Irish Sea and guarding against a long-feared south-westerly offensive by Germany via mainland Ireland. On almost every cliff top and in other locations fringing the Milford Haven waterway can be seen pill boxes, anti-aircraft batteries, searchlight batteries and other emplacements. Some of the historic Palmerstonian forts were reoccupied to house troops. Despite a quiet start to the war, Pembroke Dock suffered the shock of its first aerial bombardment on 10 July 1940, when a single Junkers Ju88 bomber came out of a cloudy sky. Attacks intensified on the docks, thankfully without much damage or any casualties, until on 19 August the Llanreath oil tanks above the town were hit and burned for eighteen days. Later in the year aerial attacks spread to other towns, including Haverfordwest. The early years of the war saw the establishment of a number of major airfields in the south of the county, including Dale, Angle, Sageston and Carew Cheriton, which had been the site of the Royal Navy airship station, RNAS Pembroke. Bill

Figure 308. The wartime defences of Pembrokeshire have left their mark on every coastal headland. On the left is the Heavy Anti-Aircraft (HAA) battery at Whetstone Hill overlooking Gravel Bay, Freshwater West, with four octagonal concrete emplacements for 3.7-inch guns. The view (below) shows a small, concrete Coastal Artillery Searchlight (CASL) emplacement (lower centre) perched on the edge of the Old Red Sandstone cliffs south of East Blockhouse Point, looking across to Rat Island (RCAHMW; left, AP-2005-2718; below, AP-2006-1160).

Richards, one of a number to have documented the wartime history of south Pembrokeshire, notes that most of the German raids on Pembroke Dock were over by the time RAF Angle and other airfields became operational. Although there has always been considerable interest in the two World Wars among local people and military historians, the major Defence of Britain Project organised by the Council for British Archaeology (CDA) between 1995 and 2002 highlighted the intrinsic value of wartime installations for a new generation of historians and archaeologists. This has helped to foster an increasing respect for the decaying remnants of Britain's wartime defences and to bring statutory protection for the best preserved and rarest examples.

THE SUNDERLAND FLYING BOATS OF PEMBROKE DOCK

Figure 309. Two former hangars of the Sunderland flying boat fleet still stand at Pembroke Dock. These are the only extant 'B'-Type hangars in the United Kingdom, designed by Air Ministry engineer N. Garnish. In the war they were cleverly camouflaged to appear to aerial bombers as a continuation of rows of terraced houses. It must have worked as they survived the war and stand as grey, gaunt reminders of former glories (RCAHMW, 2003-cs-1140)

In 1933 a Sunderland flying boat base was established at Pembroke Dock, bringing welcome investment to the remains of the historic dockyard. These large and graceful aeroplanes were the front line in the Royal Air Force's Coastal Command, one of three branches of the Home Commands along with Fighter Command and Bomber Command. The principal role of the Sunderland flying boats was photo-reconnaissance, and from 1933 onwards the crews honed their skills in the photography of targets across Pembrokeshire and further afield. The bulk of aerial photographs taken on these early sorties have not survived. Having served their training or strategic

purpose, prints and negatives were often discarded or, if stored, subsequently came to grief with the periodic disposal or accidental destruction of photographic archives. Some pre-war aerial photography by the 210 Squadron survives. Sometimes this is by virtue of the pilots and crews themselves having saved mementoes of their active service. Early prints occasionally survive in the personal collections of eminent archaeologists of the time who may have exercised professional contacts to obtain prints or even commission aerial photography. The prints of Bulliber Camp and Castlemartin Castle (Figs. 11 & 288) reproduced in

Figure 310. View of Neyland from the south in August 1950, with Sunderland flying boats moored off Pembroke Dock. This was the railway terminus as originally developed by Brunel for the transatlantic passenger trade. From the Second World War fragments of the preparations for D-Day can still be seen. These are two embarkation hards, Neyland West Hard/WN1 (A) and Neyland East Hard/WN2 (B), designed for loading two Landing Ship Tanks at a time for D-Day + 1. The hards consisted of concrete roadways leading to a rectangular hard-standing above the high tide mark (Crown Copyright MoD/1950; 540/396-0084).

this book both survived in the archives of W. F. Grimes, a key figure in Pembrokeshire archaeology from the 1920s. These survivals, along with some early airship views from the First World War, provide rare windows on Pembrokeshire's landscape from the air from before the Second World War. International bodies like the Aerial Archaeology Research Group (AARG) and the National Association of Aerial Photographic Libraries (NAPLIB) actively campaign for the preservation of such photographic collections for posterity and future research.

Figure 311. Detailed view of a Short Sunderland Mark V flying boat, moored at Pembroke Dock in 1955. Carrying a crew of ten, these four-engined reconnaissance aircraft were massive, weighing some twenty-five tons, with a range of over 2,000 miles. In flight crews engaged in observation, signalling and photography of shipping lanes and convoys from Gibraltar to Iceland and out across the Atlantic. Inside the great aircraft was a dining table and even a porcelain toilet for crews on long sorties (Copyright Reserved, Meridian Airways, Film 135, frame 18219 B, 4 April 1955).

THE BOMBING OF THE LLANRAETH OIL TANKS, PEMBROKE DOCK

An iconic moment in the twentieth century in south Pembrokeshire and a turning point in the Second World War offensive in west Wales was the bombing raid carried out on the Llanraeth oil tanks which once overlooked Pembroke Dock from the south. During the summer of 1940 the residents of Pembroke Dock and surrounding towns had been getting used to the uncertainties of day and night bombing raids, thankfully without casualties. Bill Richards (1995) relates the story of how three German Junkers Ju88 bombers launched a surprise attack on the dock on a Monday afternoon on 19 August 1940, scoring a direct hit on an oil tank holding 12,000 tons of oil. The fire burned for eighteen days, and during the

Figure 312. Looking down on disaster. An astonishing overview of Pembroke Dock and Neyland taken in early evening on 31 August 1940, with smoke still billowing from the Llanraeth oil tanks, despite some having been extinguished tirelessly by fire crews. Sunderland flying boats can be seen moored in Milford Haven, while the square-bastioned Defensible Barracks stand out in grassland above the town. The gridiron layout of the housing in the dockyard town is striking. North is to the top (Crown Copyright MoD/1940; PRU61, F/14, 17).

struggle to extinguish it five firemen lost their lives. The billowing plumes of black smoke marked the skyline and could be seen from as far away as the Devon coast. Many official and private photographs were taken of the oil tank blaze over the days it raged, but some of the most dramatic were taken by the Royal Air Force on 31 August 1940. A series of views preserved in the Central Register of Aerial Photography for Wales in Cardiff, of which four are reproduced here, were taken twelve days after the attack. They stand as a key visual record of this attack and of wartime Pembroke Dock, beset with camouflage schemes and tented encampments.

Figure 314. Defensible Barracks, Pembroke Dock. The perfect angles of the nineteenth-century barracks are still unencumbered by housing in this 1940 view, while smoke from the oil fire drifts across the top right of the frame (Crown Copyright MoD/1940; HLA/060 PRU51, F/14, frame 53).

Figure 313. The west side of Pembroke Dock, showing the angular masonry ramparts of the Seven Years War defence work, Paterchurch Fort, partially constructed in 1758. During the Second World War workshops (upper right) were ingeniously painted to be disguised as rows of terraced houses, while waterfront tanks display the bold dazzle camouflage used in the early years of the war, particularly on shipping, to break up the lines of obvious features when seen from the air (Crown Copyright MoD/1940; HLA/060 PRU51, F/14, 9).

Figure 315. The Llanraeth oil tanks from the north-west, twelve days into the blaze, with most fires extinguished but fire crews still hard at work. Fire hoses trail down from the fire, across fields to the waters of the Haven, while cars can be seen parked in the field opposite the tanks (Crown Copyright MoD/1940; HLA/060 PRU51, F/14, frame 75).

Figure 316. Vanishing industry: two contrasting views of the Pembroke Power Station looking west, the complex complete in April 1995, but virtually erased from the landscape by June 2003 (RCAHMW, 95-cs-1064; 2003-cs-1136).

In 1883 a visitor to south Pembrokeshire, Wirt Sikes, commented of Milford Haven: 'The business done here is insignificant, but the prospects of Milford Haven are, and have long been, magnificent. Here is a harbor [sic] of really grand proportions… but time has passed it by… Yet busy and hopeful brains are still at work for Milford, planning great results in the near future.' (Sikes 1883, in Ludlum 1985, 29). After decades, even centuries, of varied fortunes the industrial and financial promise of Milford Haven was only truly fulfilled with the arrival of the massive structures of the oil industry in the 1950s. The formation of the new Milford Haven Conservancy Board in 1958, which by 1960 had taken over long-standing jurisdiction of the entire waterway from the Royal Navy, oversaw the growth of the new refineries and pipelines which transformed the shores to north and south. Work began on the Esso refinery in 1957, sited on the peninsula west of Milford Haven and overshadowing the nineteenth-century fort on South Hook Point. About 3,500 people were employed on the construction site, and the refinery and massive jetties extending into the Haven opened in 1960. Soon after, BP opened its Ocean Terminal off Popton, which fed oil to Llandarcy (Swansea) via a pipeline. During the 1960s and early 1970s further refineries were established for Regent, later to become Texaco, at Rhoscrowther on the south side of the Haven, for Gulf at Waterston on the north side, east of Milford Haven, and finally for Amoco in 1973, north of Hebrandston, inland and to the north of the waterway. High-level aerial views of the waterway taken by Terrence Soames in 1958 (Fig. 275) are some of the last to show the pattern of farmland and small villages extending to the water's edge before large-scale industry arrived. But, like so many of Pembrokeshire's industries, the seemingly permanent structures of the oil industries could be hit by world fluctuations in oil prices and the effects of company mergers thousands of miles away. After years of dereliction and uncertainty the refinery sites at South Hook and Waterston are being redeveloped to hold one of two Liquified Natural Gas terminals (LNG), the other being at the former Waterston (Petroplus) refinery. The gas will be shipped from around the world by tanker, treated and converted back to its natural state at the new terminals and then pumped via massive pipelines across Wales to the British gas network (Fig. 374). Once again, large scale construction is dominating the skyline of the Milford Haven Waterway.

Figure 317. Looking north-west across ranks of storage tanks at the former Gulf refinery, Waterston (RCAHMW, 2002-cs-0522).

Figure 318. The South Hook LNG facility from the south-east in 2006, with construction in progress on five massive storage tanks (RCAHMW, AP-2006-1168).

223

Figure 319. The Irish Ferries' Isle of Inishmore *carries up to 856 cars and over 2,000 passengers on its regular sailing between Pembroke Dock and Rosslare. This view shows cars unloading in 2003, with two of the Port Authority's harbour tugs alongside (RCAHMW, DI2005-0432).*

THE CASTLEMARTIN RANGE AND THE SOUTHERN COAST

The Castlemartin Range is one of twelve Army Training Estates (ATEs) in the British Isles, covering some 6,400 acres of prime limestone coastal plateau. The principal assets of this landscape are the sheer cliffs of Carboniferous Limestone which form some of the most famous limestone coastal scenery in Britain (Fig. 273). Wave action and weathering have exploited faults in the rock and carved out caves, fissures and blow-holes, which time and subsequent collapses have turned into glorious arches, like the Green Bridge of Wales, and free-standing stacks. While some visitors will survey the cliff lines looking at the dipping limestone strata or teeming colonies of guillemots and razorbills at Stack Rocks, archaeologists are more likely to be looking for the eroded remains of coastal promontory forts, like Flimston Bay fort, or traces of early settlement inland. In medieval times this land fell within the Marcher earldom of Pembroke, and remnants of the farms and hamlets originally settled by French, English and Flemings can still be seen at Flimston and Pricaston in the central and western parts of the range. Earlier still is St Govans chapel, a medieval rebuilding of an early Christian hermit's cell, built in a cleft between high coastal cliffs. This coastline has attracted early tourists and writers from the late seventeenth century, who were awed by the majestic scenery and ancient sites along the cliffs.

In the twentieth century Castlemartin was requisitioned for military training along with other Welsh estates like Sennybridge in central Wales and the coastal ranges at Manorbier and Penally. The range was established in 1938 and used until 1945 for tank training by the Royal Armoured Corps. It was briefly returned to agricultural use after the war, but was acquired by the War Department in 1948 and pressed back into service in 1951 with the advent of the Korean War (1950-3). It remained as a specialist tank training range, often hosting German units, until 1995, when training activities were broadened to include infantry and small arms training. Historically, army ranges were seen as places where archaeological sites and historic buildings were adversely affected by the impact of training, from vehicle damage and live firing to digging by engineers and infantry. In more recent years the army has come to be seen as guardian of the landscapes it uses. Against the background of the intensively farmed lowland landscape of south Pembrokeshire, the Castlemartin range now stands as a valuable microcosm of land which has never been subjected to the damaging advances of intensive agriculture or development. Despite the impact of military training, the archaeological, historical and ecological heritage survives largely intact.

Figure 320. All that survives of Brownslade, south of Castlemartin on the western side of the range, is the courtyard of the model farm, the house having been demolished in 1976. This view shows the roofless buildings from the north-east (RCAHMW, AP-2005-2655).

Figure 321. Flimston Bay fort is one of the finest promontory forts of Pembrokeshire, with three lines of landward defence cutting off an eroding and collapsing limestone headland. Different phases of enlargement or reduction are suggested by the pair of close-set ramparts, with a third set some distance away. The interspace created could have functioned as a corralling place for stock, or as an annexe for trading, secure from the innermost enclosure. Within the fort are shallow scoops of house platforms, and it is likely that the interior was once considerably larger than today. (RCAHMW; above, AP-2005-2615; right, AP-2005-2619).

Figure 322. Panorama north-west from Bulliber Camp (centre, bottom). Also known as Castle Lady Fort, this is a very different Iron Age hillfort from the dramatic coastal promontory forts to the south. With its carefully terraced multiple defences, the fort commands the head of Castle Lady Valley, the routeway down to one of the few safe landing places for boats. Approaching up the valley, the fort is an intimidating sight and was no doubt a potent symbol of Iron Age authority for visitors arriving from the sea. The architecture of Bulliber Camp is similar to Merrion Camp, which lies nearly 4km to the east (see Fig. 24). The similarity suggests a cultural connection, or even contemporary occupation (RCAHMW, AP-2005-2650).

Figure 323. Approaching Elegug Stacks and Flimston promontory fort from the south-west in a virtual fly-past generated from LIDAR data, flown by the Environment Agency in March 2004 (© Environment Agency copyright, D0032801. All rights reserved. View generated by RCAHMW).

Figure 324 St Michael's, Castlemartin. April light illuminates the peaceful setting of St Michael's church, built against a steep slope. Uphill from the church, in the wooded area immediately adjacent to the churchyard, the walls and chimneys of the ruinous Old Rectory can be made out (RCAHMW, 93-cs-0636).

Figure 325. Buckspool Camp, a headland in the far south-east of the range, south-west of Bosherston. Two well-marked ramparts define an Iron Age promontory fort, and numerous scoops or house-platforms can be seen in the interior marking the former positions of prehistoric houses. The setting looks particularly treacherous for year-round settlement (RCAHMW, 93-cs-0622).

Figure 326. St Govans Chapel: '...the path leading down to St. Govans chapel and well, which entered soon brings you to a flight of limestone steps, worn smooth by the feet of the curious, the superstitious, and the invalid, who for ages have visited this pious seclusion'. So Richard Fenton described this remarkable thirteenth-century chapel, tucked in a narrow crevice between steep cliffs and the sea. Built on the traditional site of a hermit's cell, a holy well can also be found between stone slabs on the pebble beach below. Aerial photography is difficult, having to be timed so that the opening of the Castlemartin Range coincides with favourable offshore winds and a sun angle which illuminates at least part of the narrow gully in the cliffs (RCAHMW, AP-2005-2592).

Figure 327. Due south of Merrion are the restored medieval Flimston chapel and the ruins of the large medieval farm of Flimston, seen in an overview in 1993. The detailed view from 2005 (right) shows the main house at bottom right. First recorded in documents in the fourteenth century, the ruined house incorporates a ground-floor hall and substantial standing chimneys. The house is surrounded by farm buildings to the west (top) and to the east (foreground), where an L–shaped barn has clear medieval origins (RCAHMW. Overview 93-cs-0275; Detail AP-2005-2664).

Figure 328. The ruinous remains of the medieval house of Pricaston, seen here from the west, lie to the south of Castlemartin in the heart of the military range. Although the main house (centre) was remodelled in the nineteenth century, it has its origins in the fifteenth century and was once a fine house with well-appointed fittings and ornate dressed stonework (RCAHMW, AP-2005-2638).

Figure 329. The site of the post-medieval farm of Westland or Midland (rectangular enclosures, foreground) in the far south-east of the range near Bosherston (at SR 955 943), with the standing ruin of Eastland Cottages in the left foreground. The well-preserved field systems clearly preserve the 'S' curve of medieval open fields, and slight traces of ridge-and-furrow can still be seen despite the scars of tank training. The curved earthwork of a military blockhouse can be seen in the centre of the frame (RCAHMW, 93-cs-0618)

Figure 330. These photographs were taken during two sorties flown over Castlemartin range on the 21 August 1952. The vertical (above) shows an area of Buckspool Down, just west of Huntsman's Leap, with Buckspool Camp promontory fort at lower right. The oblique (right) looks south-east over the eastern part of the range near Buckspool farm, out to St Govans Head in the distance. In both views the surviving field systems, which are fossils of earlier elements of medieval open strip fields, have been crossed and recrossed by tank tracks. From a land management point of view, these historic images show the erosion of field banks and other landscape features by tank training. That said, much of this wear and tear appears to have been superficial, as oblique air photographs taken near Bosherton in 1993 (Fig. 329) show. (Crown Copyright MoD/1952; vertical: 540/843-5014; oblique 540/843-0015).

Figure 331. Rusting tank 'hard' targets and intersecting tracks at Castlemartin, winter 2005 (RCAHMW, AP-2005-2642).

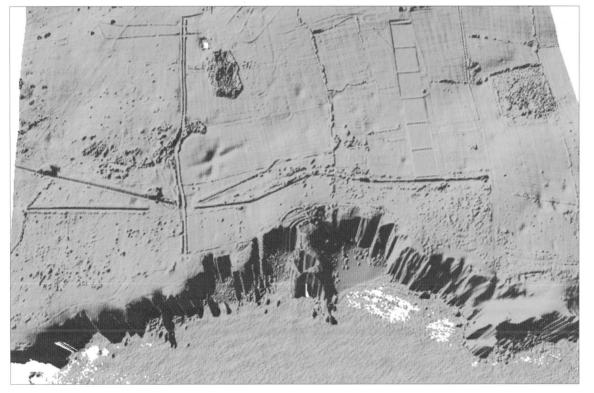

Figure 332. The extraordinarily rich archaeological landscape of the Castlemartin peninsula, captured by airborne laser in a LIDAR survey. The height of the cliffs and other ground features has been artificially exaggerated, allowing archaeological earthworks on the mainland to be seen more clearly. The sun has also been placed in the north-west, an impossibility in the real world. Certain earthworks are very clear, including Flimston promontory fort (lower centre), long ditches for moving artillery targets (centre left to right), a firing range with shooting butts (right of centre) and traces of shell craters and vestigial ridge-and-furrow cultivation across the area (© Environment Agency copyright, D0032801. All rights reserved. View generated by RCAHMW).

CHAPTER EIGHT

THE SOUTH-EAST: FROM CAREW TO CALDY

At the western end of Carmarthen Bay the Pembrokeshire coastline sweeps south, providing the settings for the resort towns of Saundersfoot and Tenby. Across the sea lies Caldy Island, whilst further to the west the coastline becomes indented with a series of spectacular cliffs, headlands and bays between Penally and the Castlemartin peninsula. A considerable part of this south Pembrokeshire coast is given over to military training activities, with long-established ranges at Penally, Manorbier and Castlemartin. The hinterland is undulating and populated by small villages, some with Norman origins. In general the soils are fertile and easy to cultivate, but in the northern part, inland from Saundersfoot, the geology is dominated by the south Pembrokeshire coalfield, with poor soils often set aside for woodland. On the west side the wooded creeks of the Daugleddau cut deep inlets towards the villages of Cresswell Quay and Carew, used to advantage by the original builders of Carew Castle and subsequently exploited by fishermen and exporters of limestone extracted from the waterside quarries at West Williamston.

Before the last Ice Age receded about 12,000 BC the present-day sea-cliffs were some way inland, forming a range of hills overlooking a wooded plain that is now Carmarthen Bay. Palaeolithic and Mesolithic hunters lived and camped in fissures and caves formed in the limestone and left stone tools and animal bones for us to study. By the Neolithic sea levels were as they are now and occasional Neolithic tombs, like King's Quoit at Manorbier, command stunning coastal views. The Iron Age coastal promontory forts are the most visible survivors of prehistory in this part of Pembrokeshire, but aerial reconnaissance has steadily rediscovered a great density of smaller forts and defended farms inland between the Daugleddau and the sea. These enclosures of earth and stone, long since levelled by the plough, reappear both as cropmarks during hot summers and, in the dark red/brown soils of south-east Pembrokeshire, as soilmarks following autumn and spring ploughing. In medieval and later times south Pembrokeshire was a fertile and productive landscape. Castles at Manorbier and Tenby were early seats of medieval power, but between Pembroke and Lydstep remnants of the rural landscape of field systems and villages survive. Some, like Jeffreystone and Jameston, have traces of radial field systems suggesting pre-Norman origins.

Saundersfoot owes its initial prosperity to industry. The harbour here served a thriving export trade in anthracite from medieval times, with the local pits eventually linked directly to the harbour by the Saundersfoot Railway, built in the early nineteenth century. The remains of this industry are fragmented, as the dismantled railway, overgrown pits and lost inclines are steadily incorporated back into farmland. Aerial photographs provide a novel way to see them again, picked out in winter sunshine or pieced together in a high-level view.

Figure 333. Tenby has been a popular seaside resort since at least the late eighteenth century, when it attracted distant visitors and the gentry classes who built many of the seafront properties. The first guides to Tenby were published in 1810, and a thriving holiday trade was boosted by the arrival of the railway in 1866. Famous visitors included Lord Nelson and Lady Hamilton, and Tenby's popularity as a seaside town has continued to the present day (RCAHMW, AP-2005-0905).

Figure 334. From promontory fort, to medieval castle, to an opulent residence for Tudor and Elizabethan lords, the whitish-grey ruins of Carew Castle, built from local limestone and later augmented with Bath stone windows, dominate the western end of a strong promontory first fortified in the prehistoric Iron Age. The castle was begun about 1100 by Gerald of Windsor, and from the late thirteenth century it was owned and developed by successive generations of the Carew family. Carew Castle was most significantly developed in two later phases. After 1480 Rhys ap Thomas, a prominent supporter of King Henry VII, remodelled large parts of the castle as a grand residence, including replacing nearly all the windows in Bath stone. Later, in 1558, Sir John Perrot added the ornate Elizabethan north wing running the length of the castle, with new rooms and a second-floor long gallery, 40 metres in length. The resulting wing, left unfinished after his arrest for treason, looks out across the millpond on the Carew River. The Civil War in 1642-8 left its mark in the refortification of the Outer Gatehouse with a V-shaped ravelin or redan, for the positioning of artillery. The magnificent setting of Carew Castle can be appreciated in this long landscape view from 1995, west across the castle to Carew Mill, thence along the Carew river to where it joins, in the far distance, the Daugleddau estuary (RCAHMW, DI2006-0354).

Figure 335. St Catherine's Island with its nineteenth-century fort, seen on a sweltering summer's day in 2005 en route from Haverfordwest Airport, across the sea to south Wales for cropmark reconnaissance. The unknown speedboat driver provides the perfect balance in the image (RCAHMW, AP-2005-0901).

Figure 336. Colby Lodge Woodland Garden. These formal and informal woodland gardens were created in the early twentieth century by the Kay family and include one of the finest collections of rhododendrons and azaleas in Wales. The gardens conceal an industrial legacy; anthracite and iron ore were mined here until the end of the nineteenth century and were originally loaded onto boats on Amroth beach, until the mines were connected by railway to Saundersfoot. Traces of a shaft can be seen in the centre of the picture, just below the central stream (RCAHMW, 2000-cs-0380).

Figure 337. Liming fields at Cresselly on a mid-April morning in 2002 (RCAHMW, DI2006-0384).

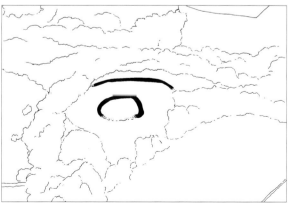

Figure 338. Continuing aerial survey brings new discoveries. An early morning flight near Redberth, in April 2002 revealed a concentric prehistoric enclosure, visible as a 'soilmark'. The ramparts of this medium-sized Iron Age farmstead show as lighter lines of stony soil, caught by the plough, against the darker brown of the field (SN 072 049; RCAHMW, DI2006-0364).

Figure 339. Iron Age defended farmstead at Myrtle Hill, Cresselly. Although the eye is first drawn to the cricket oval on the left, a far older mark appears beneath the boundary on the right. Early summer parching in 2004 revealed the dark oval of a plough-levelled prehistoric enclosure, probably an Iron Age farm, the buried ditch marked out as lush green grass growth against the grass in the rest of the field. The scale of this prehistoric farm can be judged by comparison with the school building in the top right corner (RCAHMW, AP-2004-0822).

Figure 340 (left). Park Rath or Park Camp, lying south of Cresselly Big Wood, viewed from the north. Larger than the enclosure at Myrtle Hill, Park Rath was spared by the plough. It stands today ringed with trees and protected as a Scheduled Ancient Monument. The house alongside gives a good sense of scale (RCAHMW, AP-2006-0085).

The outlines of the Pembrokeshire Coast National Park are drawn far inland to include the secluded, wooded reaches of the Daugleddau estuary, where a number of notable castles, gentry houses and quiet hamlets were built and where, in recent centuries, thriving coastal industries arose. Close to Carew the woodland has long since been cleared, and improved farmland runs down to the muddy shores of the side rivers of the Daugleddau. Away from these picturesque ruins the wooded remnants of the coastal

quarries at West Williamston remind us of the importance of extractive and other industries in providing rural employment, and modern limestone quarries can still be found at Carew Cheriton. Easily missed on the ground today are the remains of vast airfields, some dating back to the First World War. Most were hurriedly developed early in the 1940s to protect west Wales, whilst serving as springboards for squadrons of aircraft flying deep into the heart of occupied Europe.

Figure 341. Carew Castle in May 1989, with excavations in progress in the bailey by the University of Wales, Lampeter, and the Pembrokeshire Coast National Park Authority, for the Carew Castle Archaeological Project (RCAHMW, DI2006-0380).

Figure 342. Carew Mill from the north. Thought to have medieval origins, a mill at this site was first recorded in the sixteenth century. The present four-storey building dates from the nineteenth century but commands a dammed tidal mill pond of medieval origin. It is now in the care of the Pembrokeshire Coast National Park Authority and is open to the public (RCAHMW, DI2006-0345).

Figure 343. Coastal limestone quarries at West Williamston. These two views show the industrial remains of coastal quarries which open onto the south side of the Cresswell river, a side channel of the Daugleddau estuary. Limestone was extracted here throughout the eighteenth and nineteenth centuries, the stone then loaded at wharfs on to boats which travelled along a series of artificial channels to the main river. The workings were disused when mapped in 1907 and are now wooded, but the overall pattern of water channels remains striking from the air (RCAHMW. Upper view DI2006-0361; lower view DI2006-0360).

Figure 344. St Mary, Carew Cheriton, from the east in 1995, with the small village beyond. Parts of this church date to the medieval period, but the imposing tower was raised c.1500 (RCAHMW, DI2006-0344).

Figure 345. St Mary, Carew Cheriton, with excavations at the east end in progress in 1995 for the Carew Castle Archaeological Project. This long trench was designed to examine the curvilinear enclosure around the church and to examine the potential for pre-Norman monastic activity beneath the present complex. Evidence for considerable medieval occupation, including a building, was unearthed, but excavations were curtailed before potentially earlier deposits could be explored (RCAHMW, DI2006-0341).

Figure 346. Manorbier Castle and St James's church, with its medieval tower, commanding the secluded and delightful coastal valley down to the sea at Manorbier Bay (RCAHMW, 905544-15).

Figure 347. Manorbier Castle and village, with Norman strip fields beyond, seen from the south-west across Manorbier Bay, with bands of Old Red Sandstone exposed in the beach cliffs. The site of Kings Quoit Neolithic burial chamber can just be seen at bottom right alongside the cliff path (RCAHMW, DI2006-0368).

Figure 348. The graceful ruins of Manorbier Castle seen from the west in 2002, with the west range housing the hall and chapel to the right. Apparently never slighted by military attack, the castle was used in recent centuries both as a farm and an ornate private residence (RCAHMW, DI2006-0369).

Commanding a quiet, wooded valley with a view of the sea beyond, Manorbier is one of the most secluded and beautiful castles in Pembrokeshire. It is famous as the birthplace, in 1147, of Giraldus Cambrensis, who accompanied Archbishop Baldwin on a tour of Wales in 1188 to recruit for the Third Crusade. His oft-quoted writings on Manorbier describe it as 'the pleasantest spot in Wales' and provide a vivid sense of the surroundings of the castle in its heyday. He wrote: 'The castle... is excellently well defended by turrets and bulwarks... having on its northern and southern sides a fine fish pond under its walls...and a beautiful orchard on the same side, enclosed on one part by a vineyard and on the other by a wood...'. Unlike many of the more austere and ruinous Pembrokeshire castles, Manorbier contains a range of well preserved domestic and farm buildings thought to date to the seventeenth and eighteenth centuries. Two of the towers of the old castle were brought into habitation during the late nineteenth century by the owner, J. R. Cobb, through the provision of roofs and floors.

Figure 349. St Florence from the south-west on a winter's evening in 1997, showing the surviving earthworks of old medieval strip-fields, now partly ploughed out and incorporated into larger modern fields (RCAHMW, DI2006-0366).

Figure 350. Tenby from the north-west in the high summer of 1990, epitomising the extraordinary colour schemes of coastal Pembrokeshire in the summer months, to which the aerial archaeologist grows accustomed. The promontory position of Castle Hill and the advantageous positioning of the harbour below are well illustrated in this view (RCAHMW, 905529-6).

The good preservation of Tenby's medieval defences, its fine Regency and later buildings, a pleasant climate and excellent beaches have long made Tenby a destination for pleasure seekers since its birth as a resort town in the 1780s. This historic town occupies a strategically strong position on a triangular headland jutting out to sea, enclosing a sheltered harbour on the north side and linking, via a narrow isthmus, to a towering rock commanded by the remains of the thirteenth-century stone castle. Place-name evidence suggests that this site was favoured by Viking settlers – the isolated Goscar Rock on the north beach means plough-share – while documentary evidence records an earlier earthwork castle here which was captured by the Welsh in 1153. A series of raids, particularly by Llywelyn the Last in 1260, seems to have spurred the construction of the impressive town walls during the late thirteenth century. These were later refortified in 1457, when the walls were increased in height and a more substantial outer moat was constructed. These town walls today preserve a complete circuit with many

Figure 351. Tenby from the south. The curving line of St Julian's Street connects the town, left, with Castle Hill to the right and is home to Rock Terrace and Lexden Terrace. This mixture of late-eighteenth-century Regency buildings and largely nineteenth-century terraces lend Tenby its distinctive character. Winding stairs link houses to the beach (RCAHMW, DI2006-340).

Figure 352. The remains of Tenby Castle in 2002, before a new lifeboat station was built alongside the existing one (RCAHMW, DI2006-0356).

original features. Among the most impressive is The Five Arches, in fact a D-shaped barbican built to defend the South Gate through which four later gateways have been made. Within the walls Tenby is a crowded town of winding streets, medieval buildings and elegant Regency terraces which dominate the southern cliff-tops. From the air a greater sense of the town plan, including the more recent development which has spread beyond the original confines of the town wall, can be gained. The spire of St Mary's church in the centre provides a point of reference.

Figure 353. Tenby's new £5.5 million lifeboat station on the north side of Castle Hill was completed in 2005, home to Britain's first computerised Tamar class lifeboat (RCAHMW, AP-2005-0902).

Figure 354. St Catherine's Fort, on an offshore rock bordering south beach, dates from 1868-70. One of a chain of 'Palmerstonian' forts built to protect the Admiralty's ship-building yards at Pembroke Dock, this imposing structure cost £50,000 to build and was manned by 100 men and officers. Today it stands derelict (RCAHMW, DI2006-0348).

Figure 355. Tenby harbour at low water. The harbour is among the most picturesque anywhere in the British Isles. The present stone quay, built in 1848, extended a far earlier curving wall built in 1328. In its heyday during the Middle Ages the port at Tenby was one of the most important along the Bristol Channel, conducting deep-water trade with countries as far afield as France, Spain and Portugal (RCAHMW, DI2006-0347).

Caldy has a long and continuing association with the Christian church. The Welsh name, Ynys Byr, refers to what might originally have been a fifth-century Celtic *clas* on the island, dedicated to 'Pyro', its first abbot. Although no buildings remain from this early period, a fifth- or sixth-century inscribed stone in both Ogam and Latin survives inside the church. The medieval Caldy priory was founded in 1136 under the abbey at St Dogmaels, established by Robert Fitzmartin, the Norman lord of Cemaes, for an order of Benedictine monks of the abbey of Tiron in France. The walls still stand to nearly full height in places, and the priory remains in use as a place of worship by the monks.

Caldy Island had a mixed history of ownership and exploitation from the Middle Ages until the twentieth century. It was sold and resold, being used from the late eighteenth century as a source for fine limestone from the High Cliff quarry under the Kynaston family, and from the late nineteenth century as a market garden with vast greenhouses, providing produce for export to markets at Swansea, Pembroke and Tenby. In 1906 the island was purchased by an Anglican Benedictine Brotherhood which went on to build the present-day monastery, dedicated to St Samson, which stands close to the centre of the island. This great white building topped by terracotta roof tiles was built between 1909 and 1915 using limestone

Figure 357. Looking down on Caldy Lighthouse. The lighthouse was built in 1828-9, partly in response to the growing trade in limestone and coal from these parts to central and north Wales, and partly also to provide one of a series of identifiable lights at the entrance to the Bristol Channel to let ships know that this was not the English Channel (RCAHMW, DI2006-0349).

Figure 358. Caldy Priory from the north-east. Thought to have succeeded a fifth-century Celtic religious community dedicated to St Illtud, the priory dates from the twelfth to sixteenth centuries and survives remarkably intact. The thirteenth-century priory church can be seen left of centre with its slightly leaning spire. The body of the church extends to the left to join with the eastern range of the priory, which ends in the castellated Prior's Tower. Extending from the church on the right is the guest accommodation for the priory, marked by the large archway of the gatehouse. The overgrown grounds conceal former medieval fishponds and the ruins of a mill (RCAHMW, DI2006-0352).

brought direct from High Cliff quarry to the north. In 1924 the island was sold to an order of Reformed Cistercians, and around twenty monks remain in the monastery today. In addition to seven services each day, the monks keep a beef herd, make shortbread and chocolate, and sell a famous range of perfumes and toiletries inspired by the wild flowers, gorse and herbs on the island. From the air the dense green woodland which surrounds the monastery, distinct from the open pasture of the remainder of the island, equates roughly with the private monastic enclosure to which tourists are not admitted.

Figure 359. Caldy Abbey: an outstanding Arts and Crafts complex in the south Pembrokeshire landscape and the quiet retreat for a community of Cistercian monks from Chimay, Belgium. The red roofs and whitewashed walls suggest a Mediterranean scene to those passing overhead (RCAHMW, DI2006-0357).

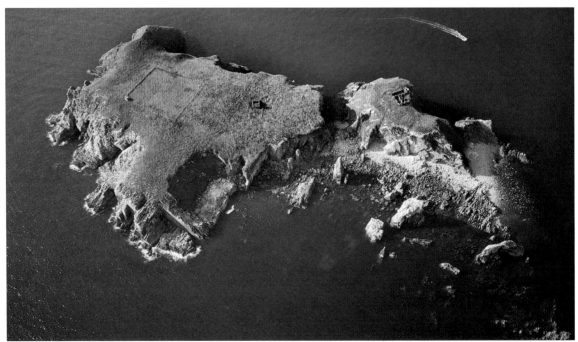

Figure 360. St Margaret's Island. To the west of Caldy, and connected at low water, this small island was once home to a chapel dedicated to St Margaret but was later heavily quarried in the nineteenth century, the chapel being converted into quarrymen's cottages (RCAHMW, DI2006-0351).

IRON AND COAL AT SAUNDERSFOOT

To the majority of visitors Saundersfoot does not look like a former industrial town. In its heyday Saundersfoot was at the centre of the export trade of very high grade anthracite won from the deep pits and shafts of the Pembrokeshire coalfield. In contrast to the medieval origins of its sister resort, Tenby, the town and harbour at Saundersfoot were largely developed during the nineteenth century. The local coalfield was first mentioned as far back as 1324, and by the middle of the seventeenth century some 30,000 tons were being exported annually from coal works around Saundersfoot, Begelly and Jeffreyston to destinations as far afield as France and Holland. Despite this apparent boom, the infrastructure for mining and transport was still at its most basic, with cart loads of coal being hauled by oxen and horses along poor country roads to the sea.

Transport improvements were long in coming, but in 1829 the Saundersfoot Railway and Harbour Co. was officially incorporated by Act of Parliament. The main four miles of railway were designed to connect the collieries at Thomas Chapel in the west to a new stone harbour at Saundersfoot, but branch lines also connected works at Stepaside, via Wiseman's Bridge to the east, and south to Moreton. The mid-nineteenth century was the heyday of Saundersfoot's industry, with new shafts sunk, a new colliery opened at Bonvilles Court, and the Stepaside Ironworks established at Kilgetty under a new company. During the 1860s anthracite production ran at well over half a million tons annually, with much of the Saundersfoot empire under the control of one man,

Figure 361. Saundersfoot harbour, seen from the north-west. This was originally an industrial harbour, where anthracite would be delivered by rail to be loaded on to ships for export. The small pier-head light on the south pier of the harbour was discontinued in 1947 after closure of the local mines, but reinstated in 1954 with the return of yachting to the harbour and the rise of Saundersfoot as a tourist resort (RCAHMW, 2000-cs-0372).

C. R. Vickerman of Hean Castle. However, stiff competition from larger, more productive coalfields in Carmarthenshire and Glamorgan put continuing pressure on the local pits. By the end of the 1870s Saundersfoot had lost its ironworks, and the majority of pits had closed. Despite this, Vickerman continued in his attempts to revive the flagging fortunes of the region. Vickerman died in 1897, but anthracite production continued at Bonvilles Court into the twentieth century, joined by an entirely new pit at Reynalton in 1914, lying to the west of Thomas Chapel; the workings were subsequently abandoned in 1921 following labour troubles. The following decades saw a rather piecemeal series of ventures to maintain existing collieries or open new workings. In 1938 the re-opened Broom colliery produced over 25,000 tons of coal, but it closed in 1939 along with the Saundersfoot railway. In 1950 the last small area of working, Wood Level colliery near Kilgetty, closed and the story of industry at Saundersfoot was over.

Figure 362. Hean Castle was built 1875-6 for the industrialist, C. R. Vickerman, who controlled the local mines in the latter half of the nineteenth century (RCAHMW, 2000-cs-0373).

Figure 363 (right). St Mary's church, Begelly (RCAHMW, AP-2006-0065).

Figure 364. The sinuous course of the former Saundersfoot Railway, still visible in the landscape to the north-west of Saundersfoot. This view shows the railway close to Thomas Chapel (village, left foreground), winding south-east towards Begelly (middle distance) and ultimately towards Saundersfoot in the far distance (RCAHMW, AP-2006-0062).

Figure 365. Begelly, from the north-east. Looking remarkably like Bronze Age burial mounds, the spoil tips from coal workings survive in improved pasture to the north of Begelly House (far left; RCAHMW, DI2006-0377).

Figure 366. Begelly, from the west, showing the former line of the Saundersfoot Railway, crossing obliquely lower left to upper right, and the line of a tramway crossing heath and field boundaries in the centre of the frame. Both served local collieries, including the Union Pit and Bushmoor, of which numerous shafts remain (RCAHMW, DI2006-0385).

Figure 367. Archaeologists usually hunt for soilmarks to reveal the outlines of buried prehistoric or Roman sites, but these dark patches in ploughed fields to the east of Jeffreystone, looking south-west, show the former positions of coal workings, now returned to farmland. Such photographs can be useful to industrial archaeologists wishing to piece together the extents of lost industries (RCAHMW, DI2006-0381).

258

Figure 368. The village of Jeffreystone, viewed from the north, is centred on its historic church, left of centre. All around are traces of the former coal industry, exposed as mounds and banks in the ploughed fields in the background and beneath woodland in the foreground, where the remains of the Underhill Wood early coal workings survive as a Scheduled Ancient Monument (RCAHMW, DI2006-0383).

Figure 369. The Stepaside Ironworks at Kilgetty, to the north of Saundersfoot. On the back of the long success of the Pembrokeshire coal field C. R. Vickerman founded the Pembrokeshire Iron and Coal company in 1847. The ironworks at Stepaside was established in the following year, and the aerial view from the north shows the surviving structures of a complex once linked by a network of railways to the wider coal field. The clearest building is the long roofless workshop to the right, once linked to a tramway. In the centre of the frame is the main complex, including the Casting House (with long shadows of its arched façade), the Engine Blast House (a box-like ruin in front of the Casting House), and a bank of limekilns on the hill behind, once served by a railway. The ground photograph by Iain Wright shows the gaunt arches of the Casting House. Production ceased here in 1877 (RCAHMW; aerial view 2002-cs-0544; ground view DI2006-1039).

Figure 370. First World War practice trenches surviving on the cliff tops at Penally, viewed from the south-east in 1991 (RCAHMW, DI2006-0376).

At intervals around the coast of Wales systems of First World War practice trenches survive as grim reminders of the training given to conscripts before their transport to the Western Front. Here, in the relatively quiet coastal grasslands of the Penally range, soldiers were given training in the construction of complex trench systems, and the surviving earthworks show many standard characteristics clearly laid out in manuals of the day. Trenches were built in parallel lines, usually three, linked by communications trenches. Two frontline trenches were supported by a third reserve trench, although, as artillery power strengthened and increased in range, changes were made during the war to the standard layout. The saw-toothed trench plan prevented shell and bomb blasts travelling along the trench. This also made it impossible to see more than ten metres along a trench, maintaining the security of the trench system even if the enemy infiltrated one particular part.

There were many reasons why practice trenches were dug on ranges across Britain at the start of the

Great War. They provided low-cost training for the one million volunteers who flocked to respond to Lord Kitchener's call. The resulting trenches could be used for combat training in the use of artillery and explosives, with trenches kitted out with barbed wire and machine-gun posts. They were also seen as a propaganda tool, showing the level of preparedness of the British army (Brown 2004).

The Penally trenches, like those in the grounds of Bodelwyddan Park in north Wales, are now preserved as a Scheduled Ancient Monument and have been recently resurveyed by Defence Estates. They stand as solemn reminders of the horror and squalor endured by soldiers who served on the battlefields of Flanders and northern France during the Great War.

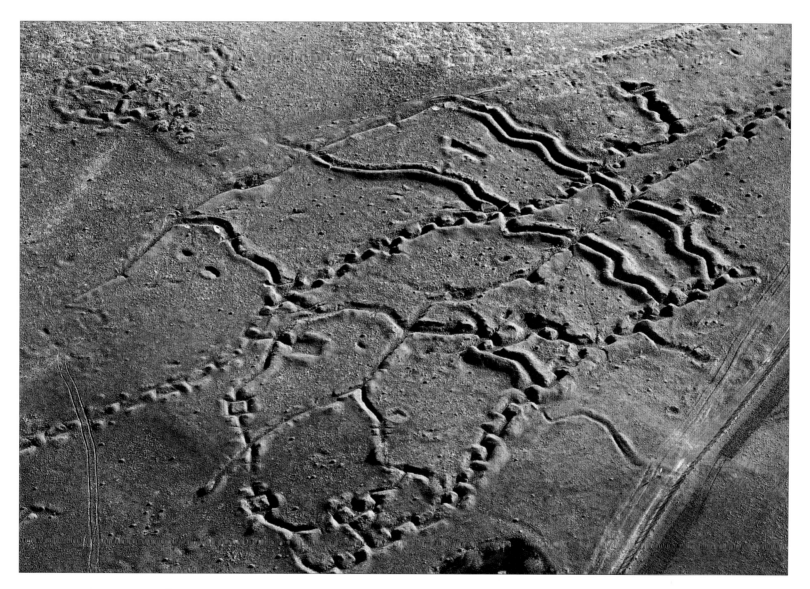

Figure 371. Penally practice trenches: a detailed view from 1995, showing the excellent state of preservation of these near-century-old earthworks and the saw-tooth trench lines. Signs can also be seen of other accommodation built into the trench lines, which could include dug-outs, strongholds, field hospitals and canteens. In places the Penally trenches are dug through the bedrock, which must have been exceedingly hard work (RCAHMW, DI2006-0374).

CHAPTER NINE

PAST PATTERNS – FUTURE VIEWS

The aim of this book has been to engage the reader in the experience of seeing the diversity of Pembrokeshire's archaeology and history from the air. Through these images the immense antiquity, and many hidden secrets, of the Welsh landscape can be better appreciated.

The pictures are silent and can be enjoyed at leisure, but aerial archaeology is an invigorating experience full of procedure, engine noise, cockpit vibration, camera checks, conversations with the pilot, pauses for air-traffic clearance, searches for hidden monuments and excitement at new discoveries revealed at extremes of light or season. In drought summers, when known and unknown buried sites can be revealed in considerable numbers as if every field had been given an x-ray, the thrill of discovery is overtaken by the need to keep pace with the recording task; booking aircraft in advance, making rapid fuel stops before heading off again, and working long into the night on returning home to write a flight report and prepare equipment for a new day. This survey process is followed by days in the office, checking discoveries with colleagues and local archaeologists, cataloguing and archiving. Only then are the most interesting discoveries visited on the ground and surveyed.

The pictures chosen for this book to represent the county in all its glorious diversity are a small percentage of the entire Royal Commission air photo collection. Technology allows us to liberate the wider contents of the archives of the National Monuments Record of Wales and place digital copies of them online, searchable by anyone with Internet access either by location, using detailed on-screen maps, or by site name or other details. At *www.coflein.gov.uk* images from across Wales can be viewed, tied to individual monument records, and compared with written descriptions and other sources.

In a county with as rich a heritage as *Sir Penfro* archaeologists and historians are looking to the next big discovery or unexpected result which will push forward our understanding of this south-westerly corner of Wales. Considerable gaps still exist in our knowledge of Pembrokeshire's past, whether they concern the true antiquity of the great coaxial field systems which cross the county from north to south, the ultimate path and destination of the Roman road, lost sites of early medieval churches and their cemeteries or even the existence of Viking settlements. Beyond cliffs and shores submerged forests, intertidal fish traps and undersea wrecks await air, ground and underwater prospection to help place the mainland in its wider context.

The people of Pembrokeshire are the key to unlocking the county's past. By making further chance discoveries, revealing lost sources through archive study or forcing investigation or preservation of unprotected monuments through local research and field survey, the entirety of Pembrokeshire's history can be steadily disentangled, reawakened and better understood. In pursuit of these goals, the aerial photograph remains one of the most powerful research tools.

Figure 372. Workmen dwarfed by the summit of a large storage tank during construction of the Liquified Natural Gas (LNG) terminal at Waterston, Milford Haven (RCAHMW, AP-2006-1185).

Figure 373. Part of a concentric Iron Age farmstead (foreground), revealed as a cropmark near Merryborough farm, east of Haverfordwest. First discovered from the air in 1996 (Fig. 245), and only visible in optimum drought conditions once a decade, knowledge of this buried site helped archaeologists to mitigate the line of the Natural Gas Pipeline when it was due to be constructed close by. Between the archaeological site and the pipeline corridor, grassed over 'evaluation trenches' (showing as dark, narrow lines) mark an early stage in the planning process, where the exact extent of the archaeology was checked and subsequently avoided. Part of the outer enclosure, a rock-cut ditch, 2 metres deep, was excavated during this work (RCAHMW, AP-2006-3311).

Figure 374. Work in progress on the Natural Gas Pipeline connecting the new terminal at Milford Haven with England; here, looking west from Tavernspite towards Lower Llantydwell farm (upper left) in June 2006 (RCAHMW, AP-2006-1649).

Figure 375. Waves breaking on Broadhaven beach, west Pembrokeshire (RCAHMW, DI2006-0591).

Figure 376. Navigable channels and algae blooms off Newport Sands, Parrog, north Pembrokeshire (RCAHMW, AP-2006-1114).

Figure 377. Farming the land: winter livestock gather in an arc on Mynydd Morvil, west of New Inn, Mynydd Preseli, where feed has been dropped on the snowy ground (RCAHMW, DI2005-0428).

Figure 378. Clouds over the Eastern Cleddau, from around 4,000 feet: looking south along the Pembrokeshire/Carmarthenshire border, marked by the wooded valley of the Eastern Cleddau, towards Llanycefn (centre, SN 096 237), with Llandissilio in the distance at upper left and a distant woodland block at upper right marking the villages of Gelli and Llawhaden (RCAHMW, 2000-cs-0486).

Figure 379. Coming in to land at Haverfordwest Airport (RCAHMW, AP-2006-3359).

BIBLIOGRAPHY AND APPENDICES

Standard sources for the entire book

There are a number of standard sources which have been consulted throughout the writing of this book and whose help and insight I freely acknowledge.

Arnold, C. J. & Davies, J. L. 2000. *Roman and Early Medieval Wales*, Stroud: Sutton Publishing Limited

Barrett, J. H. 1974. *The Pembrokeshire Coast Path*, Countryside Commission/HMSO.

Cadw, Countryside Council for Wales & ICOMOS UK 1998. *Register of Landscapes of Outstanding Historic Interest in Wales*, Cardiff: Cadw.

Carter, H. (ed.) 1989. *National Atlas of Wales*, Aberystwyth: University of Wales Press.

Charles, B. G. 1992. *The Place-names of Pembrokeshire. Volumes 1 and 2*, Aberystwyth: The National Library of Wales.

Davidson, A. (ed.) 2002. *The coastal archaeology of Wales. CBA Research Report 31,* York: Council for British Archaeology/Cadw.

Edwards, N. (ed.) 1997. *Landscape and Settlement in Medieval Wales*, Oxford: Oxbow Monograph 81.

Fenton, R. A. 1994. *A Historical Tour Through Pembrokeshire*, Haverfordwest: Reprinted by Cyngor Sir Dyfed County Council, Cultural Services Department.

Hague, D. B. 1994. *Lighthouses of Wales,* Aberystwyth: RCAHMW.

Jones, F. with Innes-Smith, R. (ed.) 1996. *Historic Houses of Pembrokeshire and their Families*, Dinas, Newport: Brawdy Books.

Lloyd, T., Orbach, J. & Scourfield, R. 2004. *The Buildings of Wales: Pembrokeshire*, London: Yale University Press.

Lynch, F., Aldhouse-Green, S. & Davies, J. L. 2000. *Prehistoric Wales*, Stroud: Sutton Publishing Limited.

Murphy, K. & Ludlow, N. 2003. *Historic Landscape Characterisation of Pen Caer, Newport and Carningli, Manorbier, and Stackpole Warren*, Cambria Archaeology, Report No. 2003/6, Project Record No. 47255, unpublished report.

Rees, S. 1992. *A Guide to Ancient and Historic Wales: Dyfed*, London: Cadw/HMSO.

Rees, V. 1976. *South-West Wales. A Shell Guide,* London: Faber and Faber.

Sikes, W. 1883. Article for *Harper's New Monthly Magazine*, reprinted as: Ludlam, S. D. (ed.) 1985. *Exploring The Wild Welsh Coast 100 Years Ago*, London: Thames and Hudson.

Whittle, E. 2002. *Carmarthenshire, Ceredigion and Pembrokeshire; Register of Landscapes, Parks and Gardens of Special Historic Interest in Wales*, Cardiff: Cadw/ICOMOS.

Additional bibliographic sources by chapter

Chapter 1

Ceraudo, G. 2005. 105 Years of Archaeological Aerial Photography in Italy (1899-2004). In Bourgeois, J. & Meganck, M. (eds.) 2005. *Aerial Photography and Archaeology 2003, a Century of Information*, Archaeological Reports, Gent University 4, Ghent: Academia Press/Ghent University, 73-86.

Ellison Hawks, R. A. n.d. (*c.*1942). *Britain's Wonderful Fighting Forces*, London: Odhams Press Limited.

Evans, J. 2001. *Pembroke Dock reflections,* Pembroke Dock: Paterchurch Publications.

James, T. 1984. Aerial Reconnaissance in Dyfed, 1984, *Archaeology in Wales* 24, 12-22.

James, T. 1986. Discovering and Monitoring Sites by Aerial Survey. In Moore, D. & Austin, D. (eds.) 1986. *Welsh Archaeological Heritage. The proceedings of a conference held by The Cambrian Archaeological Association in 1985*, Lampeter: Cambrian Archaeological Association and Saint David's University College, 137-140

James, T. and Simpson, D. 1980. *Ancient West Wales from the Air*, Carmarthen: Carmarthenshire Antiquarian Society.

St Joseph, J. K. S. 1961. Aerial Reconnaissance in Wales, *Antiquity* 35, 263-75 & pls. XXXV-XLVIII.

Chapter 2

Breeze, A. 2005. An Etymology for Dyfed, *Carmarthenshire Antiquary* 41, 175-6.

Davies, J. 1999. *The Making of Wales*, Stroud: Alan Sutton Publishing Limited /Cadw, Welsh Historic Monuments.

Davies, J. L. 2000. Roman Wales: An Introduction. In Davies, J. L. & Arnold, C. J. 2000. *Roman and Early Medieval Wales*, Stroud: Sutton Publishing, 1-140.

Davis, P. 2000. *A Company of Forts, A Guide to the Medieval Castles of West Wales*, Llandysul: Gomer.

Edwards, N. 2001. Early-Medieval Inscribed Stones and Stone Sculpture in Wales: Context and Function, *Medieval Archaeology* 45, 15-39.

Edwards, N. & Lane, A. 1992. The Archaeology of the Early Church in Wales: An Introduction. In Edwards, N. & Lane, A. (eds.) 1992, 1-11.

Gaunt, P. 1991. *A Nation Under Siege, The Civil War in Wales 1642-48*, London: Cadw/HMSO.

Green, S. & Walker, E. 1991. *Ice Age Hunters: Neanderthals and Early Modern Hunters in Wales*, Cardiff: National Museum of Wales.

Gruffydd, D. E. 1993. *Rocks and Scenery of the Pembrokeshire Coast*, Pembroke Dock: Pembrokeshire Coast National Park Authority.

Hall, D. 1987. *Medieval Fields*, Princes Risborough: Shire Publications.

Hawkes, C. F. C. 1931. Hill-forts, *Antiquity* 5, 60-97.

James, H. 1987. Excavations at Caer, Bayvil, 1979, *Archaeologia Cambrensis* 136, 51-76.

James, H. 2000. Roman Carmarthenshire, *Carmarthenshire Antiquary* 36, 23-46.

James, T. 1999. The Origins and Topography of Haverford. In Miles, D. (ed.) 1999. *A History of the Town and County of Haverfordwest*, Llandysul: Gomer, 11-33.

John, B. S. 1988. *The Geology of Pembrokeshire*, Fishguard: Abercastle Publications.

John, B. 1995. *Pembrokeshire Past and Present*, Newport: Greencroft Books.

Jones, J. G. 1998. *A Pocket Guide: The History of Wales*, Cardiff: University of Wales Press/The Western Mail.

Kissock, J. 1997. God Made Nature and Man Made Towns: Post-Conquest and Pre-Conquest Villages in Pembrokeshire. In Edwards, N. (ed.) 1997, 123-137.

Manning, W. 2001. *A Pocket Guide: Roman Wales*, Cardiff: University of Wales Press/Western Mail.

Merrony, M. 2004. Richard Fenton's 'Roman *Villa*' at Ford Revisited, *Journal of the Pembrokeshire Historical Society* 13, 5-22.

Owen, T. R. 1973. *Geology Explained in South Wales*, Newton Abbot: David and Charles.

Page, N. A. 1996. Whitland, Whitland Bypass Roman Road (SN1579 1821), *Archaeology in Wales* 36, 72-3.

Redknap, M. 2000. *Vikings in Wales, An Archaeological Quest*, Cardiff: National Museums and Galleries of Wales.

Vyner, B. 2001. Clegyr Boia: a potential Neolithic enclosure and associated monuments on the St David's peninsula, southwest Wales. In Darvill, T. & Thomas, J. (eds.) 2001. *Neolithic Enclosures in Atlantic Northwest Europe*, Oxford: Neolithic Studies Group Seminar Papers 6, Oxbow Books, 78-90.

Webster, G. 1981. *Rome Against Caratacus*, London: Batsford.

Williams, G. H. & Mytum, H. 1998. *Llawhaden, Dyfed, Excavations on a group of small defended enclosures, 1980-4*, Oxford: BAR British Series 275, Archaeopress.

Internet resources:

The historic landscapes section of Cambria Archaeology's website, www.acadat.com

Chapter 3

Evans, J. 1990. An Archaeological Survey of Skomer, Dyfed, *Proceedings of the Prehistoric Society* 56, 247-67.

James, H. & James, T. 1994. Ramsey Island Prehistoric Field System (SM 696 234 and SM 700 216), *Archaeology in Wales* 34, 52-3.

Worrall, D. 2001. Jewels in the West, *Cymru Wledig/Rural Wales*, Autumn 2001, 10-11.

Chapter 4

Crane, P. 1999. *Great Castle Head, Dale, Pembrokeshire 1999, Archaeological Excavation and Survey*, Cambria Archaeology, Project Record No. 37960, unpublished report.

Cunliffe, B. 2001. *Facing the Ocean, The Atlantic and its Peoples, 8000BC – AD 1500*, Oxford: Oxford University Press.

Hogg, A. H. A. 1973. Gaer Fawr and Carn Ingli: Two Major Pembrokeshire Hill-forts, *Archaeologia Cambrensis* 122, 69-84.

Murphy, K. 2002. The archaeological resource: chronological overview to 1500 AD. In Davidson, A. (ed.) 2002, 44-64.

Chapter 5

Baring-Gould, S., Burnard, R. & Anderson, I. K. 1900. Exploration of Moel Trigarn, *Archaeologia Cambrensis* Fifth Series, XVII, 189-211.

Darvill, T. & Wainwright, G. 2005. Beyond Stonehenge: Carn Menyn and the Bluestones, *British Archaeology*, July/August 2005, 28-31.

Darvill, T., Wainwright, G. & Driver, T. 2007. Among Tombs and Circles on Banc Du, *British Archaeology*, January/February 2007, 26-29.

Frodsham, P. 2004. *Interpreting the Ambiguous: Archaeology and Interpretation in Early 21st Century Britain, Proceedings of a conference session at the 2001 Institute of Field Archaeologists' Annual Conference, held at the University of Newcastle upon Tyne*, Oxford: Archaeopress.

Hogg, A. H. A. 1973. Gaer Fawr and Carn Ingli: Two Major Pembrokeshire Hill-forts, *Archaeologia Cambrensis* 122, 69-84.

Murphy, K. 1997. Small Boroughs in South-West Wales: their Planning, Early Development and Defences. In Edwards, N. (ed.) 1997, 139-56.

Mytum, H. 1999. Castell Henllys, *Current Archaeology* 161, 64-172.

Mytum, H. C. & Webster, C. J. 1989. A survey of the Iron Age enclosure and *chevaux-de-frise* at Carn Alw, Dyfed, *Proceedings of the Prehistoric Society* 55, 263-6.

Pearson, A. W. 1996. *Carn Ingli, circa 1500BC to AD1845: The application of geographical information systems to the study of settlement development at Newport, Pembrokeshire*, University of Portsmouth, unpublished PhD thesis.

The Royal Commission on the Ancient and Historical Monuments and Constructions of Wales and Monmouthshire 1925. *An Inventory of the Ancient Monuments in Wales and Monmouthshire VII, County of Pembroke*, London: HMSO.

Internet resources:

Alistair Pearson's research on Mynydd Carn-ingli: www.envf.port.ac.uk/geo/research/carningli/archaeology.htm

Chapter 6

Burnham, B. C. 1996. Roman road, west of Carmarthen, *Britannia* 27, 393 & pl. XVIA.

Iorwerth, D. 2005. A ruin for the future [Narberth Castle], *Heritage in Wales* 31, Summer 2005, 10-13.

James, T. 1989. Air Photography by the Dyfed Archaeological Trust 1989, *Archaeology in Wales* 29, 31-4.

James, T. 1990. Concentric antenna enclosures – a new defended enclosure type in west Wales, *Proceedings of the Prehistoric Society* 56, 295-8.

James, T. 1999. The Origins and Topography of Haverford. In Miles, D. (ed.) 1999. *A History of the Town and County of Haverfordwest*, Llandysul: Gomer, 11-33.

James, H. 2000. Roman Carmarthenshire, *Carmarthenshire Antiquary* 36, 23-46.

Ludlow, N. 2003. The Castle and Lordship of Narberth, *Journal of the Pembrokeshire Historical Society* 12, 5-43.

Page, N. A. 1996. Whitland, Whitland Bypass Roman Road (SN1579 1821), *Archaeology in Wales* 36, 72-3.

Rees, S. 1999. The Augustinian Priory. In Miles, D. (ed.) 1999. *A History of the Town and County of Haverfordwest*, Llandysul: Gomer, 55-78.

Williams, G. 1984. *Fighting and Farming in Iron Age West Wales, Excavations at Llawhaden 1980-1984*, Llandeilo: Dyfed Archaeological Trust Limited/Manpower Services Commission.

Williams, G. H. & Mytum, H. 1998. *Llawhaden, Dyfed, Excavations on a group of small defended enclosures, 1980-4*, Oxford: BAR British Series 275, Archaeopress.

Internet resources:

Sarn y Bryn Caled timber circle excavations: www.cpat.org.uk/cpat/past/neo/neo.htm

Roman road excavations at Whitland, Carmarthenshire, in *British Archaeology*: http://www.britarch.ac.uk/BA/ba6/ba6news.html

Chapter 7

Beazley, E. 1976. Milford Haven's Harbour Fortress, *Country Life,* September 16, 732-4.

Benson, D. G., Evans, J. G, & Williams, G. H. 1990. Excavations at Stackpole Warren, Dyfed, *Proceedings of the Prehistoric Society* 56, 179-245.

Copley, M. 2006. Shaped by the sea [a history of Dale], *Pembrokeshire Life,* March 2006, 12-13.

Crane, P. 1999. *Great Castle Head, Dale, Pembrokeshire 1999, Archaeological Excavation and Survey, Draft Report*, Cambria Archaeology, Project Record No. 37960, unpublished report.

Crane, P. 2004. Excavations at Newton, Llanstadwell, Pembrokeshire, *Archaeology in Wales* 44, 3-31.

Edwards, S. 2001. *The Story of the Milford Haven Waterway, The Good Times & The Bad Times,* Woonton, Almeley: Logaston Press.

Ellison Hawks, R. A. n.d. (*c.*1942). *Britain's Wonderful Fighting Forces*, London: Odhams Press Limited.

Groom, P. & Austin, L. 2005. The Iron Age at Castlemartin, *Sanctuary, The Ministry of Defence Conservation Magazine* 34, 34-5.

James, H. 2001. Castlemartin Range: The Christian Heritage, *Sanctuary, The Ministry of Defence Conservation Magazine* 30, 32-4.

Murphy, K. 1997. Small Boroughs in South-West Wales: their Planning, Early Development and Defences. In Edwards, N. (ed.) 1997, 139-156.

Murphy, K. 2002. Military Defences. In Davidson, (ed.) 2002, 76-80.

Murphy, K. & Allen, B. 1998. *Coastal Survey 1997-8, Lower Milford Haven Pembrokeshire,* Cambria Archaeology, Project Record No. 35003, unpublished report.

Musson, C. 1994. *Wales from the Air,* Aberystwyth: RCAHMW.

Nash-Williams, V. E. 1931. Roman Coins from Pembroke Dock, *Bulletin of the Board of Celtic Studies* 6, 94.

Richards, B. 1995. *Pembrokeshire Under Fire,* Pembroke Dock: Paterchurch Publications.

Saunders, A. 1989. *Fortress Britain, Artillery Fortification in the British Isles and Ireland,* Liphook: Beaufort Publications.

Saunders, A. 2001. Introduction. In Saunders, A., Spurgeon, C. J., Thomas, H. J. & Roberts, D. J.

2001. *Guns Across the Severn, The Victorian Fortifications of Glamorgan,* Aberystwyth: RCAHMW, 5-18.

Internet resources:

The Defence of Britain Project: www.britarch.ac.uk/projects/dob/review/index.html

Castlemartin Range: www.army.mod.uk/ate/public/castlemartin.htm

Chapter 8

Brown, M. 2004. A Mirror of the Apocalypse, Great War training trenches, *Sanctuary, The Ministry of Defence Conservation Magazine* 33, 54-8.

Price, M. R. C. 1982. *Industrial Saundersfoot,* Llandysul: Gomer Press.

Shepherd, A. n.d. *A Visitor's Guide to Pembrokeshire, Tenby and South Coast,* Seventh Edition. Saundersfoot: Alan Shepherd Publishing.

USEFUL ADDRESSES

Royal Commission on the Ancient and Historical
Monuments of Wales *(and* National Monuments
Record of Wales)
Crown Building
Plas Crug
Aberystwyth SY23 1NJ
Telephone 01970 621200
www.rcahmw.gov.uk

Cadw
Welsh Assembly Government
Plas Carew
Unit 5/7 Cefn Coed
Parc Nantgarw
Cardiff CF15 7QQ
Telephone 01443 33 6000
www.cadw.wales.gov.uk

Archaeoleg Cambria Archaeology
The Shire Hall
Carmarthen Street
Llandeilo SA19 6AF
Telephone 01558 823131
www.acadat.com

CBA Wales/Cymru
c/o Clwyd-Powys Archaeological Trust
7A Church Street
Welshpool SY21 7DL
Telephone 01938 553670
http://pages.britishlibrary.net/cba.wales/

Pembrokeshire Coast National Park Authority
Llanion Park
Pembroke Dock SA72 6DY
Telephone 0845 345 7275
www.pcnpa.org.uk

Central Register of Air Photography for Wales
National Assembly for Wales
Room 073A
Crown Offices, Cathays Park
Cardiff CF10 3NQ
Telephone 029 2082 3819

University of Cambridge
Unit for Landscape Modelling (Air Photo Library)
Sir William Hardy Building
Tennis Court Road
Cambridge CB2 1QB
Telephone 01223 764377
www.uflm.cam.ac.uk/

Internet resources:

Coflein: Discovering Our Past Online
www.coflein.gov.uk

Aerial Archaeology Research Group
http://aarg.univie.ac.at/

National Association of Aerial Photographic
Libraries (NAPLIB)
http://static.rspsoc.org/naplib/naplibMain.htm

LIST OF PHOTOGRAPHERS AND RESPECTIVE IMAGES

Dr Toby Driver, RCAHMW. Cover, and figures:
1, 2, 4, 6, 8, 14 (left), 16, 17, 18 (both), 21, 25, 28, 31, 34, 37, 39 (lower), 42, 43, 45, 46, 47, 52, 53, 54, 55, 56, 57, 58, 59, 61, 63, 64, 65 (both), 66, 67, 68, 69, 72, 73, 74, 76, 82, 83, 86, 89, 90, 92, 93, 94, 95, 97, 99, 100, 102, 103, 104, 105, 108, 110, 111, 112, 113, 114, 116, 117, 118, 120, 123 (lower), 124, 127, 130, 131, 132, 133, 134, 135, 137, 139, 140, 149, 154, 155, 156, 157, 158 (both), 159, 160, 163, 165 (right), 167, 168, 169, 170, 171, 173, 175, 176, 177, 178, 179, 180, 188, 189, 190, 191, 192, 193, 195, 198, 203, 209, 213, 215, 219 (both), 222, 224 (both), 225, 226, 228, 232, 233, 234, 235, 238, 241, 253, 256, 257 (lower), 259, 261 (right), 263, 265, 266, 267, 269, 270, 271, 273, 274 (both), 276, 277, 278, 279, 284, 285, 287, 289 (both), 293, 295, 297 (right), 299 (below), 301, 302, 303, 304, 306 (both), 308 (both), 309, 316 (lower), 317, 318, 319, 320, 321 (both), 322, 326, 327 (lower), 328, 331, 333, 335, 336, 337, 338, 339, 340, 343 (both), 347, 348, 349, 351, 352, 353, 355, 356, 360, 361, 362, 363, 364, 367, 368, 369 (left), 372, 373, 374, 375, 376, 377, 378, 379, 380.

Chris Musson MBE, formerly of RCAHMW. Rear cover, and figures:
3, 5, 10 (both), 24 (upper), 26, 27 (both), 30 (both), 33, 36, 39 (upper), 40, 44, 48, 50, 60, 62, 70, 75, 85, 87, 91, 96, 98, 101, 106, 107, 109, 115, 119, 122, 123 (upper), 125, 128, 129, 136, 141, 143, 144, 145, 146, 147, 148, 150, 152, 153, 161, 162, 164, 165 (upper), 166, 172, 174, 181, 182, 183, 185, 186, 187, 197, 200, 201, 204, 205, 206, 207, 208, 211, 212, 214, 216, 217 (both), 218, 220, 221 (both), 223, 227, 229, 230, 237, 240, 242, 243, 244 (upper), 245, 248, 249, 250, 251, 257 (upper), 258, 260, 261 (left), 262, 264, 268, 272, 281, 282, 283, 286, 291, 294, 296, 297 (left), 299 (left), 300, 305 (lower), 316 (upper), 324, 325, 327 (upper), 329, 334, 341, 342, 344, 345, 346, 350, 354, 357, 358, 359, 365, 366, 370, 371.

Terry James, formerly of Cambria Archaeology & RCAHMW. Figures: 24 (lower), 244 (lower), 247.

Professor J. K. S. St Joseph, formerly of CUCAP. Figures: 29, 32, 51, 80, 210, 231.

Iain Wright, RCAHMW. Figures: 81, 290, 298, 307, 369 (right).

PHOTOGRAPHIC EQUIPMENT AND MATERIALS

From 1986 to 2001 RCAHMW photographs were taken on Pentax 645 and Rollei 6002/6006 cameras, with 75mm, 80mm and 150mm lenses for black and white negatives and colour transparencies. Until 1997 Canon T70/T90 cameras were used for 35mm colour transparencies, with 50mm and 100mm FD lenses. From 2001 until 2005, RCAHMW medium format photography was taken on a Rollei 6008 Integral, fitted with 80mm and 150mm lenses. From 1997 35mm colour transparencies were taken on a Contax 167 MT, fitted with 35mm, 50mm and 135mm lenses. Digital aerial photographs taken during 2004 were on a Fuji Finepix S1 Pro. Digital aerial photographs taken from 2005 onwards were on a Canon EOS 1ds Mark II, fitted with Canon EF 28-200mm and 75mm-300mm lenses. Black and white films to 2005 were Kodak Tri-X (220) and TMax 400. Colour films to 1997 were Fujichrome 100 and Kodachrome 200, replaced from 1997 by Fujichrome Sensia 100 and Fujichrome Velvia. Automatic exposures at 1/500 and 1/1000sec were provided by the cameras. Lens hoods and UV/Skylight filters were used in all cases, with 2x yellow filters used for black and white cropmark photography.

CONTENT NOTES

Place names
Place names have been standardised in line with B. G. Charles' two volumes of *The Place names of Pembrokeshire* (1992), except Mynydd Preseli, which has been retained with an 'i' rather than a 'y', in line with prevailing usage on maps and in archaeological publications.

Building dates
Dates and other key facts about buildings have been standardised in line with *The Buildings of Wales: Pembrokeshire* (T. Lloyd *et al.* 2004) except where published dates in other established sources consistently differ with this new publication.

Figure 380. St Brides Haven, near Marloes. An historic lime kiln and site of an early medieval cemetery (upper left), together with Mesolithic flint finds close by, attest to thousands of years of coastal activity (RCAHMW, DI2005-0431).

INDEX

Within each entry references in the text are listed first, followed by Figure references.
A page number followed by 'cap' indicates that the reference is in the caption to a Figure.